"Yes, I like music, but when I was a girl the musical instruments we practiced on were the churn, the washtub, and the cradle. We didn't have much chance to play the violin or the piano."
Mrs. Franklin Powell
Pioneer of 1851

The Lockley Files

Conversations

with

Pioneer Women

By

Fred Lockley

Compiled and Edited

by Mike Helm

OREGON
COUNTRY
LIBRARY

1

First Edition
Published in 1981

Second Edition
Published in 1993

Library of Congress Catalog Card Number
81-50845

International Standard Book Number
0-931742-08-0

Published by Rainy Day Press
PO Box 3035
Eugene, Oregon 97403

Printed in U.S.A.

"After all is said and done, people are just folks, and if you feel a real and sincere interest in them, and if you are a good asker and a good listener, you will be rewarded by getting good human interest stories."

Fred Lockley
1871-1958

Acknowledgements

I would like to thank the following people for their contributions to the publication of this volume of **The Lockley Files**:

Chris Helm, for spending much of her spring vacation in a tireless search for typographical errors;

Phillip Zorich and Liz Cooksey, librarians in the Oregon Collection at the University of Oregon library in Eugene, Oregon, for introducing me to The Lockley Files and cheerily fetching them for me, volume after volume, day after day, until I had read all 58 volumes;

Donald J. Sterling, editor of the Oregon Journal, in Portland, Oregon, for his encouragement of this project at its inception.

Table of Contents

"One day we saw a big cloud of dust, and through the dust we could see hundreds of Indians riding toward us. We stopped the train, corralled the wagons, and got ready to defend ourselves. When the cloud of dust got nearer we discovered that, instead of Indians on horseback, it was a big herd of buffalo. The menfolks went out on horseback after them and killed enough that we all had all the buffalo meat we needed."

Rebecca Stevens Mount
Pioneer of 1851

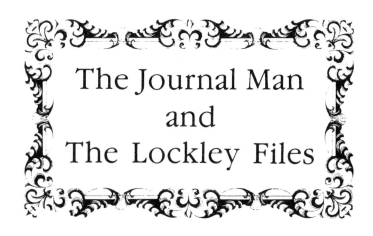

The Journal Man
and
The Lockley Files

Fred Lockley was one of Oregon's pioneer newspaper-men. He worked for newspapers in Montana and Kansas before coming to Oregon in the late 1890s, where he worked first for the **Capital Journal** in Salem. In 1905 he was in Pendleton, where he owned a 25% interest in the **East Oregonian**. Later, Lockley sold his interest in the **East Oregonian** and moved to Portland, where he worked for the **Oregon Journal**. He was known as "The Journal Man", and, for nearly 20 years, his column, "Impressions and Observations of the Journal Man", appeared daily on the editorial page of the Oregon Journal.

During his career, Lockley conducted more than 10,000 interviews with "bullwhackers, muleskinners, pioneers, prospectors, 49ers, Indian fighters, trappers, ex-barkeepers, authors, preachers, poets and near poets, and all sorts and conditions of men and women."

Today, 58 old, black, three-ring binders stuffed--perhaps by Fred Lockley himself, no one seems to know for sure--with yellowed copies of his interviews and observations turn slowly to dust behind two locked doors in the Oregon Collection at the University of Oregon Library in Eugene, Oregon. They are a rare treasure, a human view of pioneer days in the Oregon Country, recorded in the words of the people who walked to Oregon in the mid-1800s, or were born during those years in log cabins on their parents' donation land claims, and lived to tell about it in the early part of this century.

This volume, the first of four volumes of oral history by Fred Lockley in the Oregon Country Library, is a feminine view of life on the Oregon Trail and in the society building in the wilderness at its end.

"Because there were fewer things going on, everybody turned out to public affairs, like hangings, or anything of that kind."

Mrs. William Alexander
Born near Salem, 1856

Pioneer
Women

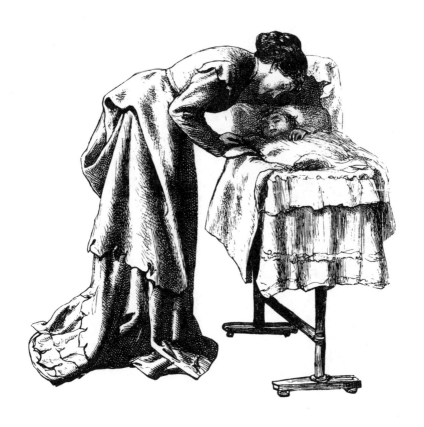

"My brother Jerry Carter Perkins was a little chap when he crossed the plains. He was playing with a rope and tripped on the rope and fell into the campfire, knocking over a large kettle of boiling water, which scalded him to death. My brother Edgar was born in the Blue Mountains."

Emma Perkins Hembree
Born in Yamhill County, Oregon, 1859

Conversations with Pioneer Women

Matilda Jane Sager Delaney

"They say I am hard and bitter. If some of the people who have life made easy for them had been through what I have, maybe they would feel bitter and vindictive, too. Nowadays, the child is everything. When I was young, children had no rights. They were to be seen, not heard, and to be seen as little as possible.

"I wrote a book recently, entitled **The Whitman Massacre.** If I had had my way would have told some wholesome truths, but my friends told me to bury the hatchet, to forgive and forget. I suppose we should forgive, but the good book doesn't say you have to forget, and as long as I live I shall never forget the injustice, the indignities, and cruelty I had to suffer when I was a helpless little child.

"When you think of those old missionaries, you are apt to think of them as saintly, long-suffering charitable people, easy to get along with, but if you had lived with them as I have, you would have another think coming. No, I am not referring to Dr. Marcus Whitman and Mrs. Whitman. I am thinking of the people who, after the Whitmans were murdered, took us, out of charity, and worked us to the limit to get their money's worth out of us.

"I was born at St. Joseph, Missouri, on October 16, 1839. I was four and a half years old when we started for Oregon. My father, Henry Sager, and my mother, Naomi Sager, died of mountain fever while we were on the journey. We seven children were cared for by the other emigrants. Captain Shaw asked the Whitmans to take care of us. Not many families would want to adopt seven orphan children they had never seen before. Would you? Dr. Whitman did.

1

"I wish I could give you a picture of the Whitman Mission—of the family life of the Whitmans, of the morning and evening prayers, of the work with the Indians, of the emigrants who stayed over that winter and the following winter, of the bathing in the river in the summer, of our walks with Mrs. Whitman, of the gathering of wild flours, of our simple meals, of driving the cows to pasture, of the routine of work and all the rest of it.

"Mrs. Whitman believed in 'Yea, yea and nay, nay'. She would point to one of us, then point to the dishes, or the broom, and we would jump and get busy with our assigned task. She didn't scold much, but we dreaded that accusing finger pointed at us. The way we jumped when it was leveled at us, you would have thought it was a gun and was likely to go off. She had the New England idea of strict discipline, and there was no danger of any of us becoming spoiled. She was a good woman, and Dr. Whitman was a man you could not help respecting and admiring.

"The events of November 29, 1847, when our foster parents, Dr. and Mrs. Whitman, and my two brothers were killed, as well as many of the others at the mission, I shall pass over. After Peter Skene Ogden bought us from the Indians we were taken to Fort Walla Walla, the Hudson's Bay Company's post, now called Wallula. From there we went in open boats down the Columbia River to Fort Vancouver and thence to Oregon City. I stayed with the Spaldings that winter and went to Mrs. J. Quinn Thornton's private school.

"The next spring the Reverend J. S. Giffin and Alvin T. Smith of Forest Grove came with their ox teams and took us to Forest Grove. A few days later I was taken by a family who had a farm nearby. They lived in a one room cabin. All the cooking was done on the fireplace. Sometimes the coals did not last overnight, so I would be sent a mile or more to a neighbor's to get a shovelful of hot coals to rebuild the fire.

"Things were crude in those days. I remember the woman I stayed with walking the floor with a toothache. They cured her toothache by knocking the tooth out with a steel punch.

"Her husband was an intensely religious man. Many of the religious people of that day were harsh, uncharitable and intolerant. He would not let me go to the school at Forest Grove, because he had fallen out with some of the people there over

2

religious differences. There was too much churchianity, too little Christianity. For the same reason, he would not let me go to the church or Sunday school. The verse in the Bible he pinned his faith to was the one that says if you spare the rod you spoil the child. He did his full duty to me in that respect. For several years I was never without welts or black and blue marks from constant beatings.

"I remember once he was going away on a trip. He told me to go and cut a thick switch. I thought he wanted it for his horse, as he was saddling up. I brought the switch. He called to me and, seizing me by the shoulder, gave me an unmerciful beating.

"I said, 'What have I done?'

"He said, 'You haven't done anything. I am going away. The chances are you will do something to deserve a beating while I am gone, and I won't be here to give it to you, so I will see to my duty before leaving.' Mounting his horse, he said, 'I will whip you as soon as I retUrn, but if you do anything to deserve a beating I will give you one you won't forget in a hurry.'

"Catherine, my eldest sister, who was 13, was asked for by a preacher at Salem. As she was the most useful, H. H. Spalding, who had charge of us, said whoever took her would have to take the baby, Henrietta, who was less than four years old. He agreed to take both of them. He had not had them long before he gave the little girl away. The people who took her gave her to someone else and she went from family to family, till finally we heard someone had taken her to California. We didn't have letters and telegrams in those days, so it took months to get word from each other. I once paid 50 cents for a letter. We heard that our baby sister was killed in California, but we never heard the particulars.

"I was eight years old when the Whitman Massacre occurred. After a few months I was given to a family near Forest Grove. In the fall of 1848 the man went to the gold diggings in California. He returned in the spring of 1849. While he was gone his wife, their little baby, and I lived with Reverend J. Cornwall. He was a good man, according to his lights, (but) he was unbusinesslike and unpractical. For example, he took a band of sheep late in the fall with the understanding that for their care he was to have half the

3

increase. He did not have any hay or feed for the sheep, so while he was away preaching that winter the ewes starved or froze to death.

"His son, George, and his daughter Narcissa, and I did the work of the farm and the house. The wolves were very hungry that winter and they used to come all around the house to get the sheep.

"The country was unfenced and the long-horned and almost wild Spanish cattle roamed at will over the country. When I went on errands I was afraid of them, for they would often tree people on foot and wait for hours at the foot of the tree. If you walked in the heavy timber you were afraid of the wolves, while if you walked in the open the cattle would see you and run after you.

"Mrs. Cornwall spent every moment she could spare in carding and spinning wool and knitting wool socks, which she sold to the miners at $1 a pair. If she hadn't we should have gone hungry.

"The winter was cold and the sheep died or were frozen to death. It was my job to pull the wool off the sheep that died and wash it in the creek. Doing the family washing in the stream by beating the clothes with a paddle on a log and rinsing them in the cold water was hard, but washing the dirt and grease out of that wool was a job that was heartbreaking for a little girl nine years old.

"In the spring of 1850 I had three months' schooling. Mr. Eells taught the school and I walked three and a half miles to and from school.

"From the time I was eight until I was 15 I was whipped so much that I got to feeling about it as one does the winter rain—that it was inevitable and was to be borne without complaint for nothing could be done about it.

"Some of the whippings, because of their severity, stand out in my memory. I remember a whipping I got that was unusually severe for going to an entertainment given at the Congregational Church at Forest Grove. The man I was staying with said it was ungodly and would teach me to desire worldly amusements and the next thing I might want to go to a regular theatre and that was the gateway to hell and damnation.

"Another severe beating I got was for going with a girl of my own age. Her name was Mary Allen. She had been born out of wedlock, so I was whipped for going with her. When she was 13 a man named Adam Wimple married her. He was 35 when he married her. He killed her within the year and set fire to the house to keep people from knowing he had killed her. Neighbors saw the fire, put it out, and found her body and saw she had been killed. Wimple was hanged at Dallas early in October, 1852.

"I remember one time the man I lived with caught his saddle horse, saddled it, and rode up to the cabin and called me out. He told me to get my sunbonnet and get on behind him, as he wanted me to go to Hillsboro with him. Children didn't ask questions in those days. They obeyed orders. As we rode to Hillsboro I wondered all the way why he wanted me to go with him. We rode to where a crowd had assembled. Presently the officers brought out a man and hanged him. I was horrified. He said, 'I brought you to see the hanging to impress on your mind what happens to people who do not mind their elders and do exactly what they are told.'

"It took me months to forget the horrible sights I had seen when the Indians killed Dr. and Mrs. Whitman and my brothers and the others, and now for weeks I woke up at night covered with the sweat of terror at seeing the man hanged in my dreams. I could see him twitch and his tongue hang out and his protruding eyes. Childhood was a time of terror and bitterness when I was a girl.

"I was whipped so much that the neighbors finally complained and they had me summoned to give evidence before the judge. The man I lived with said the neighbors should mind their own business and that he could discipline me more effectively if the judge would bind me out to him till I was sixteen. The judge was willing, but there was a dispute about my age.

"While they were settling that I married a miner from Shasta County, California, and went to the gold mines with him. He was 31 and I was 15. His name was I. M. Hazlett. During the next eight years I had five children. Mr Hazlett died and I took in washing to support myself and my children.

"Several years later I married Matthew Fultz. We had three children. We moved to Farmington, Washington, and Mr. Fultz started a livery stable. He also bought a furniture store and an undertaking business and ran the hotel. He died and I had to take care of all of the different business enterprises.

"A few years after Mr. Fultz's death I married Daniel Delaney. For the past few years I have lived with my children."

Oregon Journal
December 24 and 25, 1921

Gilead Ann Jasper Irwin

Mrs. Irwin was born in Pulaski County, Kentucky, June 16, 1839. She was 14 years old, "...a woman grown, for in those days most girls were married before they were 16," when she crossed the Missouri River on May Day, 1853, with her family on their way to Oregon. She was interviewed at her home in Philomath, Oregon.

"Well, one day we had a sick cow, so we laid over half a day doctoring the sick cow. The rest of the wagon train went on. When we started to overtake the wagon train ten or a dozen Indians rode across the road, and one, who was dressed mostly in paint, said we would have to feed him and the rest of his party. My brother Andrew said, 'Get out of the way, you ugly old devil. We don't figure on feeding a pack of lazy, no-account Indians.' We started up the oxen. The Indian ran in front of the oxen and waved his arms to make them stop.

"My brother had a long-lashed ox-whip. He could hit a horsefly on the leader's horn or cut the heart out of the ace of hearts at 15 feet. He hit that ugly old Indian a crack that sounded like a pistol shot. The blood spurted where the lash cut his flesh. The Indian turned, and my brother flicked the flesh open on his shoulder. He hit the Indian six or seven times before he had a chance to mount his horse and dig his heels in and gallop away. Every time his lash landed it brought the blood.

"My mother was crying for all she was worth. She said, 'Oh, Andrew. How could you do it? The Indians will come back tonight and kill us all.'

"Andrew said, ' There's no need of your taking on, Ma. I showed those Indians what I could do with my ox whip just now. If they come back tonight I'll show them what I can do with my rifle.'

"I guess Andrew's sample of what he could do was plenty, for they never came back."

Oregon Journal
June 28, 1925

Mollie Jett

Mrs. Jett and her husband, Benjamin B. Jett, pioneer residents of eastern Oregon and Idaho, were married in 1870, "about midway between Boise, Idaho, and Huntington, Oregon." She was interviewed at her home in Portland.

"The history as it really happens, and as you read about it, isn't at all alike. For instance, you can read in history about what a blood-thirsty chief Eagan was. Eagan visited our home frequently. He was one of the wisest and most honest Indians I ever knew. Always the white people make promises to the Indians, and always they break them. Always they crowd the Indians off their land, and always there is trouble if the Indians resist.

In the fall of 1877 the Bannock Indians on the Fort Hall reservation were going hungry. They learned that Congress had appropriated money for them, but the money must have gone elsewhere, for the Indians didn't get the food. Under the treaty, Camas Prairie belonged to the Indians, but the white men herded their hogs there, which rooted up and destroyed all of the camas, on which the Indians depended for food. The Indians tried to make the herders go away, but they wouldn't do it. So the Indians fired at them and wounded them. That started the war.

"Chief Eagan told the young men that it was folly to oppose the whites, that he had talked with the other chiefs and that in every war with the whites the Indians had been defeated. But the young men felt they would rather be killed than starve to death. Buffalo Horn was the leader of the Bannocks. He had been a scout in the Nez Perce War. The Umatilla Indians were going to fight with the Bannocks, but changed their minds and fought against them. The Umatilla volunteers attacked Chief Eagan and his men, killed Eagan and nine of his warriors and took the head of Chief Eagan and the scalps of the other Indians to Pendleton.

"I felt very sad over Eagan's death. My husband had bought Chief Eagan a Henry rifle, paying $22 for it. This was before the war, when Eagan wanted the gun for hunting.

"When we lived up there, with Bannock Indians all around us, we found them strictly honest. Whenever a calf was killed or a horse stolen by some renegade white it was always blamed on the Bannock Indians."

Oregon Journal
April 24, 1934

Vittwia St. Clair Chapman Mickelson

"No, indeed, I haven't forgotten how to dance. I danced on my 83rd birthday, to celebrate the occasion.

"A good many of the young women of today are a pampered, self-indulgent lot. For the past eleven years I have lived all alone. I do my own housework, cook, bake, clean house, do my own washing, and work in the garden, so I have no time to sit around and feel sorry for myself and indulge in nerves or tantrums.

"I was never a nagger, a calamity howler, or a complainer. I have always been too grateful for health and the possession of all my faculties to moan over my sad lot. In fact, sunshine has always appealed to me more than gray clouds or weeping skies. I not only work with my flowers, but my garden comes pretty near to supporting me. I sell eggs and chickens and with the money I buy the few things that go on my table that I do not raise.

"Tell you about myself? If you listened and wrote up all the things I could tell you you would have a book instead of a newspaper article, so I Will just give you a few highlights of my life.

"My father, Samuel Chapman, was born in England, as was my mother, Sarah Smeed Chapman. I was born August 2, 1841, in Kentucky, and I was christened Vittwia St. Clair Chapman.

"My father's people were wealthy, so he spent his boyhood in travel. My father and mother spent their honeymoon in travel in Europe. They liked it so well that they put in the first year or so of their married life in seeing the sights of Paris and other European capitals and world ports. Their first baby, a little girl, died at the age of three weeks.

"From Paris my parents went to Scotland. They lived for the next eight years at Inverness or Aberdeen. Of their 13 children, 12 lived to maturity, but I am the only one now living. Two of my brothers and three sisters were born in Scotland, my next brother in England, the next brother in New York City, the next four children, including myself, in Kentucky, and the last child at Burlington, Iowa.

"My father studied art in Europe and planned to make painting his life work, but with a family of 13 children it was necessary to turn his hand to other things to bring in money to support his family. Do you remember Captain Barckley, the pedestrian, who made a tour of the world afoot—or at least that part of the world that was dry land? He was a good walker, but poor at writing, so he sent his travel notes to Father, who prepared them for the press. These articles were published in many of the larger papers in Great Britain and Europe and brought in considerable money, so that as long as the captain kept walking my father could keep writing and the money flowed in.

"After coming to America, Father met the governor of Kentucky, who employed him to go back to England and select a herd of Durham and Devon cattle for his estate in Kentucky. Father executed this commission so well that the governor employed him as his private secretary. We lived for some time at Frankfort and later at Lexington, Kentucky.

"When I was four years old we moved to Burlington, Iowa. That was in 1845. I saw there, for the first time, some Indians. I was so frightened that I ran away and hid in some standing grain and lay as still as a quail or little rabbit. I remember a few years later seeing lots of prairie schooners going westward with mottoes like these on the canvas tops: 'California or Bust,' and 'For Oregon'. That was in 1849, when I was eight years old.

"We moved back to Kentucky in the early '50's, but just before the Civil War we moved back to Iowa.

"I volunteered for service as a nurse. What I saw as a nurse is as vivid today as if it had happened last week, in place of 60 years or more ago. I was 20 years old when Fort Sumter was fired on, and, like most young women, I was anxious to do all I could for the young men who were fighting for their convictions.

"Scores and hundreds of young medical students, as well as more experienced doctors, became army surgeons, or 'contract doctors'. This last was a great mistake. In the hospitals where I served as nurse I have seen scores of times a contract doctor amputate a young man's leg or arm that could have been saved just as well as not. Frequently they would cut off a young

9

lad's leg when all he had was a flesh wound. I would assist in the operation and of course I knew how needless the amputation was, but I could only obey orders. The contract doctors at that time received $50 for every amputation and, of course, much less for merely bandaging a wound, so they usually decided on amputation, frequently explaining to me, as a justification, that gangrene might set in, so they would play safe and take off the wounded arm or leg. The soldiers called those contract doctors the 'Iowa Butchers'.

"For a while I nursed where wounded Confederate prisoners were treated, and many a young chap who had been marked to have his leg or arm amputated was spirited away through my help.

"While I was nursing at Keokuk, Iowa, a Mrs. Astone, an Englishwoman, whose husband was in the Confederate Army, appealed to me to help her join her husband. She had two small children. I secured a skiff, and, waiting for a moonless night, we launched the skiff and started down the river for St. Louis. She cared for her two babies while I rowed the skiff. We hid during the daytime and traveled at night. She found friends at St. Louis who assisted her in rejoining her husband. I made my way back up the river to Navon, and from there I made my way home, but my career as an army nurse was over, for I couldn't explain my apparent desertion from duty.

"My brother, Henry Chapman, was eight years older than I. He was born in 1833. He was a frail and sickly child, and he was never strong. I was a light sleeper, so from the time I was a little tot I slept on a pallet beside his bed so as to cover his feet at night or give him his medicine. The doctor said a complete change of climate might be beneficial to him, so, in 1853, when I was 12 years old, he and my brother Daniel started across the plains for Oregon. Daniel got a job driving a prairie schooner for Enoch Walker, while Henry, who was 20, drove a wagon for Enoch's brother, Fruit Walker. I cried because I could not go to Oregon with my brother Henry. I remember they laughed at me when I cried and said, 'Poor Henry! Who will cover his feet and give him his medicine if I do not go along?'

"On the way across the plains, one of Fruit Walker's drivers, a man named Griffiths, quarreled with another teamster and, picking up an ox yoke, tried to brain him. Fruit Walker grabbed the yoke in time to save the man from being killed.

This made Griffiths crazy with anger, so, pulling an Allen pepperbox revolver from his pocket, he shot Fruit Walker through the groin, killing him. Fruit Walker's young widow had two small children and was expecting another shortly. My brother Henry took charge for her and brought her safe through to Oregon. Shortly after she reached the Willamette Valley she gave birth to a son who, of course, never saw his father and knew of him only by hearsay. Not long after arriving in Oregon she married Fruit Walker's brother John.

"My brother Daniel Chapman settled near Ashland. Some of his children and grandchildren still reside in Jackson County. My brother Henry went to Yreka, California, to work in the mines, but his health was so impaired that he could not do hard work, so he came back to Southern Oregon and took up a donation land claim on Emigrant Creek, seven miles from Ashland.

"During the second Rogue River War, in 1855-56, Henry, with two neighbors, was out in the hills looking for hostile Indians. He saw several grizzly bears on the hillside eating service berries. Henry was a good shot. He had a hard-shooting muzzle-loading gun. He took careful aim and shot at one of the largest of the bears. It fell in its tracks. He loaded his gun and shot another bear, which made off in the direction taken by the other bears.

"Henry, carelessly, did not reload his gun, but went up to examine the dead bear, which was a huge one. Just as he got to it the bear came to and made for Henry. Henry started to run. The bear struck at him, tearing Henry's coat nearly off. Henry ran for a tree, which proved too large for him to climb. He ran toward a smaller tree, but the bear overtook him and with one blow knocked him down and tore his shoulder blade loose. The bear with one or two strokes of his claws tore Henry's clothes off.

"Henry had heard an Indian say that if a grizzly attacked you if you 'memaloosed' the bear would leave you alone, so Henry played dead. The bear had never heard that bears do not molest dead men, for he bit my brother in the loins and back so that Henry screamed from the pain. Then the bear clawed his head and turned him over to bite his neck. My brother rammed his fist into the bear's mouth. The bear crushed the bones in his hand and wrist. Then the bear bit him through the shoulder and

11

stripped the flesh from one leg from the thigh to the knee.

"The two young men with my brother heard him scream when the bear bit him in the loins, and hurried back. They shot and killed the grizzly.

"My brother was still conscious, and as they rolled the bear off him he said, 'I'll never see Mother or Father or old Kentucky again.' Then he fainted. They thought he was dead, so they tied him across his horse to bring him in for Christian burial. The motion of the horse brought him to.

"They took him to the home of 'Daddy' Wells, a nearby settler. There was no doctor nearer than Jacksonville, so one of the boys rode at full speed to get the doctor, while Daddy Wells washed my brother's wounds and with a sack needle and twine sewed the flesh that was hanging loose back into place. When the doctor came he had to rip out all the stitches so as to wash the torn flesh better.

"Henry's neck was terribly lacerated. They thought he could not live, but he kept alive day after day and at last they decided to send him to San Francisco to secure the services of a surgeon to fix his shoulder, which was so badly shattered when the bear crunched it that the local doctor could not fix it. Even the San Francisco surgeon could not restore its strength and usefulness.

"My brother proved up on his donation claim, and in 1862 went back home by way of the Isthmus. They still call the mountain where the bear and my brother had their fight, Grizzly Butte. Come out on the porch and I will point out Grizzly Butte to you.

"In 1862, because I have always had a knack of nursing and because I loved my brother dearly and was sorry for him, I took him under my wing and did for him, earning money at whatever I could find to do to support both of us.

"Henry was restless and wanted to travel, so I bought a team and light rig and we traveled all over the middle west. I acted as traveling correspondent and field editor of one of the St. Louis papers. Later I added several other papers to my list, and made good money. Henry could do light work, so he took subscriptions for the papers on a commission basis, which brought us several extra dollars daily and helped pay expenses.

"In our travels we visited Colorado. Henry thought the climate there would help him, so I landed a position as cashier at the Southern Hotel at Trinidad. Times were flush in the early '70's in Colorado. They paid me $225 a month and board.

"I was young, good-looking, and vivacious. Scores of wealthy cattlemen or miners who had struck it rich would put up at the Southern. The rates were $10 a day and up. When they paid their bills they would toss back a $5 gold piece and say, 'Keep that for yourself, Bright Eyes,' or 'Here, Sunshine, is a gold piece to remember me by'. I took in as much from tips as I received in salary or more. Quite a few of these miners and cattlemen tried their best to persuade me to quit the state of single blessedness, but I felt that my first duty was to my sick brother. I knew he would feel, in a way, as though he were playing second fiddle if I devoted my attention to any other man, either a sweetheart or a husband, so I promised to be a sister to my various ardent suitors.

"Presently Henry became restless to be on the go, so we started by team again. Henry believed we could make big money by buying a bunch of blooded cattle. Henry got in touch with a stock man who was willing to put up most of the money, so we gathered up a bunch of cattle consisting of about 200 head and started for southern Oregon. Near the base of the Spanish peaks in Colorado we ran into a lot of grief. The Utes left the reservation and began killing emigrants and settlers and burning ranch houses. A runner came and warned us. We hurried our stock into the mountains. Henry and his partner left me in charge of the stock while they went to secure help.

"I shall never forget the lonesome night I spent. The cougars and wolves were bad there, so with a six-shooter hanging in the holster from my belt and with a Winchester on my shoulder, I kept guard over the cattle all night. We decided that it would be too dangerous to try to drive the stock through the hostile country, so we drove them down into New Mexico and sold the herd at $100 a head straight through.

"The Ute outbreak enabled me to drop back into my old job as correspondent, so I sent accounts of the Indian troubles and also travel letters to the Eastern papers.

"In work of of that kind one meets many charming people. I believe two of the most delightful persons I ever met were General George A. Custer and Elizabeth Custer, his wife. They were simple, unaffected, friendly, and most charming. Mrs. Custer always called me Pussy.

13

"I saw some rough times in the late '70's at **Trinidad**, Pueblo, and Colorado Springs. The towns were wide open and a 'man for breakfast' was a common occurrence.

"In September, 1880, 44 years ago, Henry and I came to southern Oregon. We went out to Henry's place in the foothills—the claim he had taken up near Ashland in 1855—and I divided my attention between caring for Henry and raising Percheron horses. Henry died 19 years ago at the age of 72.

"In 1890, when I was 49 years old, I married Michael Mickelson. I would not have married him, but he was sick and needed careful nursing, and I could care for him better as his wife than in any other way. Ever since I served as nurse during the Civil War people who are helpless or dependent or who need nursing have made a strong appeal to me. I guess it is the maternal instinct in me.

"Mr. Mickelson was an old-time Nevada miner. He was a silversmith and also a blacksmith. In the early days in the mines he used to get as high as $10 for shoeing a saddle horse. I married Mr. Mickelson on October 14, 1890. I traveled all over California with him for his health, but he died on October 5, 1894.

"After my husband's death I ran my brother's ranch and also my husband's. They were nine miles apart and I rode from one to the other on horseback through the mountains every day to superintend the work. I bought this place and built my home in Ashland 21 years ago. Some years ago I sold both of the ranches, as I found it hard to get reliable help to run them.

"I am 83 years—I will not say old, except in experience—and as I sit here alone of an evening, I find I have plenty to think of, though, of course, I would like to have young folks of my own flesh and blood about me."

Oregon Journal
September 1-3, 1924

Sarah Elizabeth Kinney Laighton

Mrs. Laighton was born in Iowa in 1845 and came to Oregon with her family in 1847. She lived many years in the Willamette Valley. She was interviewed at her home in Seaside, Oregon.

"You ask me as I look back at my life if I would change it in any way. I sure would. I would have been a man instead of a woman. When I was a girl I used to love to ride wild horses.

In fact, I liked to do all the things a man could do without much comment, but which were considered very improper for a girl to do. When I was a girl we had no movies, no joy rides in autos, not very many parties, but plenty of housework and mending and taking care of babies and nursing and things of that kind. It seems to me that the young women of today have a much easier time than when I was a girl."

Oregon Journal
January 9, 1922

Mrs. E. A. Hunt

Mrs. Hunt crossed the plains with her family in 1850, when she was six years old. She was interviewed at her home in Portland.

"There were four of us children who crossed the plains with them (our parents) in 1850. After coming to Oregon my parents had five more children.

"While crossing the plains all of my father's oxen died but one. In the same train with us was a man named Tinsley, who also lost all his oxen but one. Mr. Tinsley and my father went into partnership, hitched the two oxen to Father's wagon, as it was the better wagon, abandoned the goods they were carrying, except their provisions, and reached Oregon. When they got to Columbia Slough, one of their two oxen died, so all my father had was a half interest in one ox and the wagon.

"Father decided to stay on Columbia Slough. He and a man named Pullin moved their families into a cabin there and went out to secure work. Father got a job splitting rails. He had worked only a day or two when he made a mis-lick with his axe and cut off all of his toes on one foot. He nearly died from loss of blood and was lame for the rest of his life.

"I was seven years old. I had to help earn money for the family. I secured a job doing housework for a woman who was sick.

"When Father could hobble around on his lame foot he came to Portland, and Jimmy Stephens gave him a job rowing a dugout across the Willamette between Portland and the east bank, ferrying passengers. Later Jimmy Stephens built the first ferryboat to ply on the Willamette, and Father ran it.

"In the fall of 1851 we moved to a place on the west slope of Mount Tabor. Our place was located in the heavy timber and I can remember how frightened we children were when the wolves came around and howled at night or when we heard the cougars screaming. My sister Harriet Julia was born in this cabin in the winter of 1851. Father would come home every Saturday night and stay till Sunday night and then walk back through the forest along the trail to his cabin on the banks of the Willamette where he lived while working on the ferryboat."

Oregon Journal
undated

Nancy Jane Fenn McPherson

Mrs. McPherson was born in Pike County, Illinois in 1840, and came across the plains to Oregon with her father, John Fenn, in 1847. She was interviewed at her home in Portland.

"When I was 15 I married William Angus McPherson. We named our first baby William Green McPherson—William for his father and Green for Green McDonald, my husband's closest and dearest friend. They loved each other like brothers. Green used to stop at our house at noon whenever he could and take dinner with us. He was strongly southern and believed slavery was a divine institution. My husband was a strong Union man. That was one subject they avoided.

"One day Green drove up to our house, looking more serious than usual. He put up his team and came in. He and Angus sat down to dinner. I had a particularly good dinner that day. Green said, 'Fort Sumter has been fired on. The South is no longer submitting to interference with its institutions by the North. I suppose you will hold with the North, Angus.'

"My husband nodded.

"Green said, 'I am for the South. If it comes to war here in Oregon, we shall be on opposite sides. I am willing to shoot the other Yankees, but I am going to fire over your head, Angus. I couldn't stain my hands with your blood.'

"Green and my husband arose, and my husband extended his hand across the table and said, 'We have come to the parting of the ways. Goodbye, old friend.' They shook hands and left the table.

"I begged them to sit down and eat a last meal together, but they were too deeply moved. For the next 30 years they met each other without a sign of recognition. They never spoke again."

Oregon Journal

Mrs. O. K. Kronenberg

Mrs. Kronenberg, daughter of Captain Judah Parker, founder of Parkersburg in Coos County, was a pioneer resident of Bandon, Oregon.

"It was easy to make a living in those days. The cougars would frequently drive the deer down to the beach and the deer would swim out beyond the breakers and not come ashore until daylight, when the cougars had gone back to the mountains. A person with a skiff could go out about daybreak and kill a deer in the water. There were deep bayous running in from the ocean. At low tide you could get a boatload of fine oysters, which were attached to the roots of the trees along the bayous. The trees along the shore were full of ducks. They had never been shot at and you could literally pick them from the trees."

Oregon Journal
December 15, 1930

Berthine Angeline Owens Adair

Berthine Angeline Owens was the name with which she was christened, We know her best in Oregon as Dr. Owens Adair. Her father, Tom Owens, was of Welsh stock, though he, as well as his wife, were born in Kentucky. They came to Oregon in the wagon train with Peter Burnett, who later became the first American governor of California.

This wagon train, with its more than 900 souls, was the first wagon train to come to Oregon. This was in 1843. The Owens family moved to Clatsop Plains, arriving at Tansey Point on Christmas Day, 1843. The entire cash capital of the family consisted of a carefully cherished half dollar. Just ten years later, Tom Owens could draw his check for $20,000 and it would be honored at the bank.

In 1848 Tom Owens and several of his neighbors built a schooner which they named the Pioneer. It was crude in the extreme. No experienced mariner would have wanted to put to sea in it, but Owens and his neighbors were accustomed to putting up with makeshifts, so they loaded their homemade schooner with bacon, pickled salmon, cabbages, potatoes, hides, hemlock bark, and cranberries, and put to sea to go to the newly discovered gold fields in California. None of them knew much about navigation, but they decided they could learn how to sail their schooner on the way south toward the Golden Gate, and they did, and what's more, they arrived at San Francisco safely and sold their cargo at top prices.

Dr. Owens Adair was married at the age of 14, as was her sister, Diana, for in those days early marriages were the rule. At 18 she was earning a living for herself and her boy by taking in washing. She studied from 9 o'clock to midnight each night and after a year of hard study passed the examination (for a teaching certificate) and secured a school which paid her $11 a month.

In addition to teaching, she paid for her little boy's keep by getting up at 4 o'clock each morning and milking the cows at the place where she stayed. She still took in washing, doing it after school and in the evenings.

From Astoria she went to Roseburg where she started a millinery store. Within 12 months she was making $1500 a year and was able to send her son to college. Having always longed for an education, she decided to go to college herself. She decided she could be more useful as a physician, but in those days, 50 years ago, it wasn't done.

She went to Philadelphia, where she spent three years, returning to Roseburg after her graduation, the first woman graduate physician on the Pacific Coast. She sent one of her younger sisters through Mills College and sent her son through medical college.

"I bought a drugstore for my son when he had finished college," said Dr. Adair, "and selling my property in Roseburg, I found I had $8000 in cash, with which I decided to go on with my medical education. Jefferson Medical College would not admit me because I was a woman, but I went through the University of Michigan, where I was graduated in 1880. Later I became resident physician there and did post-graduate work. From there I went to Paris and London and took special work in the hospitals and also in the hospitals at Berlin and Munich. Then I felt I was in a position to meet any male physician on a par so far as medical education went, and so I returned to Oregon and began practicing in Portland.

"I had discovered in my work in hospitals that it is the women who are the sufferers from bad laws, so I decided to dedicate my life to the securing of better laws and the creation of a sentiment against the double standard of morals.

"Liquor and lust are the two enemies of womanhood and when you attack womanhood, you attack childhood and our future citizens.

"Frances Villard appointed me state superintendent of heredity hygiene for Oregon. No funds were available to carry on the work, so I spent my own money as well as my own time in creating sentiment against the saloon and its evil associations.

"When I introduced my sterilization bill in the legislature of 1907 it went down to defeat. Two years later the legislature passed it and it was vetoed by the governor. In 1911 it was defeated in the legislature by what I was told was an oversight in having referred it to the wrong committee. Two years later, in 1913, it was passed by the legislature and approved and signed by Governor West. It was referred to the people and all sorts of calumny was heaped upon the bill and its author. I am so accustomed to being abused and called a pest and a crank that I was not discouraged but went to work once more to educate the public as to what the bill was and the good it would accomplish.

"In 1917 the bill was again brought up and became a law. It has been copied by many other states. Dr. Lee steiner, Superintendent of the State Hospital for the Insane says most of the 300 insane patients on whom the operation has been performed have been greatly benefited and many of them have been discharged as cured and are making their own living and are no longer a burden to the producers and taxpayers of the state.

"I have spent years of time and thousands of dollars of my own money, but in days to come the public will realize that what I have done has been of vast benefit to the state and to humanity. My last bill, Senate Bill 174, introduced at the session just closed, which provides for the examination of all applicants for marriages as to their health and mental fitness, passed the Senate with but three adverse votes and with but nine votes against it in the House. This act provides that women as well as men shall pass a physical examination before being married. The passage of the act refers the matter to the voters of the state at the next regular election, and now I am going out on a campaign of education, so that the voters will understand the measure. If the measure is understood the people will approve it. We have too many feeble-minded people in the state already. It is unfair to the coming generation to pass on to them the handicaps of subnormal mentality or bodily ills of their parents.

"The day has come when we should have better babies as well as better calves and pigs. The farmer insists on having the best possible sire for his livestock and we should see that our babies are guaranteed health and happiness by insuring that they do not have degraded or degenerate parents.

Oregon Journal
undated

Zeruiah Bailey Large

Mrs. Large was born in Springfield, Ohio, in 1836, and came to Oregon with her family in 1845. She was interviewed at her home in Forest Grove.

"My father... was a cobbler and a justice of the peace, so he could put on half soles or join souls, whichever was needed."

Oregon Journal
February 27, 1922

Mary Geisel Blake

I would like to know how many readers of The Journal were ever held captive by Indians. I don't suppose there are more than a few such persons in the state. A day or two ago I visited Mrs. Mary Geisel Blake at her home at 1604 Alameda Drive and she told me of her captivity among the Indians in 1856.

"My father, John Geisel, was born in Germany, as was my mother, whose maiden name was Christina Bucks. They met and were married at Covington, Kentucky. From there they went to Ohio and thence to Indiana. I was there first child. I was born on St. Valentine's Day, 1843, at Hamilton, Ohio.

"When I was nine years old we came across the plains by ox team and covered wagon to Oregon. There were six of us—Father and Mother, my three brothers, John, Henry, and Andrew, and myself. Father ran a grocery in Indiana, but when we came to Portland there seemed to be enough stores to take care of the trade. We rented a house on Front Street, Portland, where we lived till 1854.

"Father then decided to try his fortune in the newly discovered beach mines in Curry County, near the mouth of the Rogue River. We went aboard a steamer bound for San Francisco. In those days the steamers for San Francisco stopped at Port Orford, a place started in the spring of 1851 by Captain

William Tichenor, who left J. M. Kilpatrick, a Portland carpenter, with eight other young men, to start a town there while he went on to San Francisco with his ship, the Sea Gull. These nine men, when attacked by the Indians, took refuge on a rock jutting out into the ocean and defended themselves successfully, which desperate fight gave the rock its name—Battle Rock.

"In 1853 gold was discovered on the beach near the mouth of the Rogue River. The gold was very fine and had to be saved by catching it on blankets in the sluice boxes or on copper plates coated with quicksilver. Father took up a claim on the beach near Elizabethtown, about 30 miles below Port Orford. Other mining towns along the beach were Logtown and Ellensburg, the latter named for Captain Tichenor's daughter, Ellen. Michael Riley, Dr. Holton, Mr. Thorp, and my father were among the first to settle at Elizabethtown. There were a store and several cabins at Elizabethtown. The first stores at Ellensburg were run by Gus and John Upton and Huntley & O'Brien. Father had a rich claim and we were doing well.

"Father hired a Rogue River Indian to help with the chores on our place, which was about six miles above the mouth of the Rogue River. Mother had a sow which had a litter of little pigs. The sow and her family of little pigs had wandered off and Mother was afraid a bear or cougar would get them, so she sent our Indian helper to look for them. This was on February 22, 1856. As it was Washington's birthday, a dance in honor of the event was given at Ellensburg. In those days when a dance or other entertainment was given usually everyone in the neighborhood attended and of course took their children. Mother had planned for us to go but she did not feel well that day, so she decided not to go.

"At midnight I heard a knock on our door. Father asked who was there, and our Indian helper responded. Father opened the door and asked him if he had found the sow and her pigs. I heard Father raise his voice and protest about three other Indians who wanted to come into the house with our hired man. They began struggling. Mother heard them and ran out to help Father. The Indians were trying to kill Father with their knives. Mother grabbed at one of the Indians. She caught his knife, but the Indian pulled the knife out of her hands and the sharp blade nearly severed her little finger. One of the Indians

21

held her while the others finished killing Father.

"The Indians took Mother and me outdoors and tied us and then went back and killed my three brothers. John was nine years old, Henry seven, and Andrew five. My little sister Anna was only three weeks old. The Indians set fire to the house after they had told Mother and me to dress and for her to get her baby. They told us we must go with them to their camp, about four miles away. It was a soft, mild night and the moon was nearly full. It was almost as bright as day, though in the moonlight things did not look natural to me. While we were going along the trail to the Indians' camp the Indians stopped near a cabin and one of them stayed as a guard to see that we did not escape while the others went to the cabin and knocked on the door. A considerable number of other Indians had joined our party and they told us we must not cry out for fear we would warn the men in the cabin. They went into the cabin and killed Mr. McClusky and the man with him. It made me feel bad to stay there and hear the men cry out and then hear their groans as they were being killed.

"The Indians took us to their village and put us into a tepee and told us to go to sleep, as no harm would come to us. The Indians had captured a colored man, who, when he saw Mother's little finger, which was nearly cut off, bandaged it very skillfully. He was very sympathetic and told Mother he thought we would soon be rescued and for her not to worry. The Indians heard him telling Mother that we would soon be rescued, so one of them came up and told the colored man not to interfere in matters that didn't concern him, and he would cure him of interfering with other people's business. So he drew out his knife and killed the colored man and threw his body into the river. It made Mother and me feel very bad and forsaken, for he was so kindly and sympathetic.

"We didn't know what the Indians were going to do to us nor how soon they might become angry and kill us. They told us to eat all we wanted and not to be worried, for they would see that no harm came to us, and they were very considerate and kind to us, but that didn't bring back my father and my three brothers that they had killed. They tried to comfort us by saying that pretty soon they were going to kill all the men in the fort and they would bring all the women and children here to be company for us.

22

"We heard them talking and telling of the settlers they had already killed. They had killed Ben Wright and taken Chetco Jennie, his Indian wife, prisoner. Ben Wright was the Indian agent. They had killed Captain Poland, who was in command of the volunteers. They had killed over thirty people and burned all the settlers' cabins and stores in that part of the country. They had flour, rice, bacon, beans, sugar, tea, coffee, and other supplies they had taken from the stores, and they urged us to eat all we wanted of whatever we wanted. Each day we hoped we should be released or that the soldiers would come and rescue us. Finally, after two weeks, we saw that the Indians had decided on some course of action in regard to us, but we did not know what.

"The settlers in the fort captured a squaw. One of the settlers, Charley Brown, went out with a flag of truce to see if the Indians would trade Mother and me and the baby for the squaw. They arranged the trade and were taken to a midway point, but the Indians claimed the white men had not kept faith. They were to give the squaw and a certain number of blankets in exchange for my mother, my baby sister Anna and myself. The Indians traded Mother even for the squaw and accepted the blankets brought for the baby, but would not turn me over without additional blankets, so the conference broke up and Mother and my baby sister went to the fort with Charley Brown and I had to go back with the Indians.

"I was afraid they would be angry and kill me, but they didn't. As I slept that night all alone in an Indian tepee, my dreams were filled with dread, for I was only 13, all alone in a camp of hostiles who were planning to kill all settlers in the coast country. I was afraid they would start with me. The next day they took me near the fort and liberated me.

"You can imagine how glad I was to rejoin my mother and how worried she had been when I had to go back with the Indians. Charley Brown had met the Indians again and arranged for my release.

"We stayed in the fort till the soldiers arrived from Crescent City and Port Orford. We were taken to Port Orford, where the settlers stayed in a big house till the Indian trouble was over. Mother and Anna and I went to Crescent City, where Mother ran a boarding house for the next few years. We came back to Gold Beach and Mother ran a boarding house there. I went to school at Gold Beach to Judge M. B. Gregory and later to Frank Stewart, who later owned and edited the **Port Orford Tribune.**

"Binger Hermann, while in Congress, secured Mother a pension of $25 a month because of Father being killed by the Indians. Two young men at Gold Beach, Colma Gillispie and Charley Strahan, thought Mother had considerable money hidden in her house. They knew she had saved money and was receiving a pension of $25 a month. One night in 1896 they went to where she lived alone and broke into the house and tried to make her tell where her money was hidden. Because she would not tell they choked her to death, set fire to the house, and burned it down.

"Colma Gillispie took Mother's pension check and tried to cash it in one of the smaller Willamette Valley towns, so he was apprehended, arrested, tried, convicted, and hanged back of the courthouse at Gold Beach. He made a confession implicating Strahan. Strahan started out in a small boat with his brother and a half-breed. The boat tipped over and all were drowned.

"The next time you go to Gold Beach you can see, by the side of the road, where our house stood in 1856, a fence around a monument to my father and three brothers who were killed by the Indians. They were cremated when the house was burned by the Indians, so the settlers made four mounds for their graves and put a fence around where the house stood. You can read on the monument their names and the manner of their death."

Many years ago in Curry County I interviewed Orvil Dodge, pioneer resident of Myrtle Point, who told me many interesting details of the Indian troubles in Curry County in 1855-56.

At the time of the uprising, February 22, 1856, in Curry County, Ben Wright was Indian agent. Friendly Indians warned Wright that Enos, a Canadian half-breed who had come to Oregon with Fremont, was inciting the Indians to rise, but Wright made light of it. He didn't think the Curry County Indians would join the Rogue River Indians, On the night of the massacre of the whites an Indian chief nicknamed Josh came to one of the settlers, Mike Riley, and told him the Indians were planning to kill the settlers that night. Riley told Josh to go home and sleep it off, for he thought Josh was drunk, he was so excited. A squaw met them and also told them the Indians were to rise that night, and she began to cry, for she had married a white man and she said the Indians were going to kill him. They thought the Indian woman was lying, so paid no attention to her.

Most of the volunteer soldiers as well as practically all the settlers had gone to a dance on the Big Flat that night to celebrate Washington's birthday, so the Indians took advantage of the opportunity and killed all the settlers they found at home and burned most of their cabins.

Wright was visiting Captain Poland of the volunteer forces. The Indians killed both of them, ate Wright's heart so they would be brave like him, threw the bodies into the river, and burned the cabin. As the volunteers were returning from the dance the Indians attacked them and killed nine. The settlers took refuge in a log fort about a mile and a half north of the mouth of the Rogue River. They stocked it with supplies from their cabins and the stores were besieged for several weeks. Small parties went out at night and picked off Indians as they found opportunity. One day a party of 15 men from the fort went out to dig potatoes. They walked into an ambush and six were killed.

A boat was sent from Port Orford with six volunteers, but in coming in over the Rogue River bar the boat was overturned and four of the six were drowned. In course of time the soldiers arrived from Crescent City under Captains Augur and Ord.

The Indians took refuge in what they called "Skookum House", built against the bluff, facing the river. Ord and Augur concealed their men across the river. Captain Relf Bledsoe and Lieutenant E. H. Meservey with the volunteers, in accordance with the plans made by the army officers, attacked the Indians from the land side at daylight. The Indians took to their boats and were met with a volley from the regulars. Many were killed at first fire. The others paddled furiously down the river, only to run, at Lobster Rock, into an ambush of volunteers who shot those who escaped down the river.

Captain Tichenor was commissioned to gather the warriors who had not taken part in the Skookum House fight or the battle of Big Bend and bring them to Port Orford so they could be placed on a reservation. He secured the surrender of 19 of the warriors on the promise of safe escort to the reservation. As he passed, with his 19 captives, the blackened ruins of the Geisel house a body of settlers concealed in the brush nearby fired at the prisoners and did not cease firing till all of the 19 were killed.

Charley Brown, who had risked his life to rescue Mrs. Geisel and her 13-weeks-old baby, was given a resolution of thanks by the citizens *and later died in the poorhouse. What was everybody's business was nobody's business, so he never received a pension.*

Oregon Journal
November 10 and 11, 1925

Catherine Norville

At Baker City there is a rather interesting official record in the courthouse which reads as follows:

"The People of the State of Oregon versus Spanish Tom. Complaint filed the 21st day of November, 1862. Warrant issued same date. Defendant brought into court 22d day of November, 1862. Kelly appointed for the prosecution and McLoughlin for Defendant. Witness sworn and testified. Mob seized the defendant, dragged him through the street and hung his lifeless body on a tree. S. Abell, Justice of the Peace."

"We started across the plains for Oregon when I was 11 years old. I was born in Iowa, and we crossed the plains to Oregon about a year after the Civil War started. My brother Dave, who was about a year and a half old, and Sarah Ellen Titus, who was also a toddler, both died on Sarah River and were buried side by side.

"We stopped at Auburn, at that time a very lively mining camp, near the present city of Baker, and Father got work as a carpenter. In November, a few weeks after we had arrived at Auburn, a man called Spanish Tom killed Mr. Desmond and Mr. Larrabee in a quarrel over a game of cards. Spanish Tom got on his horse and escaped. He was arrested in Mormon Basin and brought back to Auburn.

"At about the same time we had arrived in Auburn, Baker County was organized, and Auburn was selected as the county seat. J. Q. Wilson, who, for many years thereafter made his home at Salem, was appointed county clerk, and George Hall, sheriff.

"The sheriff put Spanish Tom in a room and put guards over him, as much to keep the miners from lynching him as to keep Spanish Tom from escaping. The miners demanded that the trial be held out in the open, where they could listen to the proceedings. Sheriff Hall deputized a number of men to prevent the crowd from lynching Spanish Tom.

"Justice Abell had Spanish Tom brought out to be examined. A man named Johnson, with a lot of miners, demanded that Spanish Tom be turned over to them. Johnson stood on one stump and urged the people to lynch Spanish Tom, while Kirkpatrick stood on another stump and urged the people to let him be hanged in an orderly manner, according to law. Spanish Tom had a chain fastened around his ankle. Some of the members of the crowd grabbed the chain and began trying to pull him away from the sheriff and the deputies.

"The crowd dragged Spanish Tom from the hillside to the main street of Auburn. Someone produced a rope, which they fastened around his neck. The men holding the rope began running down the street, dragging Tom after them. They dragged him across Freezeout Gulch, threw the rope over the limb of a tree, drew him up, and left him hanging there.

"My brother John and I saw the men hang him. He wore a blue flannel shirt, overalls, and fine riding boots.

"Later the men cut him down and were going to bury him on the hill, but one of the men that was helping to take him up to the hill said, 'Oh, hell! What's the use of carrying him clear up there? Dump him in here.' And they threw him in a prospect hole."

Oregon Journal
May 3, 1928

Mrs . A . W . Martin

Mrs. Martin was born in Spring Valley, Polk County, Oregon, on June 8, 1850. She was one of 16 children born to John Phillips and Elizabeth Hibbard Phillips, who came to Oregon with their two oldest children in 1845. She was interviewed at the home of her daughter, Mrs. Ralph Tomlinson, of Portland.

"Orpheus N. was my first child. Then came Adna Gertrude, Frances Evaline, Leroy L., Vinnie, Pearl, Leo Jerome, Charles H., Mary Essie, Vivian V., John E., Chester C., and Bessie N."

Oregon Journal
September 17, 1927

Mrs. Ellis Hendricks

Mrs. Hendricks was the oldest of the 15 children in her family. She was eight years old when she came with her family to Oregon in 1847. She was interviewed at her home in McMinnville, Oregon.

"When we reached St. Joe, my father took sick, and they

didn't expect him to live. He was a very determined man, and he said since he had started for Oregon, he would keep on going till he got there, or died on the way. They fixed up a swinging bed in the wagon so he would not get jolted by the rough roads. Mother drove the wagon. He could not eat any solid food. One of the emigrants had some sheep, so they killed a sheep and Mother made some mutton broth for Father. He rode in the swinging bed six weeks, then he finally got well enough to sit in the seat. After that he mended rapidly and was soon able to do his share of the work."

Oregon Journal
March 14, 1922

Susan Means Gray

Mrs. Gray came to Oregon during the "cholera year", 1852. She was interviewed at her home in Corvallis.

"My father died when I was about three years old.

"My mother's father, Robert Irwin, crossed the plains to Oregon in 1850 to look the country over and see if it was as good as it was cracked up to be. He found it all he had hoped for, and more, so he came back to Missouri to get his folks and move to the Willamette Valley.

"With his wife and daughter, who was my mother, and her children, he started back across the plains to Oregon in 1852. When they were traveling along the Platte his wife took the cholera and died. Grandfather took the southern route, by way of Klamath Lake. While they were camped on the Humboldt River his daughter—my mother—died, of mountain fever. A few camps farther on, my brother died.

"Grandfather took care of us children and brought us through to the Willamette Valley. I was eight years old so I remember the trip vividly."

Oregon Journal
June 19, 1925

Elizabeth Sager Helm

"My father, Henry Sager, was born in Virginia," said Elizabeth Sager Helm, when I visited her recently at her home at No. 410 Salmon Street. "Grandfather Sager moved to Ohio when my father was only 9 years old. My grandfather was born in Pennsylvania. Dr. George Sager came from Switzerland, and my father's father was his oldest child. My father had four sisters and seven brothers.

"My mother's name was Naoma Carney. Her father, John Carney, was a Baptist minister. Mother was the youngest of four children—three girls and a boy. My father was 21 and Mother 20 when they were married in Ohio. Mother was a teacher. Her people came from Vermont. I have been told that her mother's maiden name was Catherine Hastings.

"I was born in 1837. My sister, Matilda Sager Delaney, who lives in Eugene, was born in 1839, the fall we moved to Missouri.

"My people settled in the Platte Purchase, five miles from St. Joe. The oldest boy in the family was John. Then came Francisco, although we always called him Frank. My next sister was Catherine, who married Clark Pringle of Salem. I was the next, born July 6, 1837. The next, Matilda Jane, was born two years later. She married Louis Hazlet. After his death she married Matthew Fultz, and when he died she married David Delaney, son of Daniel Delaney, who was killed on his farm, south of Salem, for his money, by Beale and Baker. Louisa, my next sister, died from exposure seven days after the Whitman massacre. She had measles at the time of the massacre and in the confusion of the massacre she did not receive proper care, and died. Henrietta, the baby of our family, was killed in California. Someone had a grudge against her husband and shot at him, but the bullet hit my sister and killed her.

"We started across the plains for Oregon a few months before my seventh birthday. That was in the spring of 1844. Captain William Shaw was captain of our wagon train. He and his wife, Aunt Sally Shaw, were two of the best-hearted people I ever knew.

"My father died of mountain fever while we were crossing the plains. They buried him on the banks of Green River. He was 38 years old. Mother saw the promised land, but did not reach here. I can remember that from the summit of the mountains Mother pointed toward the setting sun and said, 'Children, look to the westward. That is Oregon. That is where we are going to make our home.'

"I also remember, as we jolted along the road, Father begged to be taken out of the wagon and left by the side of the road. After Father's death Mother took the mountain fever and was sick three weeks before she died. She said to me one day: 'Now I know why your father begged to be taken out of the wagon. It seems as if it would be easier to die than to stand this jolting.' I can remember Mother calling the children to gather around her, not long before she died. She told John to keep the children together, and she told Captain Shaw to see that we were taken to Dr. Whitman's.

"I can remember, so distinctly, our camp where Mother died. They dug a grave and lined it with willow boughs, laid Mother in the grave, and then put a lot more willow boughs over her before they shoveled the earth in.

"There was an old German doctor in our train. I don't know why I call him old—he was only 34 years of age—but he seemed old to me then. He attended Mother before her death. I remember very distinctly the first time we saw Dr. Dagon. He had a German name that was hard to pronounce, so he had shortened it to Dagon. My sister Catherine fell out of the wagon and broke her leg just below the knee. That was at Fort Laramie. Father tried to locate a doctor there, but couldn't so Father set the leg. A little later Dr. Dagon, who was with the wagon train just back of us, was located, and Father sent for him. When he came to our tent and looked at Catherine's leg, he said: 'Dot is fine. It is chust so good as I could do it myself.' This was too much for us children, and we tittered, so Mother sent us from the tent. He may have talked broken English, but if there was ever a man with a heart of gold, it was this same German doctor.

"When Father died Dr. Dagon volunteered to drive the wagon and help us to Oregon. After Mother's death, Dr. Dagon took care of us children and was both father and mother to us. Little Henrietta was only five months old, so he said the women who had little children must take turns caring for her and nursing her. Henrietta was passed from one mother to another, wherever there was a mother who had a baby about her age.

"When our oxen got poor we lightened our load by leaving all of the things we could spare. We had a big Tennessee wagon, and as the grazing became more and more scarce, even this was too heavy for the jaded oxen, so Dr. Dagon cut it in two in the middle and made our wagon into a cart. One morning I heard him calling out excitedly, and when we ran to the cart we found that in getting something out of the back of the cart he had tipped the cart over and was under the cart. Fortunately, it only bruised him.

"When we reached the Umatilla River we followed it to about where Pendleton is now located. The train camped there for a day or two while Captain Shaw went to the Whitman Mission on horseback to see if Dr. Whitman would keep us children for the winter. I remember when Aunt Sally Shaw washed us up and put on our best dresses to go to Dr. Whitman's, the tears ran down her face, and she said, 'I wonder what will be the fate of you poor little orphan children.'

"Henrietta, the baby, was not with us. Mrs. Perkins had a little baby, and she was nursing Henrietta right then, and their wagon had not yet come up. As a matter of fact, Henrietta did not reach Dr. Whitman's mission till a week after we children had arrived there. Louisa Edes, whose turn it was to take care of her, brought her to the mission.

"I have had a good many narrow escapes in my life. In crossing the plains we made a dry camp one night. I was a little tot, about 7 years old. Alvira Edes, who was nearly 16, said to me the next morning, 'Let's walk ahead of the train and find a good drink of water.' We walked along the trail for a mile or two and then decided to take a short cut up a little coulee, thinking that we would possibly strike water. Instead of that we got lost and climbed one rolling hill after another, till we didn't know which direction the road was. Presently I got so tired I couldn't travel any farther and I asked Alvira to carry me, but she was tired out, too, and couldn't do it. We walked for hours in the heat of the sun until we were almost ready to give up in despair, when, to our great joy, in climbing up one of the rolling land waves, we saw, away off in the distance, the canvas covers of our wagon train; so we forgot our fatigue and hurried forward till we came to the wagons. I told my brother, who was driving the wagon, I wanted to climb in. He told me to wait until we got to the top of the next hill, and then I could ride. This was too much for me, so I sank down by the side of the road in a disconsolate heap and began to cry. He relented and got out and lifted me up into the wagon.

"Captain William Shaw rode on horseback from our camp on the Umatilla River to Dr. Whitman's and arranged to have us stay at the Whitman Mission for that winter. Captain Shaw was to call for us the next spring, the spring of 1845, and take us to the Willamette Valley.

31

"Captain Shaw drove us to Dr. Whitman's mission. There was an irrigating ditch in front of the house. Dr. Dagon stopped the cart at this ditch, and I saw, coming from the house, a tall, matronly woman, whose yellow hair had a tint of copper. It was Narcissa Prentiss Whitman. People who didn't like her said she was stuck up, said she had red hair, but she was not stuck up and she did not have red hair. She was rather reserved, and her hair was a coppery gold. She was rather plump, weighing about 150 pounds or more.

"As Mrs. Whitman came out toward our cart, she was accompanied by a little dark-haired, dark-eyed girl who was as pretty as a picture. This little girl was Helen Meek, daughter of Joe Meek by his Nez Perce wife.

"Mrs. Whitman came to the edge of the cart and began talking with Captain Shaw. Turning to Helen Meek, she said, 'Helen, run to the mill and tell the doctor to come and see my new children.' We got out of the cart and started for the house. Mrs. Whitman noticed that my sister Catherine was still lame from having broken her leg at Fort Laramie, so she took her arm to help her into the house.

"When Dr. Whitman came into the house, he smiled at once and said to Mrs. Whitman, 'Where are the boys?'

"Mrs. Whitman said, 'The little girls are going to stay with me this winter, but the boys are going through to the Willamette Valley with Captain Shaw.'

"Captain Shaw told Dr. Whitman that my mother wanted the children kept together, so Dr. Whitman said, 'If you are going to have the girls, I must have the boys.' Dr. Whitman went out to the cart, talked to Captain Shaw, and a moment or two later he came in with my brother.

"My sister Katie had washed our clothes, and we felt very prim and respectable, but when I saw little Helen Meek, so neatly dressed and with such pretty clothes, I thought our clothes didn't look very good.

"Mrs. Whitman had us all come in to supper, and Dr. Whitman walked around the table and waited on us. We had baked pork and lady finger potatoes for supper. Dr. Whitman didn't like pork, but Mrs. Whitman raised a few pigs so she would have lard with which to fry doughnuts. When they killed a hog they usually gave the meat to the emigrants and Mrs. Whitman saved the lard. When we all sat down to the table there was a table full. There were Dr. and Mrs. Whitman, Dr. Whitman's nephew, Perrin Whitman, who was about 16, David, a little half-breed Spanish and Indian boy; Helen Meek and Mary Ann Bridger, both of whom had white fathers and Indian mothers, and we seven children.

"Dr. Whitman was a very genial, kindly man. He was fond of romping with us children, and we did not feel at all in awe of him as we did of Mrs. Whitman. She did all the disciplining in the family. Dr. Whitman was fairly tall, had dark hair a little tinged with gray, blue eyes rather deeply sunk, and heavy eyebrows, and he stooped a little. He never strolled or sauntered, he always walked as if interested in getting to where he was going. He was about five feet, ten inches in height. Mrs. Whitman was about five feet, six inches.

"We went to live with the Whitmans on October 17, 1844, and they were killed on November 9, 1847, so we lived with them for more than three years. I told you the agreement was that we children were to stay at the Whitman Mission during the winter of 1844-45. We had been there only a few days when Dr. Whitman started off on horseback to overtake the wagon train and tell Captain Shaw he need not come back in the spring to get us, as he and his wife had decided to keep us. We were with the Whitmans nearly three years before we were legally adopted. You will find certain socalled historians who dispute this because we cannot produce written papers of adoption.

"I remember one evening Dr. Whitman, or 'Father', as we children called him, was making shadow pictures on the wall. He was making, with his hands, pictures of rabbits, faces and various animals, when I noticed his fingers were crooked. I said, 'Father, what makes your fingers so crooked?'

"He spread out his fingers, looked at his hands, and said, 'They are pretty crooked, aren't they? I did that when I went back to see the great Webster.'

"One of the other children said, 'Who was Webster, Father, and why do you call him great?'

"Although I was a little girl at the time, I can see the scene as plainly as though it happened last week. Dr. Whitman was sitting there, with us children gathered around him. He had my sister Henrietta, who was only two years old at the time, on his lap. He said, "Webster is a great man. He is the one who helps the President decide questions and enforce the laws.'

"In the fall of 1847, two months before the massacre, Dr. Whitman drove down to the Willamette Valley to attend to some business matters there and also to get supplies. He drove a team of horses, while my brother John went along to drive the ox team. They brought back eight kegs of sea island sugar and a small machine to separate the grain raised at the mission, as well as a large number of bolts of calico and other cloth.

"When Dr. Whitman was at Salem on this trip he went out to Howell Prairie to see Captain Shaw. Captain Shaw told me about his visit many years later. He told Captain Shaw that he was going to adopt us and change our names to Whitman, on account of property rights. Captain Shaw told him that he had known our father, Henry Sager, well and respected him greatly and that it didn't seem right to change his children's name.

"Dr. Whitman said, 'We are going to adopt the girls and we thought it would be best to change their name to Whitman, but since you feel as you do about it, we will let them retain their own name of Sager.'

"This, as you know, was only two or three months before the massacre. Dr. Whitman had arranged to buy the property of the Methodist Mission at The Dalles for $600. Mrs. Whitman's sister, Miss Jane Prentiss, was coming out to be a teacher. She was expected that fall. A few weeks before the Indians killed Dr. and Mrs. Whitman, Mrs. Whitman was cleaning the house very thoroughly. Usually she cleaned it in the spring, so I said to her, 'This isn't spring. Why are you cleaning the house now, Mother?'

"She said, 'Don't you know we are looking for your Aunt Jane to come soon?'

"When Dr. Whitman went east in the winter of 1843 to get emigrants to come to Oregon, he visited his wife's sister, Clarissa, and tried to get her to join the emigration to Oregon. Her name is now Mrs. Clarissa Kinney. I visited her at her home in California some years ago and she told me how active Dr. Whitman was in urging his old friends and neighbors to emigrate to Oregon.

"Mary Ann Bridger was the only one in the kitchen when Dr. Whitman was killed. She told me that it was Telekout and his son Edward who killed Dr. Whitman. She said to me, 'After they killed Father, I jumped behind the stove. When they went out I climbed out of the window, climbed a fence there, and

34

came around to the front door. I ran in and said to Mother, 'They have just killed Father.'

"The morning of the massacre I heard Dr. Whitman say to Mr. Kimball, who had come into the kitchen, 'Yes, the situation looks pretty dark, but I think I shall be able to quell any trouble.' A few hours later one of the best friends the Indians ever had was dead by their own hands.

"My brother had shot a beef for the use of those at the Mission. After shooting it he came into the house to go to school. Nathan S. Kimball and Jacob Hoffman were skinning the beef and cutting it up. This was Monday morning. The school had been closed for some days on account of the measles, but it had started up again.

"Mary Ann Bridger, the half-breed daughter of Jim Bridger the scout, was working in the kitchen. Two Indians, Telekaut and Tamsuky, came to the kitchen door and, walking into the kitchen, asked for Dr. Whitman. Dr. Whitman came out into the kitchen, shutting the door into the next room, where Mrs. Whitman was feeding my sister, Henrietta. My brother, John Sager, was sitting in the kitchen winding some twine. The two Indians began talking to Dr. Whitman.

"Mary Ann told me that Telekaut was the one who killed Dr. Whitman and that Tamsuky shot and killed my brother. Mary Ann jumped behind the stove and then, running around the side of the house, came and told Mrs. Whitman that the Indians were killing Dr. Whitman.

"In a moment everything was in confusion. The children were terrorized, though Mrs. Whitman seemed calm. Mr. Kimball, holding one arm, which had been shot and from which the blood was running, came running into the room and said, 'The Indians are killing us. I don't know what the d...d Indians want to kill me for. I never did anything to them. Get some water.'

"Mrs. Whitman got a pitcher of water for him. Mr. Kimball was a religious man and ordinarily would not have sworn, but he was very much excited. Serious as the situation was, I giggled when he said, 'I don't know what the d...d Indians want to kill me for,' for I knew Mrs. Whitman would reprove him for swearing, particularly in the presence of the children.

"Mrs. Whitman and Mrs. Hall brought Dr. Whitman into the sitting room. Mr. Rogers had come in and said, 'Is the doctor dead?'

"Dr. Whitman answered, 'No.'

"Mrs. Whitman went to the fireplace to get some ashes to stop the bleeding in the doctor's head where he had been struck with a tomahawk.

Looking out of the window, I saw the Indians shooting and I said, 'Mother, they are killing Mr. Saunders'. The upper part of the door in the sitting room was of glass. Mrs. Whitman came to the door and looked out.

"An Indian that we called Frank was standing on the schoolroom step and, seeing Mrs. Whitman looking out, shot at her, the bullet striking her in the shoulder. My sister, Katie, stooped over Mrs. Whitman, who had fallen to the floor, and tried to help her up. Mrs. Whitman said, 'Go and take care of the sick children, Katie. You can do nothing for me.' In the room where Dr. and Mrs. Whitman were, were myself and my four sisters, with Mary Ann Bridger, Helen Meek, Mrs. Hall, Mrs. Hays, Miss Bewley, and Mr. Kimball.

"When Mrs. Whitman was wounded, she began praying out loud. She said, 'Lord, save these little ones.'

"Dusk came early and as the Indians began breaking the windows, Mrs. Whitman thought we had better go upstairs to Miss Bewley's room. Mr. Rogers helped Mrs. Whitman go upstairs. While Mrs. Hall and those who could helped carry the sick children up to Miss Bewley's room, Mrs. Whitman lay down on the foot of the bed.

"Mrs. Whitman said to Mr. Rogers, 'There is a gun barrel in the corner. Hold the end of the muzzle of the gun barrel over the top of the stairs so the Indians will think you have a gun.'

"The Indians broke into the house and mutilated Dr. Whitman and my brother. The Indians then broke the door to the upstairs room and Tamsuky called to Mr. Rogers to come on down, that he would take care of us. Mr. Rogers told him to come on up, but when Tamsuky saw the gun barrel, he was afraid.

"Finally, Mr. Rogers went downstairs and talked to Tamsuky and Joe Lewis. Tamsuky told Mr. Rogers that the Indians were going to burn the house and that he wanted to save Mrs. Whitman and the others. Aunt Lucinda Bewley, who was Mrs. Whitman's hired girl, and Mr. Rogers, helped Mrs. Whitman downstairs. She said to me, 'Come with me, Elizabeth.' When we got into the dining room she said, 'Stay close to me.'

"Mrs. Whitman was so weak from loss of blood that she lay down on the sofa. Aunt Lucinda put a pillow under her head and then got a white blanket which she put over her. Joe Lewis put his gun by the kitchen door and took the foot of the sofa to help carry Mrs. Whitman out. When Mrs. Whitman saw Joe Lewis she said, 'Oh, Joe. You too?'

"They carried Mrs. Whitman on the sofa, through the kitchen door. Just before they had gone out, one of the Indians had told my brother, Francis, to go along with Mrs. Whitman. As we went out of the kitchen, Joe Lewis dropped his end of the sofa, on which Mrs. Whitman was lying and at the same time the Indians standing around fired. Mr. Rogers raised his hands and said, 'Oh, my God,' and fell. My brother also fell and Mrs. Whitman, who was shot through the cheek and through the body, fell off of the lounge onto the muddy ground.

"When the Indians fired at Mrs. Whitman as Joe Lewis and Mr. Rogers were carrying her out of the house, I ran back into the house. I saw my brother fall and also Mr. Rogers, and I saw Mrs. Whitman roll off the lounge on which they were carrying her and fall on the muddy ground. My sister Mathilda also saw the killing of these three. She said she saw one of the Indians reach down, catch Mrs. Whitman by the hair, and raise her head and then strike her across the face several times with his leather quirt.

"We children stayed upstairs that night in the house where Dr. Whitman had been tomahawked. He lived for some time, for he was breathing heavily when Mrs. Whitman was carried out to be killed. Mr. Kimball had been overlooked by the Indians. He was suffering from his wound. He also stayed in the upper room with us that night.

"The children who were sick cried for water during the night, so early the next morning I went down to see if I could get some water. The body of Mrs. Whitman was lying near the kitchen door. The body of Mr. Rogers was lying not far away. I saw Edward Telekaut and asked him if he would get some water for me. He got a bucket of water and brought a dipper. As the Indians seemed to have quit their killing, I decided to go over to the Mansion House and see what was going to become of us. Mrs. Saunders met me and said, 'The Indians have promised not to kill us.' At about 10 o'clock that morning my sister Katie took the children over to the Mansion House. Helen Meek was the last to be taken over. When Katie came back for her Helen was crying as though her heart would break, for she thought she had been left.

"We stayed at the Mansion House a month. Eliza Spaulding understood the Indian language and I did also, but not so much as Eliza. Joseph Smith and James Young worked at the mill, grinding wheat for the Indians. The Indians had Eliza stay at the mill to interpret for them. I stayed with Eliza most of the time. It was cold in the mill, so we dug a hole in the straw stack near the mill and put a blanket in front of it. Eliza and I crawled in there, where we would be out of the wind, and when the Indians wanted us they would come and raise the blanket and tell Eliza to come and talk for them.

"During that month (December, 1847) the women made up several bales of calico and flannel into shirts for the Indians.

"One day Edward Telekaut came in. He had taken a bedpost and trimmed it up to use for a war club. Eliza Spalding and some of the older children were in the room where Crockett Bewley and Amos Sales were lying in bed. Crockett Bewley had typhoid and Amos Sales was also sick. Edward raised his club and hit Crockett Bewley on the head. We children screamed and ran out of the room. Edward came out and told us we must come back. The Indians with Edward beat Amos Sales and Crockett Bewley over the head till they had killed them, and then they dragged their bodies out into the yard.

"The next day Joe Stanfield, who had worked for the Whitmans several years, came with a wagon and a yoke of oxen and took the bodies away and buried them. Some days after that Joe came to the Mansion House and said the wolves were digging up the bodies of Dr. Whitman and Mrs. Whitman and the others. I went with Joe, because my brother was buried with Dr. Whitman, Mrs. Whitman, and Mr. Rogers. I noticed that he had buried Crockett Bewley and Mr. Sales in another place. Their heads were pointing to the south. I asked Joe why he had buried Mr. Bewley and Mr. Sales in a different place from the others. He said, 'Because it was easier digging there.' He had dug a grave about three feet deep.

"Joe showed me where the wolves had eaten all the flesh from Mrs. Whitman's leg from the knee to the ankle. He shoveled the grave full of dirt. Later the wolves dug up all of the bodies and when the Oregon soldiers came from the Willamette Valley they put them into a new grave near the grave of little Alice Whitman, the daughter of Dr. and Mrs. Whitman. Later, the bodies were taken up and buried in a casket, and a monument was put over them.

"On the day of the massacre, Mrs. Saunders went to the lodge of Nicholas Finley, a French halfbreed, who, with his Indian wife and family, lived in his tepee not far from the mission. He had been working for Dr. Whitman prior to the massacre. Donald Manson had gone to the Frenchman's lodge. Mrs. Saunders decided to go there and see if she could get Finley to intercede with the Indians for the lives of those who had not been killed. Steve Manson and Donald Manson were there and acted as interpreters. She told Telekaut that if the Indians would not kill the women and children the women would sew for them. Telekaut and the other Indians talked it over and consented.

At the time of the Whitman Massacre there were 72 persons living at or near the mission. Eleven of this number were sick in bed at the time. Of the 72 people 13 lived at the sawmill on Mill Creek, 18 lived in the home of Dr. and Mrs. Whitman, 27 were staying in what was called the Mansion House, and others were staying in other buildings. Of the 72 persons, 42 of them were children.

At the time of his death, Dr. Marcus Whitman was 44 years old. His wife was 39. Mrs. Helm's oldest brother, John Sager, was 17. Her other brother was 15. Her sister Katie was 13. She herself was 10, her sister Mathilda was 8, Louise was 6, and Henrietta, the baby, was 4. Eliza Spalding and Helen Meek were 10 years old. In addition to the above, the following persons were living at the Whitman Mission: Mr. and Mrs. Joseph Smith and their children, Mary, Edwin, Charles, Nelson, and Mortimer; Mrs. Rebecca Hayes and her 4-year-old son, Henry. Mr. and Mrs. Peter D. Hall and their children, Gertrude (now Mrs. O. N. Denny), Mary, Ann, Rebecca, and Rachel, the latter a babe in arms; Mr. and Mrs. L. W. Saunders and their children, Phoebe, Alfred, Nancy, and Mary; Mr. and Mrs. Nathan S. Kimball and their children, Susan, 3yron, Sarah, and Mina; Mr. and Mrs. Elam Young and their sons, Daniel and John; Mr. and Mrs. Josiah Osborne and their children, Nancy, John, and Alexander; Mr. and Mrs. William D. Canfield, and their children, Ellen, Oscar, Clarissa, Sylvia, and Albert; Crockett Sewley and his sister Lorinda; Mr. Marsh and his ll-

year-old daughter, Mary; Isaac Gilliland, Amos Sales, Jacob Hoffman, Andrew Rogers, Mary Ann Bridger, Donald Manson, Steve Manson and Joseph Stanfield, Joe Lewis and Nicholas Finley, half-breeds; James Young and David Malin.

In a letter written not long before her death to her sister Jane, Mrs. Whitman, in writing of her husband, said: "Marcus is almost always on the move. A head and heart more full of benevolent plans, and hands more ready in the execution of them for the good of the poor Indians and the white population of the country, you have probably never seen."

As soon as Peter Skene Ogden had received word by courier from Fort Walla Walla of the Whitman Massacre he started by rowboat up the Columbia River to rescue the captives held by Telekaut and his fellow murderers. Arriving at Fort Walla Walla, he summoned a council of Indians and secured the release of the captives by giving the Indians blankets, shirts, handkerchiefs, guns, tobacco, and other trade goods. The captives left Waiilatpu (the Whitman Mission) for Fort Walla Walla on December 19, 1847, after a month's captivity. After more than 11 years work for and among the Indians, Dr. and Mrs. Whitman were left buried in shallow graves to be the prey of the skulking coyotes and the timber wolves. The captives had not been gone long when the Indians burned the mission buildings.

In the spring of 1850 a jury composed of J. D. Hunsaker, A. Jackson, Hiram Straight, William Parrott, William Carson, A. Post, Sam Welch, A. Cohen, Joe Alfrey, John Dinman, John Ellenburg, and A. B. Holcomb, found the Indians who had given themselves up "guilty as charged" and Chief Telekaut, Tamahas, Quaimashouskin, Isaiachhilakis, and Klakamas were hanged at Oregon City.

"We went down the Columbia River in open boats. We reached Fort Vancouver Friday afternoon. Mr. Douglas was at the fort. We children and Eliza Spalding stayed with Mrs. Douglas. We stayed there till Monday. Mrs. Douglas offered to keep me, as I could help her with her children, but Reverend Spalding, who was along, refused to let me stay, because they were Catholics, and he was down on Catholics.

"Monday we started for Oregon City. At Portland a lot of men had come down to the wharf and when they saw us coming they fired a salute. We children tried to hide in the bottom of the boat, for we thought they were going to kill us. Captain Shaw and Colonel Gilliam reassured us and told us they were only firing the guns in our honor.

"At Green Point, Mr. Spalding and his family and myself and the rest of us Sager children got off the boat and stayed at Governor Abernethy's house. The others went on to Oregon City. Mrs. J. Quinn Thornton offered to take my baby sister, Henrietta, if she could also have my older sister, Katie. Mrs. William Roberts wanted Katie, but she did not want little Henrietta. She told Mrs. Thornton that probably her husband, J. Quinn Thornton, would be angry with her if she took the children and she thought it would be better if she herself took Katie and Henrietta, so Mrs. Thornton let her have them.

"I went to stay for a little while with Mr. and Mrs. William Johnson. Their daughter Mary, who later became Mrs. Clymer, had worked for the Whitmans awhile. Hezekiah, Johnson's daughter suggested that I go and stay with Mrs. Howland, who had recently lost her daughter. Mrs. Robb, however, wanted me, so I stayed with the Robbs. In the winter of 1848-49, Mr. Robb and William Abernethy went to the California gold mines. While they were gone Mrs. Robb and her two children and I stayed at the Abernethy home. The next summer we stayed with her father, Reverend Parrish, at Parrish's Gap, south of Salem. The next fall Mr. Robb decided to take his family to California, so Mrs. Robb got Mrs. W. H. Willson, for whose husband Willson Square in Salem is named, to take me. J. K. Gill married one of Mrs. Willson's daughters.

"I worked for the Willsons for a year. During that time I attended the Oregon Institute. For a time Mr. Fackler was my teacher and later Nehemiah Doane and F. S. Hoyt were my teachers. After staying for a year with the Willsons I went to work at the home of J. L. Parrish. Mrs. Parrish at that time was slightly deranged, but most of the time she was very good to me. Later she lost her mind entirely.

"My sister Katie married Clark Pringle, so, shortly after their marriage, I went to live with them.

"When I was 16 I went to a campmeeting on the Calapooia River. There I met a young man, William Helm, the son of Reverend William Helm. He began coming to see me, and we kept company. We were married at my sister's home. Reverend J. L. Parrish performed the ceremony. We were married August 9, 1855, 68 years ago. My father-in-law, Reverend William Helm, gave us a piece of land near the Looney Ranch, 12 miles from Salem. About a year later we moved to a farm in Linn

County, four miles from Lebanon, where we lived 17 years. From there we moved to a ranch on McKay Creek, near Prineville. After living there eight years, we sold our place and moved to a farm 22 miles from The Dalles. We lived on that place 13 years, after which we moved to The Dalles, where we lived four years. From The Dalles, I moved to Portland.

"I have had nine children, all of whom are living but my son Charles, who was accidentally killed."

Oregon Journal
July 23-27, and
September 4-6, 1923

Martha Ann Cooper Frum

Mrs. Frum, one of the First residents of Arlington, was born in Linn County, Oregon, in 1849. She was interviewed at her home in Arlington.

"My husband was born in Illinois in 1847. He crossed the plains when he was five years old. While crossing the plains a wagon wheel passed over him and depressed his breastbone. This caused his heart to shift to the right side."

Oregon Journal
September 9, 1935

Elvina Apperson Fellows

"When we reached Portland in the fall of 1847, there was a group of log cabins near the river bank and one frame house, which was owned by Captain Crosbie. The boards for this frame house were brought from Maine, around the Horn.

"I was born in Neosho, Missouri, May 20, 1837. I was one of ten children. My brother, Jacob Apperson, who lives near Dayton on a farm, and myself are the only two of the ten children still alive.

"My father, Beverly Apperson, was born in Virginia. My mother, Jane Gilbert Tubbs, was born in Tennessee. They were married in Missouri along about 1830.

"Father died on the way across the plains. He died at the second crossing of Ham's Fork. We had two wagons, so Mother had the men take the wagon bed of one of them to make a coffin. She abandoned the running gear, ox yokes, and some of our outfit, and we finished the trip with one wagon. They dug a grave in the middle of the trail and buried Father and when the grave was filled they corraled the oxen over the grave so the Indians would not find it and dig up the body to get the clothes. No, we couldn't put up a headboard, and after a few hundred wagons and the long strings of oxen and loose cattle had passed over it, I doubt if we could have located the grave.

"We came by way of The Dalles and over the Cascades by the newly opened Barlow Route, and it was a fierce road. The oldest child, William Poindexter, had died before we started, so when we reached Portland our family consisted of my mother and nine children. Mother was in her early thirties. There was Sarah, who married at 15 a man named Jenkins, went to California with him in 1849 and soon died. Then there were John and Harriet, myself, Albert, Julia, Susan, Jacob, and Milton, the baby.

"Mother had no money and had nine hungry mouths to fill in addition to her own, so she would go to the ships that came and get washing to do. She soon had all the washing she could handle, and so we got along. Then she started a boarding house. She bought a house and lot on Second Street between Washington and Stark.

"In 1851 Mother was pretty hard run to earn enough money for us to live on, so when a man named Julius Thomas, a cook in a restaurant, offered to marry me, Mother thought I had better take him, so I did. He was 44 and I was 14.

Back in 1851—that is, 70 years ago—we had slavery of Negroes in the South, and we had slavery of wives all over the United States, and saloons wherever there were enough people to make running one pay. What could a girl of 14 do to protect herself from a man of 44, particularly if he drank most of the time, as my husband did? I still shudder when I think of the years of my girlhood, when I had to live with that husband. When he was drunk he often wanted to kill me, and he used to beat me until I thought I couldn't stand it.

"One time he came to my mother's house, where I had taken refuge. I locked the door. He tried to climb in at the window, but I held it down. This enraged him so, he took out his pistol and shot at me. The bullet passed just above my head. The glass fell on me and scared me so I dropped to the floor. He looked in, saw me lying on the floor, and, thinking he had killed me, put the end of the pistol barrel into his mouth and pulled the trigger and I was a widow.

"Mother got tired of trying to meet life alone, so she married an old man who lived at Oregon City. He wanted her to support him, for he claimed he was too old to work, so Mother died pretty soon and the old man she married claimed her property, but pretty soon he died and we children got it.

"When I was about 20 I married a fine man—Edward Fellows. He was a steamboat engineer. Maybe you have heard of him. He worked for the Peoples Transportation Company. He died at McMinnville 14 years ago.

"I used to go to school, in 1848, in the schoolhouse in the woods on Clay Street. Virginia McNamee was my chum. Her father, Job McNamee, was a dairyman. Not long after the close of the Civil War the McNamees moved to Pacific City. He died here in Portland in 1872.

"My brother, who went with my sister to California, got a rich claim in the gold diggings, but, while he was sick with erysipelas, a man jumped it and made a fortune from it. My brother, John Apperson, was a steamboat captain on the Willamette. Maybe you met him in the old days. My adopted daughter Cynthia lives here in Portland. My adopted son is dead."

Oregon Journal
undated

Emma Sodergrin Erickson

"My maiden name was Emma Sodergrin. I was born in Sweden in 1847. When I was 19 I came to this country. I came to live with my sister in Mendocino County, California.

"When I came to Bandon, 48 years ago, there was but one other cabin here, and that was occupied by John Lewis, who ran a scow ferry across the Coquille River. I was married when I was 23. When my husband and I, with our three children, came to Bandon we moved into a small log cabin, 12 x 14 feet in size, and lived there for two years. We got all the supplies we used by schooner from San Francisco. We were the first family to settle in Bandon.

"John Lewis told me he wanted to sell out the ferry. W. H. Averill, who had a farm near Langlois, was here one day—this was about 1886—and I suggested that he buy Mr. Lewis' claim as well as the ferry. He said he would think it over. He came back later, saw Mr. Lewis, and he and Mr. Alberson bought the ferry and the claim from Mr. Lewis, Later Mr. Averill bought his partner, Alberson, out and sold a half interest in the claim and the ferry to George Dyer of Empire City. Later they divided their interests, Mr. Dyer taking the townsite. In those days Bandon was called Coquille Ferry. In 1873 George Bennett, with his sons Joseph and George and also a young man named George M. Sealy, came to Empire City direct from Bandon, Cork County, Ireland. Mr. Bennett was the one who suggested that the name of Coquille Ferry be changed to Bandon.

"A few people began coming in after we settled here, but not many of them had children. I had three children, and I wanted them to have the advantages of a school. I traveled up and down the Coquille and Coos Rivers, getting settlers to sign a petition for a school. The county school superintendent lived on Coos River. I went to see him and he promised to help me.

"You couldn't get any money from the county till the school was already established and running, so we took around a subscription paper and raised money to start the school. The settlers felled some trees and built a schoolhouse for me, and one of the men built a clay fireplace with a stick-and-daub chimney. I made windows out of flour sacks. They made split-log benches and split up a cedar tree from which they made a desk. I hired a squawman named Meacham to teach a three months' term of school at $30 a month. We finally started a school with 13 children. My two boys were the only white children in the school. The other 11 children were half-breeds. My son Axel, who is a gray-haired man and lives in Bandon, was of school age. Ernst, my other boy, was only 5 years old, but I sent him to school so we could draw school money for the support of the school. After the first three months the children drew money from the county. The first lock and key that was used in this county was the one I bought for the schoolhouse.

"There was no church here in those days. Occasional services were held from the top of Tupper Rock. It was a regular pulpit. Later this rock was used to help make the jetty.

"The first church to be started here was a Catholic church. Next was a Presbyterian church. Then came the North Methodist Church and the Methodist Church, South. I helped raise money for all four of them. We women gave entertainments, church socials, and took around the subscription papers to get these different churches started.

"Later my husband and I took up a ranch on which we lived for seven years. We then came back to Bandon, bought a home here, and I have lived here ever since. I am a charter member of the Rebekahs, which was organized 39 years ago. Of the eleven charter members I am the only one that still belongs to the lodge. Most of the others are dead.

"Axel, my oldest boy, lives in Bandon. Ernst lives in Nevada. Joe, my next boy, also lives at Reno. My daughter Hilda is married and lives in San Francisco."

Oregon Journal
May 8, 1927

Mary Emma Marquam Kelly

Mrs. Kelly was born in Portland, Oregon, in 1854, in her family home in the heart of what is now Portland's main business district. She was interviewed at her home, on East Franklin Street, in Portland.

"One experience I had when I was a little tot going to school has always remained very vivid in my memory. One day, when Rambo apples were in their prime, my brother Will and I stopped at the Kelly farm, where the Reverend Albert Kelly had just slaughtered a beef animal. The driveway of the barn was open, and the beef was suspended in the driveway. Mr. Kelly was skinning the beef. We were surprised and horrified, for we had never known before that people killed cows.

"When my brother Will saw the cow's head lying on the ground and learned that Mr. Kelly had killed it, he went up to Mr. Kelly and kicked him on the shin as hard as he could, for killing the cow. Mr. Kelly asked him why he kicked him, and Will answered, 'Because you killed that poor cow.'

"Mr. Kelly said, 'Don't you like beefsteaks?'

"Will said, 'Yes, I like them.'

"Mr. Kelly said, 'Didn't you know that we have to kill cows to get beefsteaks for you?'

"Will was thunderstruck, for he had never realized that beefsteaks came from cows. We went home and Will hurried in to tell Mother of what he had seen. He said, 'Mr. Kelly killed a cow. He was peeling it when we were there. Do they have to kill cows to get beefsteaks?'

"The next morning Gus and Will and started for school. I

was carrying our lunch in a basket, while Gus and Will were riding stick horses. As we went along the trail we met a big brown dog. It came up to us and sniffed at us. Gus hit him with the stick he had been riding, and said, 'Get out of our way, you big ugly dog!'

"It jumped to one side and made a funny face at Gus. I felt sorry for it, so I walked up to it and patted it on the head. As I patted it, it made bread with its paws, like a cat does, and purred as loud as a coffee mill. I said, 'Why, it's a cat.'

"Gus laughed and said, 'It's a dog. Did you ever hear of a cat as big as that?'

"It wanted to smell the lunch I was carrying, and kept putting its nose into the basket. I had to hold the basket over my head, and it reached up and bumped the bottom of the basket with its nose. Suddenly it stopped, threw its head up, listened, sniffed, and then gave a sudden jump and lit on a snag, and ran up the trunk of a fallen tree, where it could look in all directions. It leaped from the tree to the ground and disappeared, and a moment later Albert Kelly, Silas Kelly, and his son and their little dog Fiddle met us on the trail. Gus said, 'We met a big brown dog.'

"I said, 'It wasn't a dog. It was a big cat.'

"Mr. Kelly told us to show him the tracks of the cat. We showed him where it had walked all around us, and where it had put its claws in and out when it was 'making bread', and I patted it. They had guns and immediately started after it. Mr. Kelly said, 'That is the largest cougar track I have seen for a long time. Thank God that cougar ate nearly a quarter of the fresh beef that was hanging in my barn or you children wouldn't be here to tell about patting it on the head.'

"That evening when we went home we told Mother about the big cat we had met in the road and how I had patted it on the head. She said, 'Run along and play, and don't bother me.'

"A week or ten days after that Mrs. Kelly visited my mother and said, 'Weren't you nearly frightened to death when Gus hit that big cougar and Mary patted it on the head?'

"My mother said, 'This is the first I've ever heard of it.'

"She called us in and asked us, and told her we had told her about patting the big cat. She remembered about it, but at the time she had attached no importance to it, not realizing that the big cat was a cougar. After that, Mother went with us to the

47

brow of the hill, and met us there after school. Not long after that, Mr. Murhardt, a commission merchant in Portland, treed this cougar and killed it."

Oregon Journal
April 7, 1922

Mary Dunn

"We crossed the plains from East Tennessee to the Willamette Valley in 1852. I was 16 years old at the time, so of course I remember the trip vividly.

"We got to the Snake River in the evening. The men unloaded the wagons and calked the wagon beds and next morning rigged up oars or sweeps and rowed the wagon beds across the river to carry the household goods and the women and children. A man on horseback started across and called 'Sookey, sookey,' to the oxen and cattle and they followed him across the river.

"Father took over the first load of our goods in the morning, then took Mother and my younger sister over to watch them. With another sister I stayed on the opposite bank, sitting there all day in the hot sun before the rest of our goods were taken over. Father had been busy superintending the crossing and helping others, so it was dusk before he came to get my sister and me and our few remaining possessions. When we were about half way across he took a cramp in his arm and couldn't row, so we floated down the river for a mile and finally grounded on a sandbar. Father sent my sister and me up the river, where we could see the campfires a mile away, to summon help. The men came down with a long rope, fastened it to the wagon bed and 'lined it' up the river to the camp.

"We had a pretty hard time at what they called the Devil's Backbone, now known as Laurel Hill. When we came to The Dalles, 48 of the wagons in our train went down the Columbia, but 12 wagons, including our own, decided to come by the

Barlow Road. They rough-locked the wheels, cut a tree down to drag back of the wagons to serve as a brake, and let one yoke of oxen go ahead to pull the wagon down the hill, unhitching the others and leading them. Of course the women and children all walked. Two days before we made the descent of Laurel Hill an emigrant who was rather set refused to unyoke his oxen. He said his oxen could hold back the wagon on any hill. The wagon bed pitched forward and killed the man and one of his wheelers.

"As Father had traveled from Salem to the mines in northern California in the spring of 1850, he had selected a donation land claim, though, of course, he had not taken it up. It was located in the foothills of the Siskiyous, just south of Ashland. We wintered in Salem in 1852 and in February, 1853, started for southern Oregon. The stream was so high through the canyon beyond Canyonville that we couldn't go through with our wagon. Father left the wagon at Canyonville, rented a cabin for us, and he and my brother Cicero drove our cattle on through the canyon and down into Jackson County. Curiously enough, the very place Father had selected for his donation land claim was taken up by Pat Dunn, a man that we had never seen or heard of, but whom I subsequently married, so we kept the place in the family, after all. Father took up a place about two and a half miles farther south. He and Cicero built a log cabin and then came back and got us. This was in April. The canyon was still impassable for wagons, so we went to our home in southern Oregon on horseback. Father took up 640 acres at what is now known as the Kingsbury place. My son, George Dunn of Ashland, still owns this place.

"We girls were the first women to settle in that neighborhood. Barron, Russell, and Gibbs lived at the Mountain Place. Fred Alberding, Pat Dunn, and Tom Smith had a place two miles from the Mountain Place. All the men in the neighborhood called to see us. The first provisions we secured were packed in from Crescent City. They consisted of flour, sugar, dried fruit and coffee, and came from South America. It was cheaper to bring them from South America than to bring them from Oregon City.

"Father, as I told you, had taken his stock into southern Oregon. We had about 40 milch cows. We three girls milked them and Mother made butter, which was sold to the miners at

$1 a pound.

"In July, 1853, some young men from Yreka brought saddle horses and invited us girls to take a trip to Yreka, where they were going to have a big dance. They knew my aunt, Mrs. Eben Kelly, who lived there. We started at nine in the morning, rode over the Siskiyous over the trail, and reached Yreka at sunset. The streets were lined with miners who had heard we were coming and wanted to see us. We stayed at my Aunt Louise Kelly's for several days and it was a continuous reception all the time we were there. A young jeweler gave me a pair of ear-rings he made from Yreka gold dust. He pierced my ears and put the ear-rings in. That was 75 years ago, and I have never had them out of my ears since. He gave my sister Ann, now Mrs. Russell of Ashland, a pair of ear-rings, and my sister Martha a gold ring.

"On February 22, 1854, I was married to Patrick Dunn. Reverend Myron Stearns, a Baptist minister, married us. The winter before, my husband's partner, Mr. Alberding, had sold his half of the claim to Judge J. C. Tolman, so Mr. Dunn built a cabin on his half. We moved into this cabin, where my first three girls were born.

"My husband was born in Wexford County, Ireland, March 24, 1824. He came to the United States when he was four years old. They settled in Philadelphia. In 1841 he went to Illinois, where he worked in a grist mill. In 1850 he crossed the plains to California. He came to Jacksonville in 1852. Jacksonville was a rich placer district. He picked up a $300 nugget in what was later one of the streets of Jacksonville. In 1854 he was elected to the Oregon Territorial Legislature. In 1865 he was elected assessor of Jackson County and in 1872, county clerk. He also served as county commissioner of Jackson County. He never studied law, but he was often called on to settle disputes. When Jacob Ish and his brother-in-law couldn't agree on a division of their property they paid my husband $500 to go over their accounts and divide their property equally.

"We moved into our log cabin, seven miles south of Ashland, in the spring of 1853. I was 17 years old. We had not been there long when a big Indian came to our house and sharpened his butcher knife on Father's grindstone. He walked into the house in an arrogant and insolent way and, seeing Father's gun, reached for it. I was too quick for him. I grabbed

50

it, cocked it and pointed it at him. He backed out of the house with me following him. Mr. Gibbs, knowing the Indian was in an ugly mood, had followed him from the Mountain House, fearing he might do harm to us. Just as Mr. Gibbs arrived, Pat Dunn, another settler, rode up, and ordered the Indian away. He acted in a very surly manner, but went away.

"Two days later Mr. Gibbs came to our home and told us the settlers feared trouble with the Indians and we had better go to Pat Dunn's cabin, as the other settlers were gathering there. Mother, my sisters Martha and Ann, and myself went to the Dunn place. The man who went with us said laughingly, as he left us at the Dunn place, 'I will go back and bring in the wounded.' An hour or so later he came back, bringing Mr. Carter, who was shot through the arm, the bullet breaking both bones, and Pat Dunn, who later became my husband, who was shot in the shoulder. They took the bullet out of Mr. Dunn's shoulder the next day.

"The white men had killed some of the Indians and taken a number of squaws prisoners. They brought them to Dunn's house. I will never forget that night. The squaws talked and moaned and cried over their dead. The two wounded men groaned. We had fixed beds on the floor for them and given them saddles for pillows. We womenfolks were lying on the floor on blankets, and in addition to our family there was a settler and his wife there with six children. The children would keep poking their heads up to listen and I would hear the mother say, 'Keep your heads down, children. The Indians may shoot into the house and hurt you.'

"The next day an old Indian chief came and said if we would give up the squaws the Indians would give up their arms. Father took us to Fort Wagner, at Gassburg, where we stayed for several weeks. Among the settlers at Fort Wagner were the Emorys, Hellmans, McCalls, Reameses, Risleys, Rockefellers, Culvers, Simpsons, and a few others. We made our beds on the ground at night and there was just about room in the fort for us all to lie down. A company of volunteers took us from the Dunn place to Fort Wagner.

"My cousin, Isham Keith, enlisted in a company to fight the Indians. Lieutenant Ely of the Yreka Company, with 25 men, was out looking for the Indians. Several volunteers from one of the other companies, among them my cousin, were with

51

the Yreka company. They found the Indians on Evans Creek, about 15 miles from Table Rock. Chief Sam attacked them. Lieutenant Ely told my cousin and two other men to go on a high point nearby to watch for the Indians. The Indians fired at these three men and at the first fire killed my cousin and one of the other men. The Indians kept up the attack on the volunteers for several hours, killing several men and wounding four. They killed in this skirmish J. Shaw, Frank Perry, A. Douglas, A. C. Colburn, L. Locktirg, and my cousin, Isham Keith. They wounded Lieutenant Ely, John Albin, James Carroll, and a man named Shultz.

"Two days after we had left our cabin some emigrants arrived there. They camped at our place. The Indians attacked them, killing some and wounding some. One of them died on the way to Fort Wagner. John Gibbs, who was wounded, died the next day, and some of the others died at Jacksonville. , The Indians killed a span of mules, two cows, and two yoke of oxen and burned all of the grain that Mr. Dunn had raised. Later the government made the Indians pay from their allowance $750 for this damage. Isham Keith, who was killed, was the only son of my aunt, Louise Kelly, of Yreka. He was 18 years old when he was killed.

"In the fall of 1855 the Indians once more went on the warpath. We barricaded our log cabin. We covered the windows with thick planks and filled sacks with grain and piled them along the walls as high as our heads. We kept two barrels of water in the kitchen to use in case the Indians set fire to the house. Father made portholes through the logs to shoot through. Several of the settlers stayed in our cabin that winter.

"I was married on Washington's birthday, 1854. My first three children, all girls, were born in our original log cabin. Elizabeth married J. K. Van Sant. Amy married J. Quinn Willits. Amy died in 1882. Otilla married S. S. Caldwell. Quinn Willits had a brother, Rush Willits. He married Anna Tice. They had two daughters, Edna and Docia, both of whom are now living in Portland.

"In 1860 we built a home nearer the road. My son George and my daughter Ella were born in this house. Ella married Mr. Rice. She has been the Southern Pacific ticket agent at the East Morrison Street Station for many years. George lives in Ashland. George attended the University of Oregon and was a classmate of B. B. Beekman and Ed Potter of Eugene. George and Ed Potter were like brothers—in fact, they called them David and Jonathon.

"I told you that in the fall of 1853 some old friends of my father's came by way of Emigrant Creek. Among these were the Myers brothers, Cortez and Frank, three Walker brothers, Giles Wells, and some others. Father had cut some logs ready to enlarge our house. They used these logs to build a wall and stayed at our place until peace was declared in the late fall of 1853.

"My sister 'Has', or, to give her her real name, Anna Haseltine Hill Russell, lives in Ashland. For the past 50 years or so she has operated a marble works and is one of the few women in the country who is an expert at carving marble.

"I am very proud that at the last meeting of the pioneers I was made Queen Mother of Oregon, of the Pioneers."

Oregon Journal
August 24 and 25, 1927

Mrs. Carter T. Allingham

Mrs. Allingham was interviewed in Portland, Oregon.

"In 1851 Father started back for the states. He was stranded for two weeks at Panama, where he said he got thoroughly fed up eating monkeys and yams."

Oregon Journal
March 19, 1933

Maggie Baird Blakley

Mrs. Blakley was a resident of Pendleton, Oregon, at the time of her interview with Mr. Lockley.

"Mighty few wagon trains crossed the plains arriving in Oregon with the same number of wagons they started with.

"Men in those days were more or less individualists. Some wanted to travel on Sunday. Some didn't. Some wanted to lay over to recruit their oxen when they came to good pasture. Others wanted to press on. So the result was that most trains divided. On the plains the wagon train split and my father was elected captain of one section of it.

"We had a Democrat wagon, pulled by mules, for the family. We took along an extra mule just as people nowadays take along an extra tire, in case of emergency. We kids fairly lived on that mule. He was gentle and one or more of us were riding him all the time. I can remember yet how we cried when this extra mule was struck by lightning on the plains and killed.

"There were 36 wagons in our part of the wagon train. The grown folks in several of the wagons died of cholera. Father took charge of the children who had been left orphans. When a person would die they would dig a grave in the middle of the road and drive the oxen over it so that the Indians would not dig up the body to get the clothing.

"I was a little tot when I crossed the plains but I remember one of the men in our wagon train whose name was Curey. He was the most homesick man I ever saw. He was a great hand to write sad songs and of an evening around the campfire he would sing the songs he had composed during the day. Finally he went back East. He felt that he would rather starve among people he knew than to have abundance in a strange country."

Oregon Journal
October 5, 1931

Eliza McKean Hustler

Mrs. Hustler was born in Illinois in 1834. Her father, Samuel Terry McKean, "with his wife (Polly Hicks McKean) and a prairie schooner full of children...came to Oregon in 1847 and the following spring settled at Astoria, where she still lived at the time of her interview with Mr. Lockley.

"I was 13 years old when we crossed the plains in 1847, so of course the incidents of that trip are very vivid in my memory. I can still see the plains with the shimmering heat waves, the dark masses of buffalo moving over the rolling hills toward the Platte, the campfires of buffalo chips and later of sagebrush, the dust cloud hanging over our long train of prairie schooners as the oxen, with swinging heads and lolling tongues, pressed into the yokes to move the wagons slowly westward to the land of our hearts' desire. I walked most of the way across the plains, as did many of the other young folks. I remember a little baby, a girl, died on the plains. We buried her in the middle of the road and drove the oxen over her grave so the Indians would not discover where she was buried."

Oregon Journal
December 19, 1921

Lucy Ann Henderson Deady

"My maiden name was Lucy Ann Henderson. I was born in Coinson County, Missouri, February 26, 1835. My father, Robert Henderson, was born in Green County, Tennessee, February 14, 1809. He went to Kentucky in 1831 and three years later he moved to Missouri. My mother, whose maiden name was Rhoda Holman, was a daughter of John Holman, who came to Oregon with the first wagon train to bring wagons to Oregon. This was in 1843, and Peter H. Burnett was captain of the wagon train for a while, later being succeeded by Captain William Martin.

"Like Peter Burnett, my father was a very obliging man, and when a friend asked him to go on a note as security he did not like to disappoint him, so he signed. His friend could not pay the note. Neither could Father, but Father had property, while the neighbor didn't, so they took Father's property for the debt.

"My parents had sent me to Mrs. Ordway's school for young ladies at Liberty, Missouri, in the fall of 1845. This school was called the Clay Academy. When Father lost his farm he decided to go where he could have all the land he wanted for the taking, so he visited a young lawyer, Peter H. Burnett, who advised him to go to Oregon, as he himself was planning to go the next spring. I knew nothing of this until Father decided to go. Then he came for me and took me out of school, to my deep regret, for I was a very sociable little girl, and there were some very pleasant girls of my age at Mrs. Ordway's school.

"Early in the spring of 1846 the emigrants began assembling at St. Joe, Iowa Point, Council Bluffs, Weston, Elizabethtown, and Independence. About 500 wagons started for Oregon that spring, of which about 300 were bound for Oregon, while the others were going to California. While most of the emigrants were going to Oregon to secure free land, yet there was a strong political feeling, and some of the men had painted different mottoes on their canvas wagon sheets, such as '54-40—All or None'.

"I was 11 years old when we crossed the plains in 1846, so my memories of the trip are very vivid. I remember how filled with terror I was when we experienced the violent thunderstorms with the torrential rains that occurred in the Platte country. Our oxen would try to stampede, our tents would be blown down, and everybody and everything would be soaked with the driving rains. I remember with what terror I saw the Indians come out from Fort Laramie. They looked so naked and wild. The men got out their guns but all the Indians wanted was to see us to see if we would give them anything.

"Mother was baking some bread when some of these savage-looking Indians came into our camp. While she looked up to watch them, one of them came near the fire. When Mother looked back to see how her bread was coming along the bread was gone. The Indian had stolen the hot bread. Mother hoped it had burned him well, but if it did he made no sign.

"While we were stopping at Fort Laramie, the Indians gave a war dance. I was scared nearly to death. They were nearly naked, and all painted, and they jumped and yelled and brandished their tomahawks while the fire around which they danced lit up their savage faces. There was one young squaw who was really pretty. She had a shirt and skirt of beautifully beaded and nicely, tanned buckskin. It looked very pretty, but I was afraid of Indians so I didn't go very close to her.

"We went as far south as the Humboldt, from which place we worked northward to Antelope Springs, Rabbit Hole Springs, and across the Black Rock desert. While on our way to pass across the Cascades we had to cross a desert that took two days' and one night's travel. There was no water at all, so we filled every keg and dish with water so the cattle should have water as well as ourselves. We had no grain or hay for the cattle, so Mother baked up a lot of bread to feed them. When we had finally crossed the desert the cattle smelled water, and we couldn't stop them. They ran as hard as they could go, our wagon bouncing along and nearly bouncing us out. There were three boiling springs and one ice-cold spring.

"I shall never forget that camp. Mother had brought some medicine along. She hung the bag containing the medicine from a nail on the sideboard of the wagon. My playmate, the Currier girl, who was of my own age, and I discovered the bag, and so I decided to taste the medicine. I put a little on my tongue, but it didn't taste good, so took no more. The Currier girl tasted it, made a wry face, and handed the bottle back. My little sister, Salita Jane, wanted to taste it, but I told her she couldn't have it. She didn't say anything, but as soon as we had gone she got the bottle and drank it all. Presently she came to the campfire where Mother was cooking supper and said she felt awfully sleepy. Mother told her to run away and not bother her, so she went to where the beds were spread and lay down. When Mother called her for supper she didn't come. Mother saw she was asleep, so didn't disturb her. When Mother tried to awake her later she couldn't arouse her. Lettie had drunk the whole bottle of laudanum. It was too late to save her life.

"Before we had started, Father had made some boards of black walnut that fitted along the side of the wagon. They were grooved so they would fit together, and we used them for a table all the way across the plains. Father took these walnut boards and made a coffin for Salita and we buried her there by the roadside in the desert. Three days later, at Black Rock, my sister, Olive, now Mrs. Failing of Portland, was born.

"You have no idea of the confusion and uncertainty in the minds of the emigrants as to which was the best route to take. There were so many people who claimed to know all about it that gave such contradictory reports that the emigrants did not know whom to believe. A good many of the emigrants had started out with the intention of going to California, while others, meeting California boosters at Fort Laramie or Fort Bridger, changed their original plans and took the California Trail in place of going on to the Willamette Valley. Some of the emigrants disposed of their wagons at Fort Laramie and started for California with packhorses.

"L. W. Hastings had come up from California to persuade the emigrants bound for Oregon to go to California, to Sutter's Fort. All sorts of reports were circulated. Some said you had to buy the land in California while in Oregon it was free. Others said Oregon was the best climate, but it was much easier to go to California. Some advised us to take the short cut across the 45 mile desert, avoiding going to Fort Bridger. Hastings told the emigrants that he could lead them by the Fremont Cutoff, by the Great Salt Lake, and save many miles of travel.

"Many of the emigrants lost most of their oxen. I don't know whether the Pawnee or Dakota Indians stole them or whether they got homesick and started on the back track, but, in any event, many of the emigrants had to abandon a large part of their loads and get along with one yoke of oxen in place of two or three. We had six heifers, which Father yoked up in place of our lost oxen, and they brought us through to Oregon.

"At Fort Hall we were met by Jesse Applegate, Moses Harris, David Goff, and John Owens, who told us of an easier road to the Willamette Valley than the one by way of The Dalles. It was called the Southern Route, and had been laid out by a party of settlers from Polk County—Levi Scott, Benjamin Burch, the Applegates, and some others.

"The Donner party traveled with the party in which J. Quinn Thornton was traveling. They had 72 wagons. At Fort Bridger Hastings persuaded about 80 of them to go to California by way of Weber Canyon, to the Humboldt Valley. The others kept on to Fort Hall. The Donners were delayed in the Sierras and snowed in and finally ran out of food and resorted to cannibalism, few of them living to get to Sutter's Fort.

"Nearly 100 wagons followed Jesse Applegate and his party for the Southern cutoff. Levi Scott and David Goff acted as our guides, while Jesse Applegate and the others, with a lot of the unmarried men among the emigrants, went ahead to fix up the road so we could travel on it.

"Three days after my little sister Lettie drank the laudanum and died we stopped for a few hours and my sister Olive was born. We were so late that the men of the party decided we could not tarry a day, so we had to press on. The going was terribly rough. We were the first party to take the Southern cutoff, so there was no road. The men walked beside the wagons and tried to ease the wheels down into the rough places, but in spite of this it was a very rough ride for my mother and her new-born babe.

"Some weeks later we camped in the rain on the present site of Ashland. I shall never forget this place. The wood was wet and I stood around shivering while Father was trying to make a fire with flint and steel. Many years later, after I had married Judge Deady, Jesse Applegate showed me a big tree in Ashland and said, 'That is the tree you camped under in the fall of 1846 on your way to the Willamette Valley.'

"One of the emigrants in our party was named Crowley. He had lost several members of his family by death while crossing the plains, and at one of our camps another member of the family, a daughter, Martha Leland Crowley, died. Theodore Prater and Mrs. Rachel Challinor and some others from our wagon train helped bury her. They buried her beneath a big pine tree on the banks of a small stream which they christened

58

Grave Creek, and which still bears that name. The oxen were corralled over her grave so the Indians would not dig her up to get her clothing. Colonel Nesmith saw the grave in 1848 and said it had been opened and that a number of human bones were scattered about. The bones were reinterred and the grave filled in again. Mrs. Crowley, the girl's mother, later married a Mr. Fulkerson of Polk County.

"My husband, Judge Deady, used often to stop at the Bates Stage Station, on Grave Creek, to Leland Creek and the hotel's name was changed to the Leland House.

"I forgot to tell you that in crossing the stream near what was later called Linkville, now Klamath Falls, we crossed the river on a ledge of rocks that ran clear across the stream. It was called Stone Bridge.

"In coming north from the Rogue River country we followed the bed of Cow Creek. It took us five days to make nine miles. I have never, before or since, seen such rough going. The cattle could hardly keep their feet, on account of the smooth waterworn boulders in the bed of the stream, and the wagons would occasionally tip over.

"It was getting so late that at a meeting of the men of the wagon train it was decided to throw away every bit of surplus weight so that better speed could be made and so that the others should not have to wait for some one overladen wagon. One man had brought two hives of bees clear across the plains and hated to give them up, but the men of the train decided he could get along without them, so he had to leave them. A man named Smith had a wooden rolling pin that it was decided was useless and must be abandoned. I shall never forget how that big man stood there with tears streaming down his face as he said, 'Do I have to throw this away? It was my mother's. I remember she always used it to roll out her biscuits, and they were awful good biscuits.' He had to leave it, and they christened him Rolling Pin Smith, a name he carried to the day of his death.

"If you want to know what a terrible time we had coming through Cow Creek Canyon, just read J. Quinn Thornton's book, **Oregon and California.** He published it in 1849, and it tells all about our trip. Mr. Thornton was a lawyer, a sort of dreamer, not very well, very irritable and peevish. I lived with them later, when I was going to school at Oregon City, so I learned what a peculiar man he was. He was the type of man that always blames someone else for misfortunes he himself has caused. I remember one morning he came down and after breakfast he started to get up without the usual family prayers. His wife said, 'Are you not going to conduct family worship?'

"He said, 'No. I don't feel like praying. You aggravate me.'

"After great hardship and discomfort we finally made our way through Cow Creek Canyon. We came on northward, having very hard going as it was late in the year and the winter rains had started. We had been eight months on the road, instead of five, so we were out of food and our cattle were nearly worn out. We crossed the river near the present site of Roseburg by tying two canoes together and putting the wagons on them and ferrying them over.

"We had obtained some fresh meat from some trappers and a day or so later my mother's brother, Mr. Holman, met us. He had heard of our plight, so he came with food and horses to get us. We left the wagons and with Mother on one horse holding her 6-week-old baby in her lap, and with one of the little children sitting behind her, and the rest of us riding behind the different men, we started north. I rode behind my uncle, Mr. Holman. Two of the children rode with our cousin, one in front of his saddle, and one back of it.

"One family of our party had thrown away almost everything and had finally reduced their treasured possessions to one trunk. This trunk came off the horse while fording a river and was swept from sight and never recovered. I think it was lost in crossing the Long Tom, though it might have been lost in the river near the present site of Corvallis.

"At Avery's place, now called Corvallis, we stayed all night in a log cabin. Mother and we children slept on the floor, as also did some men who were staying in the cabin. I shall never forget that night. Some Indians were camped nearby and they had lost one of their number, so they moaned and groaned and chanted all night, mourning for their dead.

"We went with my uncle to what is now called Broadmead, where we stayed with an uncle who had come here the year before, in 1845. We reached his cabin on December 17, 1846, and stayed there two weeks. Father, who had come on with the wagon, did not get there until Christmas Day.

"After a week or so we moved into a cabin owned by

60

Henry Hyde. His wife was my mother's sister. We spent the winter there. There was no floor in the cabin, just earth. There was a big fireplace. There was but one room. There was a big chest and Mother filled this nearly full of clothing, and Betty and I slept in that. There were five of us children, so Father fixed up some shakedowns for beds. We lived on boiled wheat and boiled peas that winter. My mother got sick, so my Aunt Susan came to live with us and take care of Mother.

"When Mother got well Aunt Susan went to visit the Humphreys at Dallas. I begged to go along, so she took me. She told me that General Gilliam lived there and that he had a little girl about my age. I thought a general would be all covered with medals and have a fine uniform and that his daughter would be dressed in silk and lace, so I could hardly wait to get there. I was so disappointed that I cried when I saw General Gilliam and his daughter. I saw her first. She had an old dress on and was wearing moccasins. In place of wearing a wonderful uniform and having a sword, General Gilliam looked as poor as the rest of us and was just an ordinary man.

"My mother's father had come to Oregon in 1843 and was living at Forest Grove. His youngest daughter was about my age, 11. In the spring of 1847 I went to stay at their home. Harvey Clark, who had come from Vermont in 1841 as a missionary to the Indians, had settled at Forest Grove, as had a man named Littlejohn. Grandma Brown was running a little school in a log schoolhouse, which later became Tualatin Academy through the help of Reverend Clark and others. I was there until late in the fall of 1847.

"In 1848 Father built a log cabin on his donation land claim, and shortly thereafter news of the finding of gold in California spread like wildfire throughout the Willamette Valley. A good many people, including our old time friend Peter H. Burnett, went to California that fall—1848. Before long Mr. Burnett was elected the first American governor of California.

"Father waited until February, 1849, when he went to Portland and went aboard a small sailing boat bound for California. Mother said that was the saddest day of her life, as she never expected to see Father again and she would be left a widow with a brood of fatherless children.

"I was not sorry to see Father go, for we were poor and I wanted to go to school and he had told me that if he had good

61

luck he would see that I went to school. In those days there were no free schools. The last thing Father said to me was, 'Be a good girl, Lucy, and if I make any money you shall go to school.' Father came back that fall with quite a little money, so Betty and I were sent to Mrs. J. Quinn Thornton's school at Oregon City.

"In those days Oregon City was the capital of the provisional government. When Burnett resigned as supreme judge, Governor Abernethy appointed J. Quinn Thornton to the vacant judgeship. That was in February, 1847. In the fall of 1847 the settlers prepared a petition to Congress which was mailed on the bark Whiton, but Governor Abernethy decided to send J. Quinn Thornton to present the petition, so he sailed on the Whiton in October, 1847, for San Francisco and thence to Panama, Boston, and Washington. At San Jose he went aboard the United States sloop of war Portsmouth and sailed for Boston. When he returned in 1848 he brought with him some oil lamps, some fine furniture, and a lot of dresses for his wife."

Right here is a good place to tell an interesting bit of Oregon history in connection with the mission of J. Quinn Thornton. He went aboard the bark Whiton secretly, for fear the provisional legislature would take steps to prevent his departure, for he was unpopular and when it was learned that he had been appointed as a delegate from Oregon to the government at Washington, Colonel Nesmith introduced a resolution protesting against the appointment of Thornton to any office in the Oregon Country. This resolution was adopted but was later reconsidered. This vote was a tie. The speaker voted against it, so it was lost.

There was no money available to pay Thornton's expenses, so a well-to-do merchant, Noyes Smith, lent him enough flour to help him defray his expenses. Thornton sold this at San Francisco and was thus able to make the trip.

Noyes Smith, whose real name was Egbert Olcott, had been a trusted officer in a bank at Albany, New York, and had disappeared with a large amount of the bank's money. He went all over the world and finally turned up in Oregon, broke. He landed a job as a clerk in a store, prospered, and soon was a well-to-do merchant. A United States Marshal recognized him and exposed his record. He took to drink and lost his fortune and when he eventually was pardoned he went back to Albany, where he died not long after.

J. Quinn Thornton was a strange mixture of ability and overweening conceit. He was ready to claim credit for everything in sight, just as he claimed authorship of the Douglass Bill relating to the Oregon Territory. Thornton wrote: "I felt a vehement desire to multiply, in Oregon, the springs of knowledge, so I framed the 20th section of the act of Congress of August 14, 1848, giving Oregon the 16th and 36th sections of each township for school purposes."

The section for which he claimed credit was originally numbered section 18 and was a part of the Douglas Bill, prepared long before Thornton was or hand and before he knew anything about it. It read that "when the lands in said territory shall be surveyed under the direction of the government of the United States preparatory to bringing the same into market, sections 16 and 36 in each township in said territory shall be, and the same are hereby reserved for the purpose of being applied to schools in said territory and in the states and territories to be erected out of same." Probably Thornton laid claim to being the author of the bill to make the people of Oregon more resigned to his unauthorized appointment as delegate from Oregon.

Thornton was born August 24, 1810, in Virginia. He opened a law office at Palmyra, Missouri, in 1835. In 1888 he married a widow, Mrs. Nancy M. Logue, of Hannibal, Missouri. In 1841 they moved to Quincy, Illinois, and in 1846, his health being very poor, they moved to Oregon.

"Mr. Thornton wanted to keep on good terms with the prominent and influential people in Oregon, so he used to give dinners at his home not only to influential people residing at Oregon City, but also to any socially or politically prominent person who visited Oregon City. Thus we met many of the prominent men of Oregon's early territorial days. Among the girlhood acquaintances I remember best when I was a student at Mrs. Thornton's school in 1849 were Miss Abernethy, a daughter of Governor George Abernethy and who later married Captain (later General) Hedges of the United States Army and Miss Holmes, whose father was the first sheriff of the county. These girls were schoolmates of mine. Then there was a Miss Leslie, whose father, Reverend David Leslie, was a Methodist missionary. We often saw Mr. and Mrs. Robb, grandparents of E. C. Cornell of Portland, and Mr. and Mrs. Buck and Mrs. John G. Campbell, their daughter, and Colonel and Mrs. Taylor.

"Speaking of Mrs. Campbell reminds me of an odd incident. One night when Mrs. Campbell was staying at our home my mother was hurrying around to make her various guests comfortable. The men had been taken care of and Mother was arranging extra beds for the others, when she heard one of the men say, 'I wonder if there is any chance of getting a nightcap here. I can't sleep without a nightcap.'

"Mother hunted up a nightcap and, tapping on the door, said, 'I will lay this nightcap in front of your door. I hope it will fit all right.' The next morning the men were very hilarious and one of them explained to Mother that a nightcap was a drink of whiskey, not a woolen cap.

"Matthew P. Deady came across the plains in 1849, working his way across. He landed from his canoe at Portland, November 14, and after a day or so walked to Lafayette. He had no money and he needed to begin earning money at once, so he arranged to teach school there for enough to pay for his board and lodging. He taught in the school that was run by Professor John E. Lyle. At the end of the term he went into partnership in the school with Professor Lyle and made $75 a month during the rest of the school year.

"Judge Deady had to come to Oregon City to buy some school books and other school supplies and a young man in Lafayette asked him to take a letter to me. No, it wasn't exactly a love letter. It was just a friendly letter from a young man who was somewhat interested in me. Judge Deady was over six feet in height. He was ruddy-faced and goodlooking, and I was more interested in the bearer of the letter than in the letter itself. That was the first time I ever saw my future husband.

"The next year I went to school in Lafayette. Dr. and Mrs. E. R. Geary and their two daughters ran the Lafayette school in 1850. I was 15 years old, and in those days the young men began wondering why a girl wasn't married if she was still single when she was 16.

"That summer Judge Deady ran Glen O. Burnett's store at Lafayette, while Elder Glen Burnett was in California buying goods. He and I used to see each other at Christian Church services, held in a log schoolhouse near Lafayette. We all rode horseback in those days and Judge Deady was a natural horseman, just as he was a natural swimmer. He was at home in the water and equally so on horseback. We met occasionally at weddings and other social doings. My teacher, Reverend Edward R. Geary, married us on June 24, 1852.

"Reverend Geary was born in Maryland and before coming to Oregon he had been pastor of a church at Fredericksburg, Ohio. He taught for a while at Lafayette, later becoming clerk of the United States Circuit Court, then county clerk of Yamhill County and county school superintendent. When J. W. Nesmith, who had succeeded General Palmer as superintendent of Indian affairs, resigned in 1857, Mr. Geary was appointed. In 1876 he moved to Eugene, where he became pastor of the Presbyterian Church.

"Yes, I was reared a Presbyterian, but when we came to Portland we began to attend Trinity Episcopal Church. My husband was a vestryman of that church nearly 25 years. He also taught a Sunday school class there over 20 years. His people were born in Ireland and were Catholics, but Judge Deady lived and died an Episcopalian.

"In the early '50's, when I changed my name from Henderson to Deady, Lafayette was one of the important cities in Oregon. It was the county seat of Oregon's richest and most populous county and the outfitting point for many a pack train that took flour and other supplies to the mines. At one time there were more than 30 stores there and the Athens of Oregon, as it was sometimes called, was socially, commercially, and politically an important community.

"About six months after Judge Deady came to Lafayette, Judge 0. C. Pratt held a term of the District court there. That was in March, 18S0. Judge Deady had been admitted to the bar in the fall of 1847, in Ohio, so, when the court met at Jacob Hawn's hotel in Lafayette, Judge Deady, who was teaching at Lafayette, was retained in three cases tried before Judge Pratt. Two or three months after that, in June, 1850, Judge Deady was elected a member of the House of Representatives of Oregon Territory. In December, 1850, Judge Deady went to Oregon City, where I was a student in Mrs. Thornton's private school. He made many friends there with such men as Asahel Bush, J. W. Nesmith, and others, with whom we kept up a close friendship all our lives.

"After the session had adjourned Judge Deady was asked by the secretary, Edward Hamilton, to prepare the laws for publication and also to whip the laws passed in 1849 into shape and include them. This book, the first published in Oregon Territory, was at that time called **Hamilton's Code.** In the summer of 1851 he ran for the legislative council, now called the Senate. David Logan, a fellow lawyer, ran against him, but was defeated after a vigorous fight. The legislature met not long after our marriage, in extra session, so we rode on horseback to attend the session. The first night we stopped at Thurston's. We also stopped at Nesmith's in Polk County, where we met Mr. Bush, and we all rode in to Salem together. Asahel Bush was a very able and genial man. He liked to ride a good horse, and rode well.

"Judge Deady served two terms in the territorial council and at one special session. In 1852-53 he was president of the council. He had served as chairman of the judiciary committee before that. In the spring following our marriage, Judge Deady was appointed by the President of the United States to be Judge of the Supreme Court of Oregon Territory. There were three judges appointed, and Judge Deady took the southern part of the state as his circuit. He spent six months in the saddle each year covering his territory. He loved life in the open and the informality of the mining camps.

"Judge Deady and I were married at Lafayette, June 24, 1852, by the Reverend Edward R. Geary. Our wedding tour was a trip on horseback to attend the special session of the territorial legislature at Salem.

"When we came back we went to housekeeping at Lafayette in a one-room log cabin with a lean-to kitchen. I was 17 years old. I could fry meat, but I had never roasted meat. The day we went to housekeeping, Judge Deady installed in our kitchen an iron cookstove, the first one I had ever seen. We had visitors the first day we started housekeeping. Mr. and Mrs. Werner Breyman dropped in and Judge Deady invited them to stay for dinner, for he was very proud of his girl wife. I put the roast into the oven and made a big fire and the first thing I knew the smoke was pouring out of the oven at a most alarming rate. I didn't know what to do, so I called my husband. He opened the door and out rushed a cloud of smoke. He patted me on the shoulder and said, 'Don't you mind. There is plenty more meat where that came from. I will manage the stove until you learn how to regulate it.'

"The next spring we moved to southern Oregon. We traveled in a spring wagon. We stopped overnight with Judge and Mrs. R. P. Boise, near Dallas, and one night with the Averys, who founded the town of Corvallis. The next night we

66

stopped with the Esteses. The next day we got off the road and camped overnight with some men who were running a pack train. We reached the home of Aaron Rose, the founder of Roseburg, on the fifth day.

"My husband bought a squatter claim on Camas Swale, near Roseburg, and we took this up as our donation land claim. What we wanted of it I really never knew, but in any event we lived there many years while Judge Deady rode his circuit. Judge Deady organized the courts in five of the counties in southern Oregon.

"I was nervous about his traveling alone all over southern Oregon, particularly during the Indian War of 1855-56, but no harm ever came to him. Sometimes he thought he was going to be shot but he never was.

"Once he had gone to Umpqua City, at the mouth of the Umpqua River, not far from the present site of Gardiner, just down the river from Scottsburg. He had to go to Port Orford and as there was no boat going down the coast and the going was bad on the trail, he decided to walk. On his way back he was joined by Mr. Drew. They decided to walk on out and while crossing the low pass in the mountains they met two very rough looking young chaps. One of them hailed them and said, 'We are broke and must have some money. All I want is to let this pistol raise some money for me.'

"Judge Deady asked, 'How do you propose to do it?'

"The rough looking young chap said, 'Well, I will sell you this pistol, or you can loan me something on it.'

"Judge Deady said, 'If you are really in need of money I don't mind lending you five dollars.'

"This was in the late '50's. Years afterward a man came into the judge's chambers in the Federal Building here in Portland and said, 'Do you remember me?' Judge Deady shook his head. The man said, 'My name is C. H. Miller, and I am county judge of Grant County and live at Canyon City. Here is the five dollars you loaned me years ago, when I met you in the mountains on the way out from Port Orford.' Shortly after that Judge C. H. Miller published a little book of poems here in Portland which he called **Joaquin Miller Et Al,** and later another one called **Specimens.** Mr. Himes printed them for him. He signed his name to them 'Joaquin' Miller, and later he became known as the Poet of the Sierras.

"In the summer of 1857 Judge Deady went to Salem as a delegate to the State Constitutional Convention. It met about the middle of August and there were 60 men from all over the state as delegates. They elected my husband president of the convention. In 1859, when Oregon became a state, he was appointed United States District Judge and opened his court at Salem. There was a good deal of complaint by the people of Portland about having to go to Salem on all legal business, so Judge Deady went to Washington, D. C. by way of the Isthmus of Panama, and had an act passed locating the office of United States District Judge at Portland. We moved in 1860 from our farm to Portland.

"You haven't asked me about my wedding or what I wore, but I will tell you. I was going to school at Dr. Geary's school when Judge Deady was courting me. Kate Montagne was my chum and we discussed everything of mutual interest. She had many pretty dresses. I did not. I asked her to help plan my wedding outfit. My wedding dress was made of bishop lawn and was very pretty. Kate and I made it. The waist was pointed in front and fastened in the back. It had a Dutch neck and was trimmed with folds of the dress material and silk ribbons. I did not wear a veil, but I wore a white ribbon in my hair. I had white kid slippers and white kid gloves. My bonnet was of straw and was lined with white silk and had broad streamers.

"Judge Deady was asked to prepare a code for Oregon in 1862 and in September, 1863, it was adopted. Later he prepared a code of criminal procedure and a justice's code. He prepared an act incorporating the City of Portland, which was passed by the legislature. At the request of the legislature he prepared a compilation of the laws of Oregon. This is known as **Deady's Code,** and it had over 1100 pages. In 1874, with Lafayette Lane, he revised this code.

"When we came to Portland we bought a home pretty well out, at 7th and Alder Streets. We had four children—Edward, Paul, Mary, and Henderson Brook. Two or three years after we came to Portland—this was about 1863—my husband's annual salary had shrunk so through the depreciation of greenbacks that we were having to live on about $800 a year, greenbacks being about 55 cents on the dollar. He was offered $40 a month to serve as the Oregon correspondent of the **San**

Francisco Bulletin. He wrote a letter each week, consisting of comment on men and events in Oregon. He also wrote articles for the **Overland Monthly.** He kept this up four or five years. In 1867, 1868, and 1869 he held circuit court at San Francisco three months of each year. In 1876 he was appointed a regent of the University of Oregon and was president of the board for many years.

"My husband was born May 12, 1824, in Talbot County, Maryland. He was the eldest of five children. His father, Daniel Deady, was a native of County Cork, Ireland, and was a teacher. His father came to the United States in 1823 and married Mary Ann McSweeny, whose father was also a native of County Cork. She was born at Baltimore. His mother died of consumption when she was 38 years old. This was in the spring of 1834, when Judge Deady was ten years old.

"In 1841 he fell out with his father and left home and became apprenticed to a blacksmith named John Kelly. He lived with the Kellys the four years that he was learning the trade of blacksmith. He received $3 a month for the first year, $4 a month the second, $5 a month the third, and $7 a month the fourth year. After serving his apprenticeship he went to school a while and later taught at $22 a month. While teaching school he read law and was admitted to the bar in the fall of 1847. He started across the plains for Oregon in the spring of 1849 and saw Portland for the first time on November 14, 1849.   We moved to Portland in 1860, where my husband continued to live until his death. I have lived here continuously for the past 62 years."

Oregon Journal
January 24-29, 1923

Valeda W. Smith Ohmart

Mrs. Ohmart was born in south Salem in 1865, in the same house where her interview with Mr. Lockley took place in 1934.

"Unlike Tabitha Brown, who founded Pacific University, Orris Brown wasn't very religious. The Pawnee Indians robbed them of almost everything they had when they were going back to the States in 1845. One of the men of the party killed a skunk, which they cooked. Dr. Elijah White started to ask the blessing over the skunk, but Orris Brown said, 'I won't stand for any blessing being asked over a skunk. It would be too much like sacrilege. If the Lord is as good as you say he is, he would furnish us better meat than a skunk, so we'll eat it and neither thank Him nor complain to Him about it. You'd better save your blessings until we get some deer meat or something fit to eat.'

Oregon Journal
March 1, 1934

Minerva Jane Thessing Oatfield

Mrs. Oatfield was born in Dayton, Oregon, in 1852. She was interviewed at her home on Oatfield Road, between Milwaukee and Oregon City.

"Like Doctor Owens Adair, I am a firm believer in sterilization of the criminal insane and the mentally unfit. Anyone who will visit the Oregon Insane Asylum and the feeble-minded institution, or talk to Dr. Lee Steiner and other authorities, will be converted to this belief.

Oregon Journal
June 21, 1926

Aeolia F. Royal Oberg

Mrs. Oberg was born in Wilbur, Oregon, in 1863. She was interviewed on the Oberg farm in Portland.

"My father and mother crossed the plains by ox team in 1853. Father went to Jacksonville, which at that time was the metropolis of Southwestern Oregon and one of the livest mining camps in the West. James Cluggage had deeded a lot at Jacksonville to the Methodist Church. Father would go into a saloon where a lot of miners were gambling and where stacks of $20 gold pieces or pokes of gold dust were on the table, and would hold a service. The saloonkeepers were glad to have him take up a collection and go, for while Father was praying, the miners, out of respect to him, would not drink or gamble. By making rather frequent visits to various saloons Father soon collected enough money to build the church."

Oregon Journal
February 23, 1935

Inez Eugenia Adams Parker

Mrs. Parker came to Oregon with her father, Dr. W. D. Adams, in 1848. She was interviewed at her home in Seaside, Oregon.

"When my husband, W. W. Parker, was a member from Clatsop County of the Oregon Legislature in 1856-57, he introduced a very modest temperance measure, which was promptly and contemptuously voted to be 'thrown under the table.'

Oregon Journal
October 21, 1928

Lucinda Adeline Clarno Evans

"Clarno is named for my father, Andrew Clarno. When we moved there, in the '60s, we didn't do much writing, because it cost 50 cents to get a letter or send one. They came by express. Joaquin Miller ran an express between John Day and Walla Walla. He and a man named Mossman used to carry letters and gold dust. They took the gold dust from Canyon City up to Walla Walla and carried letters both ways.

"My father was born in Iowa, October 11, 1820 . My mother, whose maiden name was Elinore Jones, was born on May 5, 1827. There were six girls and three boys in our family. My sister, Laura MacDonald, who lives at Clarno Bridge, on the John Day, and myself are the only ones of the family now living. I was born in Illinois on December 8, 1858.

"My father was drafted, but he paid a substitute to take his place in the Civil War, and we started for the Pacific Coast by way of the Isthmus of Panama. My father's two brothers, George and William Henry Harrison Clarno, had crossed the plains to California not long after gold was discovered out there. Father decided to join them in California.

"We started out from New York on board the Aerial. We were in sight of an island—I don't know whether it was Cuba or some other island down that way—when a ship started toward us. The captain of our ship tried to get away, but the other ship fired at us, and the mainmast fell to the deck. A lot of women passengers began screaming and pretty soon the Confederate ship Alabama caught up with us.

"We had some soldiers on board, and when the sailors from the Confederate ship came aboard the ship they took the guns away from the soldiers and threw them overboard. There were two boys—little chaps, not over 14 or 15—in uniform. One was a drummer and the other a fifer. The Confederate sailors told them to throw their fife and drum overboard, but neither of the boys would do it. The fifer broke his fife and

71

threw it on the deck, and the drummer boy broke in the head of his drum, so they wouldn't get them. Some of the men who had come aboard us went down in our engine room and disconnected some pipes so the steam all ran out, and they threw our sails overboard. They went into the captain's office and took all the money he had in the safe, and some of the sailors made the passengers give up their money.

"A fishing boat came out and told Admiral Semmes that there was a United States man-of-war on the other side of the island.
Captain Semmes was going to land the women on the island, take the men prisoners, and burn our ship, but when he found out that the captain of our ship was a Mason he changed his mind and didn't do it. His boat, the Alabama, was built in England in the summer of 1863. He captured 62 different vessels, most of which he burned at sea. The Alabama was sunk by the Kearsarge, June 19, 1864.

"After the Alabama had left us our engineers fixed up the engines and we went on to the Isthmus of Panama. We crossed the Isthmus and took another boat for San Francisco. My father's brother Henry met us in San Francisco and took us to his ranch. My brother Frank got a job herding sheep, and my father and my brother John got a job putting up hay on a cattle ranch. We stayed in California three years.

"My father and brother were working for a cattle man named Marsh. He had some trouble with his cowboys, who were Mexicans. He hitched up his team and went to town to get money to pay them off. The team with the buggy came back to the ranch, so they went out to look for Mr. Marsh. They found him by the side of the road. He had been killed. They didn't know whether the cowboys had killed him because they were mad at him, or whether someone had killed him for his money. Anyway, instead of looking for another job, my father decided to come up to Oregon.

"Father and Mother and I rode in the wagon, and John and Frank and my sister Jennie rode on horseback and drove our loose cattle. We wintered at Wilbur, in southern Oregon. We children went to school to the Umpqua Academy. Professor Royal, or 'Limpy' Royal, as they called him, was the principal. Father and the boys got work on nearby farms.

"My mother's cousin, Miss Branson, had married Mr.

72

Cosper. We drove from Wilbur to Empire City, so Father could size up the coast country, and from there we drove to Cosper's place, between Salem and Gervais. Father told Mr. Cosper he was broke, so Mr. Cosper furnished money to him, and Father bought cattle. Father drove this band of cattle across the Cascades by way of McKenzie Pass. He finally found a place he liked, on the John Day, so he took up a homestead, bought some school land, and took up a timber culture claim, so altogether he had around 1000 acres. Mother, with us children, went up to The Dalles by boat, and from there by wagon to Antelope.

"Our place was 12 miles east of Antelope. We had to keep our horses tied to the cabin so the Indians wouldn't steal them. They ran off our stock. Three times they stole our stock, so Father had to plow with a team consisting of an ox and a horse.

"Mr. Lockwood, whose son, Chauncey Lockwood, lives at Salem, had a stage line. He boarded with us one winter. He let Father have two oxen for wheelers, and Father and my brother John broke four yoke of young steers. John, who was about 14, drove a freight wagon to the gold mines in Idaho.

"One time when Father was out looking for stock he saw dust, so he climbed up on a small butte and with his field glasses watched the Warm Springs Indians having a battle with the Snake Indians. The Warm Springs Indians licked the Snake Indians.

"One time when we were out of beef, Father and Frank crossed the John Day and killed a beef. Father saw a Snake Indian who was acting rather suspiciously, so he captured him and brought him in. He fed the Indian and decided to let him go. The Indian said to him, 'Take your women and children away. The Indians are coming here to kill you.' So we went to Maupin's at Antelope.

"I was married March 6, 1887, to W. A. Evans. My husband has been a conductor or motorman for P. E. P. Company for the past 26 years. He ran on the Irvington Line for quite a while, but now he is on the St. Johns Line."

Oregon Journal
April 23, 1929

Mrs. U. J. McConnell

Mrs. McConnell was born in Jo Davies County, Illinois in 1845. She was interviewed at her home in Sherwood Oregon.

"We crossed the Missouri River in the spring of 1852 headed for Oregon. My mother, whose maiden name was Susanna Smith, died of cholera while we were camped on the Platte River. Father had put in a false bottom in the wagon and he used the boards from this false bottom to make a coffin in which my mother was buried.

"My mother's mother, Mary Smith, was along. She also died of the cholera. We had with us also my father's father, John Gregg. He also died and was buried on the plains. Two of my father's sisters were along, so when Mother died they took care of us children."

Oregon Journal
undated

Mary Jane Heater Judy

Mrs. Judy was born in Mount Pleasant, Iowa, in 1849. At the time of this interview, she had lived in Oregon for more than 81 years.

"When Father and Mother started across the plains they had two children—my sister, Margaret Elizabeth, and myself. Father and Mother had ten more children after they came to Oregon."

Oregon Journal
March 15, 1932

Sarah Brown Keyes

Mrs. Keyes was born in The Dalles, Oregon, in 1856. At the time of the interview, she had lived in or near Mitchell, Oregon, for more than 60 years.

"We had a small cloudburst here day before yesterday. As you see, Mitchell is located in the hills, and when there is a cloudburst up in the hills, Bridge Creek, from a small stream, suddenly turns to a roaring torrent. The lower end of Mitchell has been wiped off the map twice by cloudbursts."

Oregon Journal
June 19, 1929

Mary Elizabeth Munkers Estes

"I was born at Liberty, Missouri. My friends call me Aunt Elizabeth. My maiden name was Mary Elizabeth Munkers, and I was born April 8, 1836. My father, Benjamin Munkers, was born in Tennessee. My mother, whose maiden name was Mary

Elizabeth Crowley, was also born in Tennessee. They had eleven children. I was the third from the last, and I am the only one of the family left. Two of the children died at Liberty, Missouri. There were eleven of us who came across the plains—my father and mother and their nine children.

"I was ten years old on April 8, 1846, and we started to Oregon on my birthday. We met the other emigrants who were going to Oregon at St. Joe, Missouri. There were about 50 wagons in our train. Three of my brothers were married and had outfits of their own. My sister Jane was also married. She married Green MacDonald.

"When we first started, we had about 100 wagons, each pulled by three yoke of oxen. We also had 50 Durham cows and five saddle horses. Captain F. Martin was in charge of the train, but after we had traveled a while our train split in two parts, and Ben Simpson, father of Sam L. Simpson, the poet, was our captain. Our wagons traveled near Ben Simpson's wagon, and when Mrs. Simpson was doing the washing or making bread or doing other camp work I used to take care of her baby, Sam.

"My mother traveled clear across the plains lying on a bed in the wagon. We had five wagons, each pulled by three yoke of oxen. We also had 50 Durham cows and five saddle horses.

"The thing I remember most distinctly about the trip is fording the streams and crossing rivers on rafts. Where we couldn't obtain driftwood to make rafts, and where there was no timber, we took the wagon beds off the running gear and used them to ferry the women and children and the goods across. Where we found good grass and water we would often stay a day or two to rest the oxen. While the oxen were grazing the women would wash all the soiled clothes that had accumulated, and the men would fix up the wagons and make necessary repairs, while some of the younger men would go hunting to bring in fresh meat. Oftentimes we had to travel long after dark to keep from making a dry camp. I was ten years old and was interested in everything, and as I could see better afoot than when in the wagon, I walked most of the way. At first it was very hard on the women to have to cook the meals without wood, but they soon became experts in cooking over sagebrush or buffalo chips.

"I remember while we were camped on the Platte the whole sky became black as ink. A terrific wind came up, which blew the covers off the wagons and blew down the tents. When the storm burst upon us it frightened the cattle, so that it took all the efforts of the men to keep them from stampeding. It stormed all night. It would be dark as Egypt one moment, then there would be a vivid flash of lightning when everything would be bright as daylight. It seemed as if the sky was a huge lake or an ocean and was slopping over. The rain came down in bucketfuls, drenching us to the skin. There wasn't a tent in the camp that held against the terrific wind. The men had to chain the wagons together to keep them from being blown into the river. As the storm increased in violence the wind would catch our bedquilts and other light things and blow them away. Finally, in spite of efforts of the men, the cattle stampeded. It took all the next day to round them up and get things fixed up to go onward.

"Fortunately, we had no cholera, and the Indians made no trouble for us, though at one time a big band of Indians in all the glory of war paint and feathers charged down on us, and we thought we were going to be wiped out, but their head man told us that they were on the warpath against another tribe of Indians and they meant no harm toward white people.

"There were about 1200 or 1500 people who came across the plains to Oregon in 1846, and possibly 1000 who went to California. It was a rather dry season in 1846, so a great many of the larger wagon trains split up into smaller ones. If you will talk to the old pioneers you will find that some very influential men came to Oregon in the emigration of 1846. Hugh L. Brown, who, like my father, was a Tennessean, was in our company. He settled on Calapooya Creek, in Linn County. The town of Brownsville is built on his place. Captain Blakely, who lived to be over 100 years old and whose descendants are scattered all over the west, was also in our train. Among others who became well known in Oregon and who came across the plains that year was Elijah Bristow of Kentucky, who settled at Pleasant Hill in Lane County. Fabritus R. Smith of New York state was another. He settled near Salem. Smith Collins, who settled on the Luckiamute River in Polk County, was still another. Mr. Collins married Douglas Wyatt's daughter. They had 12 children. Mr. Collins was born in Virginia. You must have met J. L. Collins of Dallas. He was 15 years old when he came to Oregon.

"Among others who came that year were John Baker,

Reverend J. Cornwall, J. T. Rainey, Virgil K. Pringle, for whom the Pringle neighborhood, south of Salem, is named; Alphonso Boon, whose daughter Chloe married Governor George L. Curry; W. P. Breeding, one of Salem's early blacksmiths; F. W. Geer, who settled near where Butteville was later built; J. D. Holman, Joseph Waldo, Martin Vaughan, and Rice Dunbar. Then there were the Kennedys, Colvers, Fays, Crumps, Campbells, Zumwalts, Wallings, Coxes, Davidsons, Hoyts, Lownsdales, and a lot of other equally well known people.

"We came by way of the newly opened Barlow Trail. When Father reached the Willamette Valley he was anxious to secure a place already improved, so he could move Mother into a cabin at once. Mother was an invalid and had stayed in bed all the way across the plains. Father had 30 yoke of oxen and a large herd of Durham cows, as well as a large amount of money, so when he found a 640 acre claim on Mill Creek, near Salem, for which its owner, Jack Anderson, would take $1000, he bought it and moved Mother at once into the double log cabin.

"In addition to the cabin there was a log barn, ten acres of the 640 had been plowed, and part of the place was fenced. My father had brought half a bushel of peach stones with him from Missouri. He planted these and soon had a fine orchard. He also planted some apple trees. I remember in the early '50s he sold 100 bushels of apples, getting $14 a bushel for them. When we first came to Oregon money was so scarce that when you bought anything you paid for it in barter. Father used to accept, for what he sold, wheat or peas at $1 a bushel. The peas were dried and were used to make pea soup or to make coffee. Sea island sugar or molasses was used for sweetening.

"As I told you, Mother was an invalid and stayed in bed in the wagon all the way across the plains. Under her bed Father had built, just above the bed of the wagon, a long flat box, in which he brought to Oregon over $10,000 in gold and silver coin, so we were considered very well-to-do, for that time. Four of my brothers—Marion, Riley, Ben, and Tom—went to California when gold was discovered there. Tom was only 14 years old, Ben was 16, and Riley 19. Marion died in California.

"I often think of the people who were in our wagon train and what became of them and how their families are scattered over the west. The Crowleys settled in Polk County, as did the Fulkersons. Glen Burnett, who was our wagon train preacher, lived in Polk County for a while and also in Yamhill County. The Finleys and the Kirks, the Browns and the Blakeleys all settled in Linn County. Ben Simpson, with his family, settled at Salem.

"I was married in November, the year I was 15. I married Albert Davidson. I lived with him three years and then went back to live with my folks. I had two children, Thomas and Mary. Reverend William Roberts, one of the early missionaries, was the minister who married us, and L. F. Grover, who later became governor of Oregon, was one of the guests at my wedding. I was married to John Estes on December 4—I don't remember the year, but I was about 22 years old. We had three children—Benjamin, John, and Alice. All of my children are dead, but I have three grandchildren and eight great-grand-children.

"Mr. Estes and I came to Portland in 1858. He bought a half a block facing on Broadway, just across from W. S. Ladd's home. My husband worked for his brother, Levi Estes, who had a sawmill. Among our neighbors were the Glens, the Powells, and the Carsons. No, I didn't visit the Ladds, nor the other well-to-do people here, because I was pretty much of a hand to stay at home and do my housework. My son was a playmate of Willie Ladd. If there was sickness anywhere, I was glad to help them out. In fact, whenever there was a birth, a death, or sickness, you could usually count on finding me there, for I was considered a good nurse, and in those days Portland was a village and the people were very simple and friendly. Everybody knew everyone else.

"We stayed in Portland until about 1861. My mother needed me at home, and so my husband sold out our half block here in Portland for $1700 and we went to the old homestead near Salem. In those days when a man and his wife took up a claim the man owned 320 acres and his wife owned 320 acres. My mother deeded one-half of her half to me. That gave me 160 acres. My sister Isabel had married Henry Boon, who ran a bookstore in Salem. It is now called the Patton Book Store. My mother had given Isabel the other half of the claim, so when I bought Isabel out I owned 320 acres.

"One of my most distinct memories of Salem is of the big flood in the winter of 1861-62. Almost all of Salem was under water. Lots of people who had been driven out of their homes by the high water stayed in the courthouse. No, the high water didn't wash away any bridges across the Willamette, because in those days they didn't have any bridges. They crossed in ferryboats. After the high water in December, 1861, came the deep snow, which stayed on the ground for nearly six weeks. That winter was certainly a hard winter, particularly on stock.

"I lived at Salem over 20 years. I moved to Portland some years ago to live with my niece, Mrs. Charles M. Cox. Her husband was with Feldenheimer's Jewelry Store many years. He was a brother of Dr. Norris Cox. My niece's maiden name was Minnie Munkers. Some day if you will come and visit me again I will tell you more, but that's about all I can think of today.

Oregon Journal
March 21 and 22, 1923

Jane Straight Bingham

Mrs. Bingham was a resident of Canemah, Oregon, at the time of this interview.

"One of the most vivid recollections of my childhood is of seeing the Indians who had murdered Dr. Whitman and his party hanging with the black caps over their heads on the gallows at Oregon City. They were hanged by the sheriff, Joe Meek. In those days people did not have grand opera, or even the movies, so they came from all over the country to witness the hanging of these Indians."

Oregon Journal
July 6, 1922

Mary Thompson Epple

"I was born in Johnson County, Missouri. My father's name was Squire M. D. Thompson. He was born in Tennessee. My mother, whose maiden name was Sarah Baldwin, was born in South Carolina. They were married in Tennessee in 1840. I was the second of their three children and was born on October 3, 1842.

"When I was a girl we always had men teachers. Usually our teachers were preachers. They preached for the love of it, and taught school to make a living. There wasn't any school near our place, so I went to school at Columbus, 12 miles from our farm. I boarded, my room and board costing five dollars a month. Yes, that sounds pretty cheap, but in those days eggs were only five cents a dozen, butter was ten to fifteen cents a pound, milk was about ten or fifteen cents a gallon, bacon was only five or six cents a pound, and other things accordingly.

"Most of the people in the country at that time were people of moderate means. Not many of them were able to afford to own slaves. My father and his brothers owned slaves. When Father died, in 1848, Mother sent the slaves he had left her back to his family, for Mother, though she was born in South Carolina, didn't believe in slavery. All of my father's men folks fought in the Confederate Army, but my brother had been brought up by Mother with an intense love for the Union and with a dislike for slavery, so he fought in the Union Army.

"I was married on August 11, 1858, to David Murdick. My husband enlisted in the Union Army, and the last letter I got from him was from Helena, Arkansas, in 1863. He was marked on the rolls of the Army as missing. I suppose he was killed and buried where he fell, without anyone knowing who he was. They didn't have identification tags in those days, as they did during the World War.

"Before the breaking out of the Civil War conditions were very much disturbed along the Kansas-Missouri border. Feeling about slavery was so intense that it caused a great deal of bloodshed. After the war started it seemed as if fighting was a sort of free for all. You didn't know whether you were going to be killed by the Confederate soldiers or the Union soldiers or the bushwhackers or some neighbor who had a grudge against you. For the most part, the men folks slept out in the brush at night. No one trusted anyone else. If you spoke in favor of the Union cause, some neighbor would report it to the bushwhackers, or, if you spoke in favor of the Confederates, the word got out, and the Union sympathizers swooped down on you .

"Some of the Union people in Johnson County went to Leavenworth and asked for help. Captain Jim Lane and Captain Jim Jennison came with a lot of mounted men and stayed in Johnson County twelve days. They got a list of Confederate sympathizers and of the bushwhackers and they burned their houses and barns, ran off their stock, and did what they called 'foraging'. They escorted about 300 Union families to Kansas. They escorted our family to Aubrey, on the state line. We were there from January 12 to March 8. Captain Jennison was mighty unpopular with the Confederate sympathizers in Missouri. They called his soldiers Jennison's Jayhawkers, though their real title was the Seventh Kansas Regiment.

"A man named Charles W. Quantrell, who was born in Maryland in 1836, organized a band of guerrillas, or bushwhackers, as they were called, from among the men of Jackson, Clay, and Cass Counties, Missouri. At first they stole horses and waylaid ammunition trains. General Jim Lane, who was in command of the Kansas Militia, tried to capture Quantrell, but Quantrell always seemed to be able to escape and turn the tables on the regular soldiers. Cole Younger and Frank and Jesse James were among Quantrell's best men.

"As my husband was serving in the Union Army, I had gone home to stay with Mother and had gone with her to Aubrey. One morning, in the spring of 1862, just about sunrise, we heard a knock at the door. Mother and I went to the door to see what was the matter. I can remember how startled and scared I was when we opened the door and two horses stuck their heads in the door. The men on the horses spurred them and made them put their heads in the door and at the same time the men pointed their pistols at us and said, 'Where are your folks?'

"My brother-in-law heard the commotion and came running downstairs from his bedroom. They took him prisoner and made him go with them. My brother, my cousin, and a young man friend of theirs were still upstairs. They wanted to leave the house and run to escape, but three men in a house nearby had started to run away and been shot and killed, so Mother told them to stay where they were.

"One of the men who had taken my brother-in-law had said that Captain Quantrell was raiding the town, so Mother said, 'I am going to go and see Quantrell.'

"Quantrell had about 40 bushwhackers with him. He had a lot of the men folks rounded up, his soldiers having formed a ring around them. Mother went to where the soldiers were and said, 'I want to see Captain Quantrell.'

"Captain Quantrell stepped up to Mother and said, 'I am Captain Quantrell. What can I do for you?'

"Mother said, 'I have three young men at my house. One of them is 20 and the other two are 19. I don't want your men to kill them or hurt them.'

"One of Quantrell's men said, 'Go and get them.'

"Mother said, 'What are you going to do with them?'

"Quantrell turned to the man, motioned for him to be still, and said to Mother, 'Bring all three of the young men at your house here, and I'll talk to them. If their names are not on my list, I'll see that they are not hurt.'

"Mother went back to the house, returned with the three young men, and after Quantrell had talked with them a while, he let them go.

"In a little while Quantrell's men began scattering through the town, breaking open stores and taking what they wanted. They gathered up all the horses and stock in town. By this time they had broken open the saloon and most of them were pretty noisy and boisterous. Finally, they left town, driving the stock in front of them.

"We decided to move to a safer place, so we went to Lawrence, Kansas."

Charles William Quantrell was born at Hagerstown, Maryland, on July 20, 1836. While he was a boy the family moved to Cleveland, Ohio. He and his brother, several years older, attended the public school at Cleveland. The father had died shortly before they moved to Cleveland, and Mrs. Quantrell died after they had been in Cleveland a year or two. The older brother quit school and went to Kansas, where he secured work. Charles Quantrell was a very studious boy, so he decided to secure an education. He earned his way, while attending high school, by doing odd jobs in Cleveland. In 1856 his brother wrote him from Kansas, saying he was going to California and he asked Charlie to go with him. Charles Quantrell had been looking with longing eyes toward a college education, but he gave up this plan and went to Kansas, where he joined his brother.

At this time Charles William Quantrell was 20 years old. He and his brother bought a team and wagon, outfitted it, and started for their trip across the plains to California. As neither of the young men had taken sides with either the Jayhawkers or the Border Ruffians, they anticipated no difficulty.

A few days after they had started they camped one evening on the banks of the Cottonwood River in Kansas. Not long after supper they noticed a party of horsemen coming toward them. The two Quantrell boys walked out toward them, the older one waving a white handkerchief to show they were friends. The horsemen were a small body of Captain Jim Lane's Jayhawkers. Disregarding the waving white handkerchief, they fired a volley at the two Quantrell boys, killing the older one instantly and wounding Charles W. Quantrell seriously. They hitched the horses to the Quantrell wagon, threw the tent on, and left the two Quantrell boys, both dead, apparently, on the prairie. Charles W. Quantrell did not regain consciousness till next morning. He lay beside the body of his dead brother for three days before he was able to crawl to the banks of the Cottonwood to quench his thirst. A Shawnee Indian, passing by, stopped and bound up the wounds of Charles Quantrell and buried his brother. The Shawnee Indian took the wounded man with him and nursed him back to health. Quantrell swore to avenge his brother's death. From a quiet, studious boy, he became a bloodthirsty, merciless assassin. He lived only for revenge.

"When Quantrell and his men raided Aubrey and my mother appealed to him for the lives of my brother, my cousin, my brother-in-law and a friend of theirs who was staying at our home, Quantrell's men were rounding up the Union sympathizers. Some of the men folks fired at Quantrell's men. Quantrell's men attacked them. They took refuge in a house not far from ours.

"It happened that Bill Cody (whose house we were renting) was at Aubrey when Quantrell made his raid. He was one of the number of men who had fired on Quantrell's men. The bushwhackers killed the men who had taken refuge in this house, all except Cody. He escaped, mounted his horse, and, though they pursued him, he outran them. He came back to town that same night, after Quantrell's men had left.

"We decided that things were too strenuous in Aubrey, so we moved to Lawrence, Kansas. My brother got work driving a freight outfit to Fort Union, New Mexico. We left Lawrence on August 18, 1863. Three days later, Captain William Quantrell, with 400 bushwhackers, raided the town, killed over 150 people, and burned many of the buildings.

"Conditions were so bad in Kansas and Missouri during the war that you didn't know when you went to bed whether you would wake up the next morning dead or alive, so we went to Peru, Nebraska. My husband, who was in the union Army, dropped from sight in Arkansas, and I have never heard of him from that day to this. I don't know whether he was killed in battle or died of his wounds or what became of him. I started a millinery store at Peru, Nebraska.

"On June 25, 1868, I married George F. Epple, who had come from Germany ten years before. We had seven children. My daughter Carrie married E. F. Redd of Pendleton. Rozene is a teacher here in Portland. Lillian married Robert Renn of Pendleton. They live in Spokane. Mary lives in Portland. Sarah died. Edith married Fred Ross of Yakima.

"After I married Mr. Epple, we moved to Eudora, eight miles from Lawrence, and later moved to Lawrence, where my husband carried on his business of making pottery. He was a hand turner. We lived in Lawrence for 20 years. In 1890 we came to Pendleton, to be with my daughter, Mrs. C. F. Colesworthy. We lived in Pendleton 20 years, coming down to Portland in 1910.

"It's too bad you never happened to interview Fred Eggert, the shoe man, here in Portland. We left Lawrence three days before Quantrell's raid, but he was there at the time. He was a clerk in Duncan's Drygoods Store. One of Quantrell's men told him to open the safe. He said, 'I don't know the combination.'

"One of the other men pointed his gun at him and said, 'Let's kill him.'

"The other man said, 'Oh, he's just a boy. Let him go. Don't kill him.'

"So they didn't."

Oregon Journal
April 24, 1929

Mrs. W. C. Kantner

Mrs. Kantner was born in Linn County, Missouri, in 1856. This conversation took place on the train between Portland and Salem.

"We started for Oregon in the spring of 1865. My brother, William Wesley White, was captain of the wagon train. He became a pioneer of Wallowa County and lived at Enterprise for many years. There were over 100 wagons in our train. I was nine years old and my memories of the trip across the plains are very vivid.

"I will mention but one incident of the trip. On account of the danger of having our stock stolen, we kept guards on duty with the cattle all night long while crossing the plains. One night one of our party, a Baptist minister, started out to take his turn as guard. It was about midnight, and the night was cold. He decided to wrap his blanket around his shoulders to keep from getting chilled through. His son saw a stealthy figure approach. He waited till the moon came out from behind a cloud and, seeing that the approaching figure was wearing a blanket, he took careful aim and fired. As the blanketed figure pitched forward the young man called out, 'That Indian will never steal any more stock.' And ran to see if the Indian was dead. When he found he had killed his father he nearly went crazy. The dead man had been a general favorite in the wagon train and had preached on the Sunday preceding his death. We buried him in the roadway and scattered the ashes of our campfire over his grave and drove the cattle over it so the Indians would not find the grave and dig up the body."

Oregon Journal
undated

Alma Howe

Mrs. Howe was interviewed at her home in Hood River.

"The Indians, for 30 years or more, called me 'the law-maker'. They used to come to me to settle their troubles among themselves and their disputes with the white people. For 25 years Indian George was a regular visitor at my home, and he has eaten hundreds of meals at my house. He was one of the last of the Wasco Indians. His mother was a Nez Perce, his father a Wasco. When Oscar Stranahan died, Indian George said, 'Oscar a good man. Too bad he dead. But we still got Mrs. Howe.' He was celebrated all over the valley for his ability to foretell the weather. He was about 90 when he died. Some years ago, when I was very sick, the Indian preacher held meetings every night, which all the Indians in the neighborhood attended, praying for my recovery. I think that paid me for all the meals I have furnished the Indians and all the trouble I have taken for them."

Oregon Journal
undated

Jeanette Love Esterbrook

"I was born December 29, 1855, on Fall Creek, in **Lane County, Oregon**. My father, David S. Love, was born in Philadelphia. My mother's maiden name was Helen Marney Stewart. Father crossed the plains to Oregon in 1853. Robert and Henry Pittock, and George Meyers, who started one of the first salmon canneries on the Columbia, and also my father's brothers, John and James, were members of this wagon train.

"My father was a journeyman carpenter at Memphis, Tennessee, when words of the discovery of gold reached him in the fall of 1848. He went at once down the Mississippi to New Orleans and in the fall of 1848, with some others, took passage on a sailing vessel for San Francisco. This vessel was delayed by constant gales while going around the Horn and was also delayed in South America. After meeting storms and calms and other delays, it finally reached San Francisco in the fall of 1849, having been eleven months on the way.

"After mining for a while in California, Father heard of the rich gold strikes in Australia, so he went to Australia, where he mined for a while. From Australia he returned to the United States, going to his home at Allegheny, Pennsylvania. My mother's people, like my father's, were Scotch. Mother's people lived at Pittsburgh, Pennsylvania. Father met Mother first when she was seven years old. Father and Mother were both in the same wagon train crossing the plains in '53. Mother had her 18th birthday, which was on June 22, 1853, while on the plains. Mother was born in 1825 and Father in 1828.

"My mother's father, John Stewart, started across the plains with his wife and four daughters, two of whom were married. There were over 100 wagons in their train. Some distance beyond Salt Lake, when the wagon train was pretty well strung out, some of the wagons took the fork in the road that led to Salt Lake. This was in the forenoon. The rest of the wagons came on and did not notice that some had turned off, so continued the trip until it came time to camp that night. My mother's half-sister, Mrs. James Stewart, with her family, was with the part of the train that had turned off toward Salt Lake. Her little girl, Jessie, who was seven years old and who was a twin of John Stewart, was riding with my mother's mother. This little girl didn't see her folks again for two years, for the wagons that had headed for Salt Lake wintered there and went

86

on next spring to California.

"After the train had divided, my folks met someone who told them there was a shorter way to the Willamette Valley by what was later known as the Greenhorn Cut-off. This was supposed to take them into the head of the valley near Eugene. They crossed the summit of the Cascades between Summit Lake and Diamond Peak. They found there was a trail but no wagon road, so they had to make a road. The trail took them to the headwaters of the middle fork of the Willamette River. They were almost out of provisions, their cattle were worn out, and the wagons were almost racked to pieces. Martin Blanding started on ahead to go to the settlements on the other side of the Cascades and secure help. He was found at the foot of Butte Disappointment, near the present town of Lowell, almost starved to death. He told them of the emigrant train he had left and also that they had been out of flour three weeks and were very short of provisions. A settler rode all night, visiting the farmers around there, securing provisions and help to go to the aid of the stranded wagon train. Robert Tandy was first in the search party to reach the emigrants. He found part of them at Big Prairie, near the site of the present town of Oakridge. The emigrants were taken to Eugene and parceled out among the settlers. My mother's father and mother, her sister Agnes, and herself and her nieces, Jeanette Stewart Warner, and Jessie Stewart, were taken by the Bowman family, at Pleasant Hill. They were guests there for some time.

"My mother's father bought a relinquishment claim on Eall Creek, where Fall Creek Post Office is now located. My father bought a relinquishment from John Brattian farther up this same creek. Father hired my mother to stay with his mother, as she was almost an invalid as a result of the hardships suffered on this trip. This, of course, was before my father and mother were married. While Mother stayed with Mrs. Love, my father went up the valley, where he got work at his trade as a carpenter.

"Mother told me that that first winter the only flour they had was what they ground from wheat in the coffee mill. Father and Mother were married on February 2, 1855. They bought a few sheep. Timber wolves were abundant in those days, as well as bears, so they brought the sheep up at night and put them in a pen. One evening, when I was two years old, Mother left me with Grandmother Love while she went out to bring the sheep up. They were half a mile away. Unknown to my mother, I toddled out to follow her. Mother went to the top of the hill about half a mile from our log cabin to see if she could locate the sheep. Just as she got there six big timber wolves came toward her. She backed away from them, and when she had got 100 yards away she turned to run and fell over me. She grabbed me up and started to run with the wolves following her. She said she never ran so far nor so fast before, and it seemed she never would get to the cabin.

"The Christmas before I was two years old my grandfather started, with a few Christmas presents, for my Aunt Mary's cabin. She lived between our place and Grandfather's place, which was about two miles from Aunt Mary's. Aunt Mary knew he was coming with the Christmas presents for the children, so when he did not arrive she became anxious and gave the alarm. There was snow on the ground, but the wind had blown the snow over his tracks. For two weeks the men hunted for him, but from that day to this his disappearance has remained an unsolved mystery.

"It is surprising how bold the timber wolves were during the winter, when game was scarce. My brother Walter was born on January 15, 1858. A neighbor, Mrs. Bagley, was staying with Mother. When Walter was three or four days old three big timber wolves came close to the door and began howling. Father went out to drive them away, but they snarled and snapped at him and wouldn't go. Mrs. Bagley grabbed up the ax and, brandishing it, charged the wolves, and they ran away.

"My people crossed the plains to Oregon in 1853. They came out here to take up land, but every one of my relatives bought squatter's rights of settlers who had already taken claims. When my brother was eight months old, and I was two or three years old, my father and mother left us with her mother and her sister Agnes while they took my father's mother to her son John, who had a tinshop in Jacksonville. The care of Grandmother Love and the children was too much for Mother. Her son John was not married, so he hired the widow Harris and her daughter Sophia to keep house for him and to take care of Grandmother Love. John later married Sophia. Their daughter Mary married John Hanley at Jacksonville. Their son George McKay Love married Fanny Dowell, and their other two chil-

88

dren, John and Maggie, died of smallpox during the epidemic that took so many lives in Jacksonville.

"When I was five years old we moved to Springfield. We were there during the big flood of 1861-62. My mother's mother kept house for us and took care of the two boys while Mother and I went to school. Miss Mary Brattain was the teacher. Mother had never had much opportunity to go to school and this was the first good chance she had to study grammar and some of the other things she wanted to know about.

"My father had a carpenter shop, where he did cabinet work, near the millrace. Walter and I went to his shop one day. He told us to play in the shavings and sawdust and not get in mischief while he worked. Presently I missed Walter, who was about two or three years old. The last I remembered of him was seeing him throwing sticks into the millrace. There was a log close to the shore, so I crawled out on the log and looked to see if I could see him under the water, but I couldn't find him. My father was working upstairs in the cabinet shop. I crawled up those 30 steep steps and told him I couldn't find Walter. Father and the other men hurried down and in a moment or two they discovered Walter lying in the bottom of the millpond, which was about 15 feet deep. One of the men dived and brought Walter up. Everyone told Father that Walter was dead. Father wouldn't give up. Mother rubbed Walter's legs, and Father worked his arms up and down and rolled him and held him up to get the water out, and did everything he could. It was nearly three hours before Walter finally showed some signs of life and finally came to. He grew up, was married, and had a large family, but he was always a little deaf from having been under the water.

"In the spring of 1861, when we were living in Springfield, my aunt Ellis brought her three children to our house, and also her sweetheart, William Pennington. I was only five years old, but I remember distinctly their marriage in our home. They went away on horseback on their wedding journey, leaving my aunt's three children, Hugh, Agnes, and James, with us.

"Next spring came the big flood, after the hard winter of '61-62. The water came into our house, so we had to live in the attic for three days. Finally someone came in a boat and took us to Skinner's Butte. That same spring Father built a boat 32 feet long and rigged up a sail for it, and my father and mother, my uncle and aunt Pennington, with my aunt's three children, Mr. Powers, my two brothers and I, sailed down the Willamette to Oregon City. They hauled our boat around the falls and then we sailed down to Portland, where we stopped for several days while Father bought supplies. From Portland we sailed down to the mouth of the Columbia, sailing by day and camping on the river bank at night.

"At the Cascades we hired teams to haul our boat to the upper Cascades. At The Dalles, Father bought a wagon and some oxen and we started for the Salmon River mines. This was when there was so much excitement about the rich gold discoveries around Lewiston. While we were camped at the site of where Pendleton was later built we met some men coming from Auburn, in what is now Baker County. As this was much nearer than Lewiston and the men said the mines were as rich as those around Lewiston, Father and Mother decided to go to Auburn.

"In those days the road beyond Pendleton followed the side of the hill. Father thought he would take a short cut and head directly for the mountains, but the wagon mired down so he had to unhitch the oxen and fasten them to the back of the wagon to pull it out. In doing this the wagon was upset and one of the front wheels was broke and all of Mother's dishes fell out of the copper kettle, to Mother's great disgust. We had to stop at the agency for a week to make a new wheel for the wagon.

"We had a hard time getting over the Blue Mountains. We got caught in a hard storm and the cattle wouldn't face the driving hail. We later camped not far from where the town of La Grande was later built. In crossing Rock Creek, which was high, the oxen got tangled up and Father had to wade out to get them straightened up. In doing so he was washed down the stream and nearly drowned.

"We finally reached Auburn on June 1, 1862. Father and Mother started a hotel in a tent. Mother did the work while Father built a log hotel in which we kept boarders all that summer and winter. Father hired Ole and Maggie Olson to help do the cooking and wait on the table. About 2000 people wintered in Auburn the winter of '62.

"That fall, in November, two men were stabbed in a dispute while playing cards. They had quarrelled over the game, and the two men had walked out of the saloon, when they were followed by Spanish Tom, who stabbed them and then ran away. The Spaniard was arrested at Mormon Basin and was brought back and turned over to Sheriff Hall. Captain Johnson demanded that the trial of Spanish Tom be held out on the hillside, where the miners could be present.

"While the trial was going on someone grabbed the chain fastened around the Spaniard's ankle and began pulling at it, while the sheriff and his deputies tried to hold Spanish Tom. They got the Spaniard away from the sheriff, put a rope around his neck and started off at full speed. When they struck Freezeout Gulch, his head struck a log and his neck was broken. They put the rope over the limb of a big tree, pulled Spanish Tom up, and left him hanging there. They dragged him past our hotel. Father tried to make us go in, but we saw the whole thing."

Oregon Journal
September 14 and 15, 1927

Mrs. C. Alderson

Mrs. Alderson came with her parents and five of her 12 siblings to Oregon in 1852. She was interviewed at her home in Portland.

"When I was ten years old—that was in 1852—we started across the plains by ox team for Oregon....When we reached The Dalles we stayed there for a week, during which time Father sold our oxen and wagons. Father wanted Mother to go down the river on the log raft with our goods. My mother refused to go on the raft. She said to Father, 'We have crossed the plains together, we have lived together 34 years, and I am not going to be separated from you now.' So Mother and I walked down the trail with Father, who was driving our cows from The Dalles to the Cascades."

Oregon Journal
undated

Catherine Thomas Morris

"I suppose I really ought to start this interview with telling you where and when and why I was born. My name before I was married was Catherine Thomas, and I was born in Nodaway County, Missouri, on June 27, 1841. I suppose I ought to begin feeling like an old woman, but I don't. In spite of all the scolding and lectures my children and grandchildren and great-grandchildren give me, I go along serenely and do about as I please. It's pretty hard to improve a person and make them change their ways after they are my age. As far as that goes, I can't see that the present fashions or ways are any improvement on the times when I was a girl, 75 years ago. The flappers of today have their necking parties, compared to which our play games, as we young folks used to call 'Drop the Handkerchief', playing 'Postoffice', and other kissing games, were innocent. However, I am not much of a hand to tell other people how to live their own lives. That's a job each person has to decide for himself or herself.

"You want me to get back to the time we crossed the plains? First, I'm going to tell you about my father and mother. My father's name was Turpen T. Thomas. He was born in England. My mother's maiden name was Nancy Curl. They were married in Indiana and I am the fifth of their nine children.

"I went to school for two short spells before we crossed the plains to Oregon, 77 years ago. I didn't get much chance to go to school, for I spent quite some time when I was a girl on the go.

"In the spring of 1849 Father hitched up the oxen to our prairie schooner and we took the old Santa Fe Trail and went down into Texas where we visited my mother's sister for about a year. In the summer of 1850 we headed north again and went back to Missouri. Next spring —that would be the spring of 1851—Father yoked up the oxen again and we started for the Willamette Valley.

"We had two well-built wagons. The fact of the matter was, we had to, because there were eight children in our family, so it took one wagon to hold our family and the other wagon to carry our provisions and bedding. Because Father had had considerable experience in traveling on the plains the other folks in the wagon train elected him captain.

"There were around 100 wagons in our train. About 25 young chaps got jobs with the different emigrants driving a team for their board. There were lots of young girls in the train, to say nothing of the children. I was only 10 years old, but I certainly can remember vividly the skylarking and good times the young folks enjoyed around the campfire.

"There was one young chap, along about 20 or thereabouts, whose name was Steve Devenish. He was an awfully jolly, likeable chap. All the girls liked him. He was quite a cut-up and a great hand at joking.

"One day some Indians came to our wagon train and, like most Indians, they were very anxious to get hold of some of the white girls for wives. When Steve found what the chief wanted he pointed to one of the prettiest girls in the bunch and asked the chief what he would pay for her. The chief offered ten horses. Steve and the chief bargained back and forth and finally the chief raised his bid to 20 horses. Steve said, 'Sold. She's yours.' All the girls and young fellows thought this was a great joke.

"Next day the chief caught up with us and turned 20 head of horses into our loose stock and demanded the girl. Steve explained that he was joking, that white people didn't sell their women for horses, that a white man didn't have to pay anything for a wife and sometimes she was dear at that price. The Indian couldn't see the joke. He became angry and demanded that Steve carry out his bargain. Finally the girl's father and my father, the captain of the train, sent the Indian about his business and we went on.

"That night the Indians swooped down on us and stampeded our stock. Father was left with two wagons and not an ox, a mule, or a horse to move a wheel. The father of the girl that Steve had jokingly sold also lost his stock. The men made up a party and started out to overtake the Indians. When they caught up with them the Indians met them with a volley of arrows and one of our men was badly wounded, and as the Indians outnumbered our party the men came back.

"After rounding up all of the cattle, horses and mules in the party, they found they would have to abandon at least half of the wagons. The women-folks certainly felt bad to see their treasured possessions left. Mother had to leave all of her treasured possessions, including her linen tablecloths, napkins, bed quilts and towels and other things that she had spun and woven herself. The only keepsake that mother was able to sneak out of the wagon was a six-pound flatiron that her mother gave her for a wedding present. All of the contents of the 50 wagons was burned with the wagons, so the Indians wouldn't get them.

"The father of the girl who had been sold to the Indian chief was furious. He got his gun and was going to kill Steve, because he and his wife lost all their stock and had to abandon one wagon with most of their heirlooms and keepsakes. The men-folks held the father of the girl so he wouldn't kill Steve, but he swore that the first chance he got he would kill him, as the world would be better off to be rid of a fool that would play such a joke on the Indians and cause the loss of the livestock and more than 50 wagons.

"The men had a meeting and decided not to kill Steve, because he had not intended to bring such a calamity on the wagon train through his practical joke. They figured that another such joke would wipe them clear off the map, so they had better not take any chances. They passed a sentence of banishment on Steve and told him he would have to strike out alone and that if he tried to return to the wagon train he would be killed.

"The loss of more than half of our wagons meant that every child over ten had to walk. I was one of the ones that had to walk, and we walked for the next two months, nearly choked by dust, as they made us walk about in the middle of the wagon train, so the Indians couldn't swoop and get us.

"When Steve struck out from the wagon train the morning we moved out, after we had burned the 50 wagons, all the girls gave him their lunch so he would have provisions for the next few days and wouldn't starve. We all cried, because we liked Steve. The men-folks held the father of the girl that Steve had sold till Steve got out of sight, and he went away at a good lick. The hostile Indians were all around, so we knew we were seeing Steve for the last time. The men that had tried him for his practical joke told him that he would have to head south for California and not to come to the Willamette Valley as there was no room in Oregon for him.

"We all felt pretty bad for a few days after Steve had left. We hoped that he wouldn't fall into the hands of the chief that he had played the joke on, for fear Steve would be tortured. We hoped the Indians would kill him quickly.

"In a week or two our shoes and stockings were worn out. The country was full of crickets. Someone told me that they could sting like bees, and every time one lit on my bare legs it made me jump like a jackrabbit.

"A good many years after we had reached the Willamette Valley my brother went up to the Idaho mines. Just about dusk one evening he stopped at a miner's cabin and asked if he could stay all night. The miner invited him and after he got a good look at him said, 'Isn't your name Thomas?' My brother told him it was.

"The miner said: 'I crossed the plains with you and your people. At least, I came part way across the plains with you. After the Indians stole our stock they made me leave the train and strike out alone for California. Naturally, I expected the Indians to kill me, but by traveling off the road and watching like a hawk I dodged the Indians and overtook a wagon train that was bound for California. They took me in and I mined for a few years in California.

"After the Indians had stolen a good part of our stock another bunch of Indians rode up to us and demanded a beef, flour, bacon and coffee as rent for the grass our stock ate while passing through their country. Father had the men corral the wagons and get out the guns.

"We had very heavy canvas on our wagon, so heavy that when the Indians shot arrows into it the barb of the arrow would stick in the canvas and not go clear through.

While the Indians and the men were disputing one of the Indians thrust his hand under the wagon cover to steal some bacon from our wagon. Mother saw his hand and came down as hard as she could with the butcher knife, across his knuckles. He let out a yell, and a moment later our wagon cover was in flames. Another Indian had set fire to it. The men and mother put the fire out, so it only burned one corner. One of the men struck the Indian over the head with his gun, and, I guess, broke his skull. They dragged the Indian to one side of the road and got ready to shoot the other Indians, but they lit out, and after awhile we pulled out. For several nights after that the Indians would shoot at our stock, and quite a few arrowheads buried themselves in the canvas of our tent, but the guards ran the Indians off every time they came around, so they finally gave it up.

"Pretty soon we ran out of food, so we sent word to the soldiers at The Dalles. They sent a pack train to meet us. They issued to each person four pounds of flour and some bacon, and to the older folks coffee.

"At The Dalles we found, in addition to the government troops, a blacksmith shop, a store, and two saloons. It wasn't much of a place in those days.

"Ours was the first wagon train that season to go over the Barlow Pass. The men had to cut away the down timber from the road and repair the road. The Hood River Loop is a pleasure trip now, but I wish you could have seen it when we came down Laurel Hill 77 years ago. We tied a heavy rope to the back axle of the wagon, wrapped the rope around a tree and the men who were holding the rope inched the wagon down Laurel Hill by letting the rope out a little at a time. Each wagon had a single yoke of oxen with a man at the head of each ox to keep shoving back on its face or by its horns, so they would hold the wagon back.

"When we got to Foster's, which we reached on August 20, the man whose oxen Father had hired had to have his oxen, so Father got an Indian pony and rode down into Linn County to see my mother's brother, Jim Curl, who had settled in Linn County in 1847. He had raised three good crops of grain and had some fat young oxen. He drove up and got us and took us to his place, six miles from Scio. He had picked out a land claim for us, about a mile and a half from his place, so we moved on it and Father soon had a cabin up.

"I cannot hope to explain to you how happy we all were. Father and Mother and all eight of us children had crossed the plains in good health. We children were particularly happy, for, instead of having to strike out each morning and walk barefooted in the dust, where we stubbed our toes, stepped on cactus and watched that we didn't step on any rattlesnakes, we were in a country where the grass was belly-deep for the cattle and when the sea breeze made it wave it looked like waves of changeable green silk. We didn't have to worry about the Indians running off our stock. No longer did we have to eat bacon, beans, and camp bread, and not get as much of them as we wanted, for here we had found a country of beauty, where we could have all the vegetables we wanted, where the hills were full of deer, and the streams full of trout, where, when we looked to the westward, instead of seeing nothing but a long winding train of prairie schooners with a cloud of dust hanging over all, we saw waving grass and vividly green fir trees. We looked up at a blue sky with white clouds and to the eastward we could see Mount Hood, clean and clear and beautiful and so so wonderful that it almost took your breath.

"Just before sunup Father would go out on one of the

game trails and would be back in time for breakfast with a deer slung shotpouch fashion over his shoulders. All the settlers around the forks of the Santiam used to go out in the fall and kill wild hogs. The hogs had got away from the early settlers and lived on mast wherever there were oak trees.

"We girls soon found we had to be careful about going out on the prairie unless we were on horseback, for the country was full of widehorned Spanish cattle as wild as deer and as savage as wildcats, but within a few years the men-folks had killed off most of these wild cattle.

"For my 13th birthday I was given a spinning wheel. This was in 1854. Mother was a good hand at carding wool. People used to bring in their wool, and we washed, carded, spun and wove it on shares, so we soon had plenty of clothes. Mother used alder bark to dye the cloth brown and oak bark to dye it butternut color. We had no nails, so the men-folks used an auger, and pegs made out of oak, to build the houses.

"The first school I went to was at the home of Mrs. Delphine Hamilton. She was a New York lady who had brought out some schoolbooks. She took 12 of us children and taught us in her home.

"Later the settlers got together and put up a regular schoolhouse out of logs. Professor Easop A. McInish taught school for' several years. He charged $10 a term for each pupil. The children came from as far as ten miles away. Some of the young men were 20 years old and the girls 16 or 17. I think they did as much sparking as studying. He kept a bunch of heavy hazel switches in the different corners of the schoolhouse, so wherever he was he could get one right away, and he sure knew how to use it. In the summertime the opening that served for a window was left open, but in winter time the window was covered with oiled foolscap paper in place of glass.

"I remember one day an Englishman came to visit our school. The teacher invited him to make a talk. He said, 'I don't 'old with girls going to school. All the heducation a girl needs is to know enough to go into the 'ay and gather heggs and all the figgering she needs is to know enough to weigh butter.'

"No, my folks wouldn't let me go to dances. They held that the devil was in the fiddle and that if a girl danced, she was dancing her way to hell.

"I guess human nature hasn't changed much. The girls of

that day liked to pick out their own husbands as well as they do today, in spite of parental objection. One of my girl chums had a fellow that her folks thought was a kind of harum-scarum chap that wasn't good for anything but hunting and fishing. They liked each other, though, so he arranged to bring a couple of saddle horses and hide them in a grove near her place. She watched her chance, sneaked out, and they rode lickety-clip to the Willamette River, where they caught a boat, intending to go up into Washington Territory and get married. When the folks on the boat learned that they were eloping, one of the passengers said he was a preacher and would marry them, so they didn't have to go to Vancouver, but got married right on the boat. They came back, settled down, and after their first baby came someone told them the passenger that had married them wasn't a preacher at all but was just a practical joker, so they hunted up a sure-enough preacher and got married again.

"I was 16 when I was married. My husband's name was Lee Morris. Becky Morris, who was crowned queen of the Linn County Pioneers at Brownsville recently, is my sister-in-law. She and I married brothers. My husband and I were married on Sunday at my parents' home. The Rev. W. R. Bishop performed the marriage ceremony. We didn't have to have any license in those days and some folks tried to argue with me that any contract entered into on Sunday is illegal, but our contract of marriage turned out pretty well, for we had ten children, nine of whom are still living, to say nothing of 35 grandchildren and 45 great-grandchildren.

"We were married in 1857 and in 1859 we moved up east of the mountains. We lived the winter of 1859 in a blockhouse in Wasco County. We took up a place on Three Mile. My husband and my brother, Newton Morris, hauled the first load of freight for the government to the Warm Springs Indian Agency.

"Each generation thinks that it is a great improvement on past generations. In a way I suppose this is true or we would make no progress, but in some ways I cannot help thinking that, as busy as they were, the pioneers of Oregon had more time to be kindly, thoughtful, and considerate than the people of today. When I was a girl, if a woman got sick she didn't have to hire a trained nurse. Her neighbors came in, did the housework, took her children to their homes to care for till she was well, brought her home-made bread and jellies and other things, and if a man met with an accident or was sick, all the men in the neighborhood would put in his crop for him or reap his grain, making it a day's picnic, just as if they were going to a house-raising. If he was out of wood they would haul wood and cut it up, and in every way the neighbors showed a spirit of helpfulness and service.

"In these days many families have no children and others have one child. In those days there were usually from 10 to 15 children in the family so that children had no chance to grow up spoiled and selfish. They had to learn to share their things and to help each other. Both the boys and the girls had certain duties that they had to perform, so they had very little time to get into mischief. Because we were so busy with our work we appreciated all the more the occasional social gatherings and parties we went to. It seems to me that the children of today are so blase'—so much is done for them.

"In 1862 my husband wanted me to go back to my folks in Linn County, so he could go to the mines at Bannock City, Idaho. After he had tried his luck mining awhile he came back to the Willamette Valley, bought some emigrant wagons and for the next four years freighted to the mines. He built a store at Bannock City. He did not make what would be considered big money in these days, but nevertheless we were able to save a good deal of it, for there were less things to spend money on. We didn't buy any radios nor automobiles and we didn't feel it necessary to turn in our old prairie schooners for a new model. Our oxen weren't six-cylindered but if you gave them time enough they usually arrived where they started for. If you will look back over an account book kept by some old pioneer you will not find any payments made for rent, gas bills, electric lights, milk, butcher bills, fuel bills nor many other such expenses as the housewife of today has to meet. I used to cook over the fireplace and I have cooked many a meal and darned many a sock by the light of a grease light. We used to save the bear fat or elk grease and with a twisted bit of rag and a teacup of grease, we had a light that might not have been very stylish but it served the purpose.

"After my husband quit freighting to the mines we lived in the Willamette Valley for a while and then moved back to eastern Oregon and ran sheep and horses on Juniper Flat in

Wasco County. It hardly seems possible when I look around my home in The Dalles now, that I knew it 77 years ago, when there was only one store, a couple of saloons, a blacksmith shop and some soldiers.

"My grandchildren and great-grandchildren are all getting good educations. I suppose that's a good thing to do, but I often wonder, after everybody gets educated, if there will be anybody left to do the real work and make a living for the rest of them. Every year the government or the state or the county or the city gives jobs to more people and, of course, that means that taxes go higher and higher till it's an expensive luxury to own a farm or other property."

Oregon Journal
August 8-11, 1928

Caroline Augusta Dix Kamm

Mrs. Kamm's father came to Oregon as a missionary in 1838. She was born at Lapwai, "which is now part of Idaho, but at the time of my birth was located in Oregon," in 1840. She was interviewed in Portland.

"My brother, John Henry Dix Gray, was born March 29, 1839, at Lapwai. He was the first white child to be born west of the Rocky Mountains."

Oregon Journal
December 23, 1931

Violet Ann Brown Kersey

Mrs. Kersey was born "on the old Salem state road between Dallas and Salem, about one and a half miles northeast of Dallas," in 1851. She was interviewed at her home in Dallas, Oregon.

"My father was a man of great force of character. He had good judgment and he thought he could pick out a husband better than could, but as I had to live with the man who was to be my husband I decided to do the picking myself."

Oregon Journal
September 2, 1930

Rebecca Larkins Jones

Mrs. Jones was born in Old Waconda, Oregon, in 1850. She was interviewed at her home in Brooks, Oregon.

"When I was 16 the young man who later became my

husband would hitch up his father's wagon, put a board across the seat, and take me driving. No, I suppose it wasn't so speedy or stylish as the automobile, but it served the purpose just as well. So far as that goes, an ox team and prairie schooner served every purpose of love-making and courtship.

Oregon Journal
August 3, 1922

Harriet Elizabeth Tuctness Bailey

"I was born in Dallas County, Missouri, June 8, 1849. My father, James Tuctness, was born in Tennessee. My mother's maiden name was Pamelia Baker. She also was born in Tennessee. Father and Mother were married in Missouri. I am the only one of their seven children now living.

"We crossed the plains to the Willamette Valley in 1853. I celebrated my fourth birthday on the plains.

"Father took up a donation land claim of 640 acres near Parrott Mountain, in Yamhill County. The first winter we were here we lived in Mr. Zumwalt's cabin. Father put in that winter getting out sawlogs for Mr. Zumwalt.

"Father built a cabin on our place in the spring of 1854. The first year or two we couldn't raise a garden. The deer would come in at night and eat up the lettuce and carrotts and other vegetables. Father used to put out salt on a block of wood near our house. The deer would come there to lick the salt. Father would lie in the fence corner and shoot a deer whenever we needed meat. There were lots of grouse and pheasants on our place.

"We children had to walk four miles to the Pleasant Hill School. We only had one three-months' term each year, and that was in summer.

"My brothers died young, so my older sister and I had to take their place on the farm. We gathered the wheat and oats, tied it in bundles, and shocked it. I used to drive the harrow when Father was broadcasting grain. I also milked the cows. Mother said she didn't want her girls to be farm hands, so she taught us to cook, to make soap, to spin and weave and to do other housework.

"I was married on June 12, 1867, to George S. Bailey. My husband was born in Tennessee. He came to Oregon in 1865. He was 13 years older than I. We bought 100 acres of school land near Butteville at $1.25 an acre.

"We started our married life simply. I cooked over the fireplace and we slept in a home-made bedstead made of poles and my husband made the kitchen table and the benches that served us for chairs.

"We had some sheep. Mother had taught me how to card the wool and spin it, so my husband would shear the sheep and I would wash the wool, card it, spin it, and weave cloth. I still have my spinning wheel. When I was a girl, at home, we used to spin the wool thread and make socks. We sold these knitted socks for 50 cents a pair. Socks were accepted at the stores in exchange for groceries at 50 cents a pair. The stores shipped them up to the mines and the storekeeper usually got 75 cents a pair. The miners had to pay $1.50 a pair. Just as beaver pelts and wheat were legal tender at one time, so there was a time in the Willamette Valley when socks were as good as legal tender. The merchants used to ship bales of them up into eastern Oregon and into Idaho.

"My mother used to tan deer hides and make buckskin gloves. Harvest hands, stage drivers and men working with the cattle used to buy all the gloves my mother could make. My mother was a master hand at making shoes. She made shoes not only for herself and my father but for us children. I never had a pair of store shoes till I was grown.

"When I was a girl I belonged to the United Brethren Church. The Congregationalists built a church near our place, so I went there, but they couldn't raise money to pay the preacher, so that church shriveled up and died. For the past 25 or 30 years
have gone to the Methodist Church.

"My mother worked hard all her life. She died when she was 87 years old.

"My mother's brother, Endymion Baker, crossed the plains the year before we did. He came in 1852. He started to take a place that joined Portland but he didn't like the idea of having to drink river water, so he took up a place on a small stream three or four miles from Sherwood. Yes, I suppose he could have dug a well if he had taken a claim joining Portland, but he didn't think that was worthwhile when he could take up a place with running water on the farm.

"Not many young girls nowadays can quilt, nor, for that

102

matter, are many of them good cooks. They can't even take care of babies when they get married. They have everything to learn after they get married. Girls of my day and generation were trained to be wives and homemakers, not to drive cars and play contract bridge."

Oregon Journal
undated

Mrs. Robert Judson

Mrs. Judson was born near Halls Ferry, Marion County, Oregon, in 1855. She was interviewed at her home in South Salem.

"My parents had four children when they started by ox team across the plains for the six-months trip to Oregon. John, who was about a year and a half old, died near the Blue Mountains. Ellen, who was a few months old, died not far from where the city of Pendleton now is. Mother's brother, many years later, took the map Mother had made showing the location of the graves of her two babies and went up there to put headstones on the graves. He could locate only one of the graves, and it was in a field planted to wheat, so he couldn't tell just where the grave was."

Oregon Journal
June 27, 1922

Mary McGhee Day

"My maiden name was Mary McGhee. My father, Reverend John Wesley McGhee, was born in Virginia, April 29, 1821, and was the fourth generation of McGhees born in Virginia. My mother, whose maiden name was Cordelia Miller, was also a southerner. Her mother was a native of South Carolina and her father of Kentucky, while she was born in Missouri.

"Father and Mother were married in Missouri, December 10, 1840. The stories of opportunity and adventure in California were too much for my father, so in 1850 he went to the California gold diggings. In 1851 and 1852 he preached at Yreka and at other mining camps in northern California. The discovery of rich diggings here at Jacksonville and the removal of most of his congregation from northern California to southern Oregon caused him to come to southern Oregon.

"In 1852 he took a claim in Sams Valley. He had not been there long when Chief Sam came to him and said, 'You are a

Bible man. I don't want you to be killed. Go away for a little while. My young men are going on the warpath. The white men insult our women and kill our men. I cannot hold the young men in our tribe in check.' A little later the first Rogue River War, that of 1853, was raging.

"Father went to Salem and took up a donation land claim, six miles southeast of Salem, next to the claim of Sam A. Clark, the editor, historian and author. He went back to the Rogue River country to serve in the war, but before he went he wrote to Mother to come to Oregon.

"I was born in Missouri, November 22, 1841, so I was 12 years old at the time we came to Oregon. There were three of us children. We came by way of the Isthmus of Panama. Mother took the Panama fever while at the Isthmus. She died about 300 miles south of the Golden Gate. We three children had to see her dropped over the side of the boat and buried at sea.

"I had seen St. Louis and New Orleans, so when we landed at Portland it seemed to me a very insignificant little village and I doubted if it would ever amount to much.

"At Oregon City we met a man who knew my father. He took us to Salem with him on the boat and had his son drive us out to Father's place. Father didn't know which boat we were coming on, for Mother had no way of letting him know. He said to me, 'Where is your mother, Mary?'

"I said, 'She was buried at sea three days before we got to San Francisco.'

"Mother being dead, Father had no way of caring for us, so he arranged with Tabitha Brown of Forest Grove for us to stay at her boarding school. Mrs. Brown was a Vermonter, the widow of an Episcopal clergyman. She was well educated, badly crippled, a good manager and very strict. The girls who stayed with here had no opportunity to be vamps or flappers.

"Professor Marsh was president of Tualatin Academy. Judge Shattuck was one of my teachers. The older students taught the primary grades. My brother Melville and Henry Spalding were the only boys in Mrs. Brown's school. They were both small. Martha Spalding, who was the daughter of Reverend H. H. Spalding, the associate of Dr. Marcus Whitman, looked after her brother Henry, while I cared for my brother Melville.

"I spent two years at Tualatin Academy, meeting the

Walkers, Eells, Smith, Griffin, and other missionary families. In 1859, when I was 18, I entered Willamette University. The following year I taught school to earn money to continue my work at college. In 1861 I resumed my work at Willamette and graduated in 1863 in the class with Lucy Ann Lee, daughter of Jason Lee. I took up teaching as my life work. I taught my first school in Moore's Valley, in the foothills near North Yamhill. I taught in a log cabin owned by Governor Woods. He and my mother were cousins.

"Among the early pioneers who settled in Polk County were the Hydes. Aaron Hyde was one of the early day teachers in Portland. He married Rachel Whitaker. My father met his widow, Mrs. Rachel Hyde, and married her.

"Silas J. Day was a miner and lived at Jacksonville. He was appointed a delegate to the Odd Fellows Grand Lodge at Salem. The ladies of the Methodist Church of Salem gave a strawberry festival for the delegates. President T. M. Gatch of Willamette University was an Odd Fellow. He came to me and said, 'Mary, I want you to meet a friend of mine from southern Oregon.' He introduced me to Mr. Day.

"A little later, Reverend C. C. Stratton, a graduate of Willamette University, said to me, 'Mary, I want you to meet a friend of mine from southern Oregon, and he, also, introduced me to Mr. Day.

"Later in the evening Sam May said, 'Mary, I want you to meet...'

"I said, 'I know him already. His name is Silas Day. He is a miner and lives at Jacksonville.'

"Mr. Day called on me the next day. We did our courting by letter. Reverend C. C. Stratton performed the marriage ceremony.

"I forgot to tell you that before I was married I taught at the select school at Albany under Judge Flinn. When Albany College was founded Dr. Monteith, Professor H. K. Warren, and I were the first teachers.

"I have lived at Jacksonville since 1871. When I came here Jacksonville was the metropolis of southern Oregon. Medford was undreamed of and Ashland was a little sawmill and gristmill town. Today there is a larger population in our graveyard than in the city itself. Most of the old pioneers are asleep on the hillside."

Oregon Journal
July 6, 1922

Elizabeth Shepard Holtgrieve

"I had three brothers and three sisters. I am the only one of our family left. I celebrated my 88th birthday a few days ago.

"I was born on Brush Creek, about 15 miles from Rome, in Jefferson County, Iowa, October 16, 1840. When my father, Henry Shepard, moved to Iowa, in 1837, the Indians had not yet been moved from there."

I have interviewed many pioneers who, like Mrs. Holtgrieve, were born in Iowa. People from Iowa seem to be great travellers. You will find them wherever you go. When the Iowa people living at Los Angeles have their annual picnic, you would think that most of the population of Iowa lived at Los Angeles.

The state of Iowa itself is almost as much a traveler as its people, for it was originally owned by France. In 1762 it was ceded to Spain. In 1800 it was ceded back to France. In 1803 it was ceded to the United States, and for the next two years was a part of the District of Louisiana, but was under the government of Indiana Territory. In 1805 it became a part of the Louisiana Territory. In 1812 it was made a part of Missouri Territory. From 1821 to 1834 it was what was known as the unorganized territory of the United States. In 1834 it became a part of the Michigan Territory. In 1836 it was made a part of Wisconsin Territory. It was a part of Wisconsin Territory when Mrs. Holtgrieve's father moved there, in 1837. In 1838 the Territory of Wisconsin was divided, the Western
division being named Iowa, which is a Winnebago word meaning, "The Sleepy Ones." In 1840 Iowa Territory applied for admission into the Union as a state, but, because of disputes as to the boundaries of the territory, it was not created a state till 1846.

"Two years after my father moved to Iowa, in 1837, his father, Charles Shepard, and his mother, whose maiden name was Sarah Springstein, came with three of their sons—Charles, James, and Joseph—to Iowa. My father was born at Dewaynesburg, in Schenectady County, New York. My mother, whose maiden name was Elizabeth Mattern, was born on November 14, 1811, in Hesse-Darmstadt, Germany.

"One of the Christmases of my girlhood that I remember particularly well was that of 1849, when I was 9 years old. I remember it because my mother died just a week before

Christmas. Another thing that makes me remember it is that Father and the neighbors were all talking about going to the California gold diggings. Father didn't go, because Mother died, but two of our neighbors did.

"In the fall of 1851 my father, with my sister Nancy and myself and my Uncle Joseph and Aunt Louisa Shepard, and with two young men, Ellis Straway and Martin Hoffman, went to St. Joseph, Missouri. Father hired Martin Hoffman to drive one of the wagons across the plains. We had two wagons, six yoke of oxen, three milch cows, and a saddle horse. My sister Nancy hired out to a family to cook for them. My uncle and aunt, with Ellis Straway and Martin Hoffman, got work for the Indian agent across the Missouri River from St. Joe. My aunt did the cooking for the three men. Father turned the cattle loose on the river bottom of the Missouri across from St. Joe. I spent that winter with a family named Hanna, who had come from Iowa with us. My uncle and aunt, the Hannas, and Ellis Straway were to go across the plains with us, but when it came time to start, in the spring of 1852, they had heard so much talk about people dying on the plains or being killed by the Indians that they backed out and started home. They went by boat to St. Louis and from there by team to Iowa. Martin Hoffman and my father brought the cattle across the river to St. Joe and put them in a corral. They had wintered in good shape, but after they were put into the corral someone stole our three cows.

"Three young men who wanted to go to Oregon asked Father if they could go with him. They dickered back and forth and Father agreed to take them across the plains for $10 each. We started on April 27, went up the Missouri to Westport, which is now Kansas City, and there we joined a train of emigrants. Dr. Bonner was captain of the train. His half-brother, Mr. Eddy, was his assistant. Two days after we had started from Westport we were joined by two men who were driving horses in place of oxen. They were planning to go to California. They traveled with us. After we had been traveling about two weeks three Indians came to our camp and asked if they could sleep under one of our wagons. Next morning we gave them breakfast. They traveled with us for three days. The third night they stole all the horses in the wagon train. We never got them back. Mr. Kane, the man who was driving the horses, the man who was going to California, had to buy a team of horses from some French horse traders we met.

"I became very fond of a little girl in our wagon train whose name was Elmira Eddy. She took the cholera and died of it and was buried on the plains. Martin Hoffman, who was driving one of our wagons, also took the cholera, but he recovered.

"About three days' travel the other side of the Boise River, another wagon train overtook us. In this train was a young woman named Lucinda Nelson. The two trains camped together for the next three nights. There was a minister in the wagon train, the Reverend Mr. Coston. Father suggested to Miss Nelson that they should take advantage of the minister's being with them and get married. Father and Miss Nelson had known each other for two or three days, so they were married on the banks of the Boise River, and she brought her things over to our wagon.

"About five miles east of The Dalles we came to a wagon standing at the side Of the road and found there were seven children, the oldest a girl of about 13. Their father and mother, James and Mehala Fitzgerald, had died and they didn't know what to do.

"It was late when we got to The Dalles. Father heard that the army officer there was looking for someone to run the hospital so he looked the matter up and took the job of running the hospital for the winter. There was only one patient in the hospital, a woman. She died the night we moved in, and we didn't have any more patients all winter. There were two rooms in the hospital. We hadn't been there long when a family named Gardner moved into the hospital, so we had to move into one room and let them have the other. My sister Nancy worked for a family named Coston, all winter. They lived at the Cascades.

"I spent my twelfth birthday on the plains cooking dinner at our camp between Boise and The Dalles. In the spring of 1853 Father took up for his donation land claim a beautiful, grassy, level meadow about two miles west of The Dalles, near Mill Creek. Just above our place was an Indian camp. Father put in a garden. The Indian chief who was camped above us told us that Father had settled on their grazing land, and that they had lived there and used it so long that the oldest Indian couldn't remember when they weren't there. Of course, Father didn't want to give up the place, so Mark, the Indian chief, went to Major Alvord at The Dalles and asked him to make us get off their land. Major Alvord sent some soldiers to help us move our things off the Indian's land. The soldiers and the Indians moved our household goods down to the river bank.

"The Nelsons, my stepmother's people, had taken up a place south and west of Portland, just over a high hill later known as Council Crest. Father decided to go there. Captain Baughman was running a flatboat on the river. Father went to see him at The Dalles to find out what he would charge to take us down the river. Captain Baughman stopped and took our household goods on board his flatboat, and that night he tied his flatboat at his place on the north bank of the Columbia about a mile above the Cascades. As it looked as if it was going to rain, the captain and my father carried our household goods into Captain Baughman's house. It was raining next day, so Captain Baughman said we could stay at his home until the storm was over. Meanwhile, he had to make a trip to The Dalles.

"It rained off an on for the next two or three weeks. Captain Baughman moved one family named Smith and another one named Joslyn, who settled at what is now White Salmon. Captain Baughman told my father that he could show him a good claim two or three miles from the Cascades, and that Father could make a good living cutting wood on it to be sold to the steamers or shipped to The Dalles. Father went to look at the claim and liked it, so he took it up. My father worked that summer, helping to build a boat at what is now Cascade Locks. A man named Bush was the owner of the boat, and it was finished and ready to be launched in September. It was launched on September 12, 1853, and they held a big celebration. Everybody in that part of the country attended and came to the big dinner, and, of course, they had plenty to drink.

"We moved onto our claim, living in a tent all summer. In the fall Father and some other men cut logs and built a log house. Father hired these men to cut cordwood, which he stacked on the riverbank. My sister, while we wintered at The Dalles in 1852, worked for a family at Cascade Falls, Washington. On January 24, 1853, she married Francis M. Vanderpool. They were married at the home of Mr. and Mrs. Bush, the man Father had worked for helping to build the boat. After my sister was married she worked at the boarding house at Cascade

Falls. A few months after she was married, her husband, **Mr.** Vanderpool, went up to Umatilla to work, while my sister went down to Portland, where she worked for the next three years. After three years, Mr. Vanderpool came back and he and my sister took up a place later known as the Bevins place. It joined my father's place. The Stevenson Cemetery is now located on the Vanderpool place.

"In the spring of 1855 my father decided to go to Portland to buy some fruit trees to set out on our place. He told me I could go along and visit my sister Nancy. I was between 14 and 15 years old. Father rowed down the river in a skiff. When we came to the head of Government Island the River was so rough that Father rowed to the lee of the Oregon shore. It was getting toward sundown. Father was figuring on stopping all night at the Davis Place, near Vancouver, but that was five miles farther down the Columbia. We saw a man coming down to the river to get a bucket of water. Father hailed him and said, 'Can we stay all night?'

"The man said, 'I am baching, and not very well fixed to take in company, but if you can make out with what I've got, you're welcome to stay.'

"We spent the night there. He said his name was John Dodd.

"When he found out I was upwards of 14 years old, he said he had a friend, named Henry Holtgrieve, who was looking for a wife. He asked Father when we would be back. He said he would arrange to have his friend there to meet me. We went on to Portland. Father bought his fruit trees. My sister arranged to get off for a little while, so she came back with us. Father hired a flatboat and a young Indian to row it, or sail it if the wind was right. When we were ready to start out of Portland, Mr. Marble and his family, who were moving to Salmon Creek, back of Vancouver, towed our flatboat as far as the Brown place, where the Union Meat Company is now located.

"We stopped at Mr. Dodd's place, on the Oregon shore, five miles from Vancouver. Mr. Holtgrieve was there and he and Father talked the matter over and said he would be up the next week to our place to marry me. He and Mr. Dodd came up to our place, at what is now Stevenson, the following week, and we were married by Matteson Morris, the justice of the peace.

"On our wedding journey down the Columbia from our place we came in a skiff, staying the first night at the Hamilton place and the next night at the Riggs place. The third night we got to my husband's claim. I was 14 and my husband was 28. We were married on his 28th birthday. At first we had very crude furniture. We slept in a bunk made of poles, and had home-made stools and tables, but later my husband went to Vancouver and bought a bedstead and three chairs. Two years later we built a larger house and he bought fallen maple leaf furniture in Vancouver—a table, a stand with drawers, and some chairs.

"Some time ago you wrote up Henry C. Leiser, who lives on his father's donation land claim four miles above Vancouver, on the banks of the Columbia. He was born in Wisconsin in 1848 and came across the plains on 1851. Before our house was finished—this was in 1857—his father and Henry came to our place to stay all night. They had with them the body of Mrs. Lieser, Henry's mother. They put the coffin, with Mrs. Lieser in it, in the front room on a workbench that the carpenters had not yet moved out. My husband went to her funeral, though I couldn't get away on account of my babies. Henry Lieser was a little boy then, about nine years old. Later he went to college at Forest Grove and became a teacher. Afterwards he studied law, was admitted to the bar and practiced law in Vancouver.

"My mother died 1849. Father and my stepmother took up a place on which the town of Stevenson, Washington, was later built. They lived on this place from 1853 to 1863, at which time my stepmother died. During the ten years of their married life they had seven children—Henry, Richard, James, William, Embracilla, Ellen, and Melissa.

"My husband and I lived on the Columbia, five miles from Vancouver. I milked cows and made butter which we sold to the army officers at Fort Vancouver. We had a small lake on our place, and sometimes this lake was fairly black with ducks and geese. At other times it was white with swans. The swans used to pass over in great flocks and would frequently light on our lake. We had all the deer meat, geese, ducks, swans, salmon, and trout we could eat. I haven't seen a flock of swans for years.

"In those days I knew everybody as far up the river as Cascade Falls and down the river as far as Columbia City. In coming up or down the river my friends would usually aim to make our place by nightfall and stay overnight. I am about the only one left who used to live along the river there in the '50's.

"I was married on March 18, 1855. The following year the Indians attacked the Cascades. My sister was visiting me, when one day we saw the Bell and the Fashion, two river steamers, coming past our place with their flags flying at half-mast. Our place was just across the Columbia from Lewis Leiser's place. He had a woodyard, where the steamers stopped to take on wood. John A. Williams rowed across the river from our place to see why the flags on the boats were at half mast. He came back and told us that the Indians had attacked the Cascades, had killed Mr. Sinclair and some other men there, and that all the settlers between the mouth of the Sandy River and the mouth of the Willamette River were advised to go to Portland, while those on the Washington side of the river, from Cape Horn on down, should go to Vancouver. My husband went out to warn the settlers, and upon his return he went to Vancouver. While he was gone, warning the settlers, most of the people along the river passed him in their skiffs on the way to Vancouver. Among the people he met were Mr. Hamilton and his family, and a man named Pierce, who had been shot by the Indians. The following day we saw the Jennie Clark, which had come down from Portland with volunteers. It was headed for the Cascades, but after going up the river a short distance they came back and stopped at Vancouver.

"My husband's sister was at the Middle Cascades. I was afraid that my father, my stepmother, and their two children had been killed, but they wrote me later that as soon as they were warned Father took his rowboat and started across the river. The river was rough, as the wind was blowing strongly from the east. They had forgotten to take a dipper or a pan along to bail the boat, so my stepmother had to use her sunbonnet to bail out the boat. She couldn't bail it out fast enough, so the boat sank before they reached the Oregon shore, but they all managed to get ashore. The steamer Mary came along and took all the women and children, including my stepmother and her two children, to The Dalles.

"Lieutenant Philip Sheridan and the other soldiers had a battle with the Indians, killed some of them, and later hung some of the ones they had captured.

"I lived on our donation land claim near Vancouver from 1855 till 1886, at which time we moved to the Long place, on Columbia Slough. My husband died in 1896. My oldest daughter, Emma, married Zachariah Fitzgerald. He was one of those children that I told you about, whose father and mother died on the plains, leaving seven little children, the oldest of whom was 12 years old. My next child, Oceana, married Alfred Baker. They live in Portland. My son Charlie lives with me. Mary is dead. My next child, John, is farming our old place near Vancouver. My daughter Arie is dead. My youngest boy, Benjamin, is farming our Columbia Slough place. Henrietta, the baby of the family, married Alonzo Miller. Though I have celebrated my 88th birthday, I find that my memory is as clear as it was when I was a girl, particularly about incidents that occurred in my girlhood and when I was a young woman."

Oregon Journal
November 14-16, 1928

Marilla R. Washburn Bailey

"I was born in New York state, December 22, 1839. My maiden name was Marilla R. Washburn. My father, Alfred Washburn, and my mother, whose maiden name was Mary Jane Farrington, were born in New York state.

"My mother's people were among the first settlers in America. They were Quakers. Her grandfather and her father wore Quaker knee breeches with buckles at the knees. I remember very dinstinctly Grandfather always said 'thee' and 'thou'.

"Father was born in 1811 and Mother in 1812. There were 14 children of us—12 boys and 2 girls.

"We moved to Chicago in 1842. Father ran a transfer depot and a livery stable. He did draying and rented sleighs and carriages. I guess if some of our early-day neighbors in Chicago who died during the '40's could come back and take a look at Chicago as it is today they wouldn't know the place.

"In the fall and winter of 1851 a great wave of excitement, the Western fever, swept over all that part of the country. Nearly everybody was talking about the Willamette Valley, the Puget Sound country, or California. Father decided to go to Oregon. He made a contract to bring four families across the plains, he to furnish wagons, teams, and drivers for a stipulated amount. The contract he made was all right as far as it went, but it didn't go far enough, because the families he brought out were to pay him on arrival in Oregon, but it turned out that none of them had the money and, while all of them promised to pay later, none of them ever did.

"We started with five wagons. Father brought out some blooded mares. One of them was a fine Morgan mare. Two of our wagons were drawn by horses, the other three by oxen.

"Two days before we came to Chimney Rock the cholera struck us. Seven died in our train that night and four the next day. A young man in our wagon train named Hyde went out as a guard for the stock that night. When he left, after supper, he seemed perfectly well. When the guard was changed at midnight Mr. Wood brought his body back to the train. He had been taken with severe cramps and died within two hours.

"My brother and I both took the cholera. Mother gave us all the hot whiskey she could pour down us and put flannel cloths soaked in whiskey, as hot as we could bear them, on our stomachs. This cured us.

"Father was a veterinary surgeon. He had brought a lot of medicine for horses and cattle, and also the family medicine chest. My mother was a good practical nurse. In fact, she had to be, to raise 14 children.

"Shortly after my brother and I had the cholera we lay over half a day at Chimney Rock, and when we pulled on the next morning we had a new brother. Father and Mother had started across the plains with 12 children, so now, with our baby brother Melvin, there were 13. Another child was born after we came to Oregon.

"We crossed the Missouri River at St. Joe. There were 72 wagons and eight light buggies in our train. There were 170 men, women, and children. Captain Berry, the captain, took mountain fever and could no longer serve as captain, so my father was elected captain. Dr. Kellogg, one Of the members of our train, always claimed that Captain Berry had yellow fever, but others thought he had mountain fever. Just after the Fourth of July some of the members of our train took smallpox and four died of it.

"My brother, Henry, just older than I, who was 14, was a fine horseman and an expert swimmer. When we reached the Snake River Father told Henry to take the stock across, where they could get better pasture. The horse Henry rode became frightened in the swift water and began faunching around and got into deep water. When my brother tried to get him back in the shallower water he reared up, threw Henry off his back, and kicked him in the head. We stayed there two days searching for my brother's body. Henry was drowned just above Salmon Falls. Mother wrote a notice and fastened it to a board beside the road, asking anyone who found Henry's body to bury it and notify her. The next spring we got a letter from a man named Llewellyn, who had settled above Salem. He said he had found Henry's body and buried it. He sent Mother the things he had found in Henry's pockets. Just before leaving Chicago a chum of Henry's had given him a small horseshoe for good luck. Before we left home Mother wrote our names in indelible ink on strong pieces of cloth and sewed them inside our clothes. Mr. Llewellyn cut from Henry's jacket the label with his name on it and the little good luck horseshoe, and sent them to Mother.

"Just behind us was a train from Michigan. When the Indians attacked them they corralled and fought the Indians off, but four men in the wagon train were killed.

"We used to see a cloud of dust rising and Father would call out to get ready to divide the train. Soon we would hear a low roar, like the sound of surf, and then we would see a big herd of shaggy-haired buffaloes, their heads held low, running at a slow, lumbering trot to the river to drink. They wouldn't stop for anything, so we gave them the right of way. Several times we had to divide our train to let them through.

"We ate buffalo meat and antelope. Some of the families ate sagehens and jackrabbits, but we kids didn't like them and would go hungry before we would eat them.

"When we got to The Dalles Father sold his blooded mares and his stock to the government. In those days there was a fort at The Dalles. Father left his five wagons there, intending to go back and get them later, but he never went back. We went from The Dalles to the Cascades on a flatboat. There we caught a small steamer for Vancouver. We stopped at Vancouver four days and then went to Portland, where we lived till 1854.

"My most vivid recollection of that first winter in Oregon is of the weeping skies and of Mother and me also weeping. I was homesick for my schoolmates in Chicago and I thought I would die. We knew no one in Portland. We had no use for

Portland, nor for Oregon, and were convinced that we never would care for it. We stayed in Portland till 1854, when Father took up a donation land claim near what is now Kelso, Washington.

"I was married at Kelso shortly after my 15th birthday. My first baby, Amanda, was born in Fort Smith, in Cowlitz County, in 1856. The settlers had gathered in the fort there on account of the danger from the Indians. This was during the Indian War of 1855-56. I married John Black, who was born in Ireland and who had a farm near ours. We were married by a justice of the peace.

"In 1856 my parents moved to Olympia. When Amanda was 5 months old I put her into a basket, hung it to the horn of my saddle, and went to Olympia to visit my parents.

"There used to be a trading station named Monticello, where we traded. Later Seth Catlin started a store. His place was called Freeport.

"I lived on our farm, five miles from Kelso, 25 years. All of my ten children were born on the farm. I had five girls and five boys. Four of my daughters and one son are still living.

"Forty-five years ago I moved to Portland. I ran a rooming house and took boarders on Yamhill Street, to support my children. Twenty-five years ago I went to Rossman, British Columbia, and for the next four years I worked as a practical nurse. There I met and married Orrin E. Bailey, a clerk in the hotel. We moved to Ferry County, in northern Washington. We used to trade at Midway, just across the line. Sixteen years ago we moved to St. Johns. My husband works in the woolen mills.

"I am 87 years old and as I look back to my girlhood I cannot help thinking how much more is done for the girls of today than was done for the girls of my day and generation. They have liberty that in our day was undreamed of.

Sometimes I wonder if the girl of today is as self-reliant, self-sacrificing and as useful as girls were when I was a girl.

"I was married at 15, and was not only a good cook and housekeeper, but I knew how to take care of babies, from having cared for my brothers and sisters. I had ten babies of my own and never had help. I could paddle my canoe on the river or handle the oars in a rowboat as well as an Indian. When my husband was away I could rustle the meat on which we lived, for I could handle a revolver or rifle as well as most men. I have

116

shot bears, deer, and all sorts of smaller game. I used to take my revolver out and shoot the heads off grouse and pheasants. In fact, I became so expert with a revolver that at 50 to 100 feet I could beat most men.

"During the early days I lived in tents, in log pens, and in log cabins. The modern mother would think twice before she let her 15-year-old daughter move out on a tract of timber, miles away from any other settler, where she would have to kill the game for meat, cook over a fireplace, take care of the children, make soap and make clothes for the children. In those days we could not run into some handy store to get supplies.

"My first baby, Amanda, born at Fort Smith, Cowlitz County, in 1856, was married when she was 15. Her first child was a girl, whom she named Laura. Laura's first child was also a girl, who is now 13, and who, by the by, is my great-granddaughter. I hope I may live to see my great-granddaughter married and have a child, so I shall have a great-great-granddaughter."

Oregon Journal
March 3 & 4, 1926

Samantha Ann Carter French

"Yes, I guess I can qualify as a pioneer of The Dalles. The first time I stopped at The Dalles was in 1852. At that time, of course, I had no idea that I should later go back to The Dalles and live 47 years in the same house. My maiden name was Samantha Ann Carter. My twin sister's name was Miranda Jane. Mother certainly selected good old fashioned names for us. My sister Miranda Jane, now Mrs. Hinkle, lives at No. 1055 Cleveland Avenue, Portland.

"I was born on August 8, 1850, in Iowa. My father, Robert Carter, with my mother, my two older brothers, Amos and Will, my twin sister and myself, started across the plains for the Willamette Valley in the spring of 1852. On the Platte Father took the cholera and died in a few hours. My brother Amos was only ten and Will was eight. With these boys and her twin girls, hardly more than babies, Mother pressed on to Oregon.

"When we reached The Dalles, Mother sold her outfit and was paid for her oxen and wagon in gold. Part of this money was a $50 gold slug. The little boat running between The Dalles and the Cascades was laid up for repairs. While we were camped on the river bank someone came into our tent and stole my mother's bag, in which she had all of her records and family papers.

"Mother hired a man to take us to the Cascades in a flatboat. Mother's brother, William Howard, with his family, and our family, shared the expense of the flatboat. The flatboat ran upon a snag and filled so that we barely reached the shore before it sank. My uncle had a daughter 17 years old who was sick with mountain fever. As we were coming down the river we went ashore at what is now White Salmon, where she died. My uncle made a rough coffin for her and dug a grave. Just as he was about to lower her into the grave two men came up and volunteered to do it for him.

"At Oregon City Mother shared a cabin the first night with a family who had come some time before. The next morning her $50 slug had disappeared. Mother decided not to take any chances by staying there another night. The woman urged her to stay and said there were so many rough characters around that it would be unsafe to stay in a cabin alone and that someone would come and get the rest of her money. Mother found a small log cabin that had been used to store grain in. She rented this and cleaned it up and we moved in. Mother told my brother Amos to take Father's gun and she would take the ax, and if anybody attempted to come in, to shoot when she gave the word. Late that night, Mother heard someone prowling around the cabin, and presently the latchstring was pulled and someone began to open the door gently. Mother said, 'Amos, point your gun at the door and shoot when I give the word.' The door was hastily closed and the intruder disappeared. Mother was sure it was the woman at whose home we had spent the previous night, who had come back to get the rest of her money.

"Charles Adams, who had started out in our wagon train with his wife and six children, lost his wife shortly after reaching Portland. He and Mother were married in 1853. This made a family of ten children for Mother to care for, and before long she had two more.

"We think the men who worked in the old days from daylight to dark had a hard time. Mother worked from daylight to midnight. She cooked for her family of 12 children over the fireplace, made her own candles, and, in addition to sewing for her husband and her big brood of children, she took in sewing

118

for neighbors who could afford to pay for it. I doubt if many women worked harder than my mother. She lived to be 76.

"They took up a donation land claim five miles south of Oregon City. After proving up they sold it and moved to Albany. My stepfather bought a farm in Benton County, just across the Willamette from Albany. When my brother Amos was 14 he went to work in a bakery at Oregon City and learned the trade. He followed this, and did prospecting and mining, practically all his life.

"Last week I got word that my brother Amos, who was 84 and lived at Copperfield in the Seven Devils Mountains, was sick with pneumonia. I went up there and found he was in bed with the flu, so I brought him to Portland. He is staying with my twin sister Miranda.

"We moved to Albany in 1858. When the high water in the winter of 1861-62 caused the Willamette to rise so that it flooded our farm, we moved to Salem.

"I was a student at Oregon Academy. Miss Draper, who later married Arthur Nicklin, was my teacher. My sister Miranda and I were registered under the name of Adams, though my brothers retained the name of Carter. My stepfather, Mr. Adams, conducted a draying business at Salem from 1862 for some years. Later he ran a store at Salem. In 1871 he went east of the mountains, going into the stock business at Antelope. When we were at Salem we lived on Court Street. Our property adjoined the lot on which the Methodist Church was built. Our next door neighbor was J H. Moores, father of C. B. and Allie Moores."

Oregon Journal
May 4, 1926

Lura Homsley Gibson

"How did I happen to meet my husband? I was out on the porch feeding the homeliest hound pup that ever traveled on four legs. A young chap in a soldier's uniform rode up to the gate and asked me where Joe Ingalls lived. I told him that Mr. Ingalls lived on the next farm. He said, 'I am going there to visit him. He is my uncle.'

"This was during the Civil War, and this young chap had

on a blue uniform with brass buttons and you know how girls fall for a uniform. He told me that Joe Ingalls had married his father's sister. He also told me that his name was George Gibson and that he and Sam Taylor were on a furlough and were stationed at Fort Vancouver. The woman I stayed with was quite a matchmaker. She gave George Gibson and Sam Taylor tickets to a dance to be held at Frank Newman's. The two soldiers were doubtful of being able to attend the dance, as, they said, they had no girls. She said, 'One of you can take Lura Homsley and the other her sister Sarah.' George Gibson and Sam Taylor went on up to Polk County to visit friends, but got back in time for the dance. George Gibson borrowed Bill Kaiser's team and carriage and the four of us went to the dance at Frank Newman's. Georqe came back from Vancouver to see me. You know how it is in war time—a soldier never knows where he's going to be sent next—so George suggested we get married. George and I were married on December 23, 1864, and my sister, Sarah, married Sam Taylor.

"My husband came across the plains in 1852. I was born in Missouri in the spring of '49. My father thinks it was in May. We lost our family Bible while fording a stream coming across the plains to Oregon in 1852. The wagon tipped over and the Bible got lost out, so I never have known what day to celebrate my birthday.

"There were three of us children who started across the plains with my parents. The oldest two children—Georgiana and Lycurges—died not long before we started for Oregon.

"My uncle Jeff Homsley and my uncle Wash Homsley both owned slaves. A slave girl named Winnie, owned by my uncle Jeff, did the housework for us. My mother liked her, but for some reason Father had no use for her and naturally didn't take any pains to conceal his feelings.

"One day when Father and Mother went to town they left Winnie to take care of the two oldest children. I have an idea that Mother had taken the younger children with her. In any event, when they got back home Georgiana and Lycurges were both dead. Winnie, the slave girl, had poisoned them to get even with Father. Winnie was young and strong and good-looking, so Uncle Jeff figured it would be foolish to have her hung, for he would be the loser, so he sold her 'down the river'. In those days the worst punishment you could give a slave was sellinq them 'down the river'. He sold Winnie to a slave owner in New Orleans.

"My father and mother, with us three younger children, started from our home in Missouri with two wagons drawn by oxen for the Willamette Valley. My mother and the baby died at Laramie, Wyoming, of the measles. They were buried by the side of the road. When Father buried Mother he found a piece of sandstone. With his jackknife he scratched deeply on this sandstone this inscription:

'Mary E. Homsley, died June 10, 1852, aged 29'. I lost all track of Mother's grave and supposed that the site of her grave had either been built over or plowed up, but 73 years after Mother was buried, Dr. Grace Raymond Hebard, professor of history at the University of Wyoming, wrote me a letter saying that the Wyoming Historical Society had put up a monument over Mother's grave and that at the services more than 500 people were present, that the mayor of Laramie, Wyoming, was in charge, and that Mother's grave had been banked with flowers.

"My father died September 6, 1908, at the age of 94.

"When Father came to Oregon in the fall of 1852 he took a donation land claim in Clackamas County, on Elliott Prairie. We went to school with the Elliott girls. One of them married Captain Apperson of Park Place. The other married Captain Sanburn, who died recently.

"After my marriage my husband and I lived with Father on Marks Prairie. Father bought for us the old Doc Giesy place. This was also known as the Joe Ingalls place. We came from Pomeroy, Washington, to Portland 22 years ago. I have ten grandchildren and ten great-grandchildren.

"Some time ago you wrote an article about an interview you had with Tom Brents, Congressman, of Walla Walla. My sister and I lived at his mother's place while we went to school. This was in Clackamas County. There was Tom, Jim, Becky, Adelaide, and Sarah Brents. Naturally, living in the family with them we became very fond of them. Tom Brents was an awful cut-up. Tom and most of my other girlhood friends have taken the oneway trail."

Oregon Journal
August 12, 1932

121

Mary Robinson Gilkey

"I was born three miles south of here (Dayton, Oregon), on March 7, 1846. My father, Benjamin Robinson, came across the plains by ox-team in 1844. He was born in New York state in 1814 and moved to Illinois in 1833. From there he went to Missouri, where he found everybody talking about going to Oregon. He got the Oregon fever also. Joel Chrisman hired him to drive one of his wagons. Propinquity is the cause of many a marriage, and it was so in this case, for my father married Elizabeth J. Chrisman, Joel Chrisman's daughter. When they reached The Dalles, Reverend Waller wanted my mother to stop there and teach school, but she decided to come on with the rest of the family to Oregon City. My mother's family spent the winter of 1844 at Oregon City.

"Grandfather Chrisman took up a donation land claim of 640 acres two miles southeast of Dayton. His son Gabriel took up a claim adjoining on the east. My father took up the claim that adjoined on the south. His son-in-law, William Logan, took up the claim that adjoined on the west. Samuel Campbell, and Labon Marin, his sons-in-law, took up claims adjoining these, so that my grandfather and his family owned six square miles of land in one body. I still own part of the old donation land claim. Joe Marin also owns some of his father's original claim.

"On April 14, 1845, my mother, Elizabeth J. Chrisman, who was 26 years old, and my father, who was 31 years old, were married in the log cabin of my mother's parents on their donation land claim. They were married by Enoch Garrison, a Methodist minister, who had taken up a claim near Amity. This was the first marriage in this neighborhood. I was their first child and was born in the old log cabin on our claim. As a child can remember our mud and stick chimney on the outside of our log cabin. I can also remember my mother stooping over the fireplace frying venison in the long-handled frying pan or taking the coals off the old Dutch oven to see if the bread was done. Father made our bedsteads. They were made of poles.

"One of the earliest recollections of my childhood is of Father coming to the door of our log cabin riding a horse and leading a pack horse. This was in the spring of 1849. He kissed me good-bye, and Mother told me he was going away off, to be gone a long while to mine for gold in California. Mother and I and the new baby went to live with my uncle, William Logan. Father came back after awhile from the California gold fields with less money than he had taken there.

"As I told you, I was the first child. John, the next child, who was a baby when Father went to the gold fields, died at the age of 20. Eliza, the next child, married J. B. Stillwell. Araminta, who came next, died when she was a little girl. We children took what they called in those days the 'putrid sore throat'. Ruth, my sister, died of it. I was expected to die.

"In those days they knew nothing of contagious diseases and when a child had diphtheria all of the neighbors would come with their children to the house to visit. The result was that within a few days or weeks there would be many funerals. When my sister Ruth had the putrid sore throat my brother John and I also had it. Mrs. Odell helped nurse us. Father Wilbur preached Ruth's funeral sermon.

"My uncle, William Logan, sold his farm to General W. H. Odell. General Odell married Samuel Thurston's widow. They lived here for some years.

"Mrs. Odell was born in Maine. She influenced my life more than any other person. The first carpet I ever saw was in her home. The first potted plant I ever saw was at Mrs. Odell's house. The pioneer families owned but few books, and the first library I ever saw was at the home of Mrs. Odell. They were books that her first husband, Samuel Thurston, had got in Washington, D. C., when he was a delegate in Congress from Oregon. I remember how astonished I was when I stayed at her house to dinner and she handed me a napkin. I did not know what it was. I had never seen one before and did not like to use it for fear I would get it soiled.

"Mrs. Odell taught school two terms. One evening as she came home from school I saw she was carrying a plant she had dug up. I asked her what she was going to do with that wild flower. She said she was going to look in a book and see what its name was. I remember how profoundly astonished I was to think someone had written this plant's name in a book. I couldn't understand it. That was my first introduction to botany.

"Next to my mother, I never loved anyone so much as Mrs. Odell. She was tall, had blue eyes, had auburn hair, and had a pleasant voice.

"I love to think of the old days, and I like to treasure the old home-made furniture. I have always kept the old home-made cradle, made for me, and in which all of my brothers and sisters were rocked to sleep. It was made from an oak tree cut from the Goodrich donation claim. He used to make home-made cradles, split-bottom chairs, and other homemade furniture for his neighbors.

"Recently, Dr. George Odell died here and was buried in the Odell Cemetery near Dayton. General W. H. Odell, who is now about 96 years of age, was here from Portland to attend the funeral. His father and mother and all his brothers and sisters are buried here. He is the last survivor of the Odell family.

"The first dress I ever had stands out vividly in my memory. Mother washed and carded the wool, spun it, and wove the cloth and made the dress for me, while Dr. Danforth made me a pair of shoes with cloth tops and rawhide soles.

"Joel Palmer, whose son William still lives here in Dayton, was one of our earliest friends. He was tall, of medium build, had a heavy shock of gray hair, and was a fine looking man.

"The first school I attended was at Lafayette. Dr. White was my teacher. Matthew Deady, later a distinguished judge, was also a teacher in the Lafayette School at that time. Mrs. Deady and my aunt were intimate friends. Among the teachers I remember best in my childhood were Virginia Olds and William Alexander. I believe the latter is a cousin of C. B. Moores of Portland. My father was school director for over 30 years. Later I was a student at Lafayette Academy, in which Ed Cartwright and W. B. Nichols were teachers. Mrs. Duniway, who lived at Lafayette, taught there a while. Later we went to Portland Academy and Female Seminary. Father came in every Friday night to get us and drove us to Portland again every Monday morning. I remember that Julius Moreland, J. B. Cox, and Eva Polk and some others were graduated the year we started.

"Later I went to Willamette University. Dr. Wyeth was president at that time. Lucy N. Lee, daughter of Jason Lee was preceptress, and F. H. Grubbs, whom she later married, was one of the teachers. Waife, their daughter, is with a printing company in Portland. I was graduated in 1866. There were 19 in our class.

"Among my schoolmates that I remember with a great deal of pleasure were H. H. Gilfrey, who for the past 40 years or so has been reading clerk in the United States Senate, and Sam Simpson, Oregon's sweet-voiced singer, who was not only bright as a dollar, but very popular with his fellow students. He married Julia Humphrey. I was present at their wedding. Other fellow students whom I highly esteemed were Neamiah Butler of The Dalles, James and Joe Sellwood, Helen Williams, who married Milton Stratton, a brother of Rev. C. C. Stratton; William Wyeth, Ella Starkey, who later married Bob Bybee; and Frances McFarland, who became the wife of Sylvester Simpson.

"One of my girlhood chums of whom I thought a great deal was Martha Forrest. She was 15 when I was 13, so I looked up to her and thought what she did was just about right. One day she failed to come to school and when I asked what had become of her, her people told me that an old bachelor there, Nick Day, had proposed to her and that her people thought it was an excellent match, so she had married him and gone to southern Oregon. I thought it was a dreadful thing for her to go away all alone with that old man and stay with him.

"Several days later Martha's brother proposed to me. Remember, I was only 13 years old at that time, yet a great many of the girls in that day were married a 13. I told him I didn't care to get married—that I wanted to know something, that I wanted to come and go as I pleased, and later I wanted to become a teacher. I told him Mrs. Odell was my ideal and wanted to be like her and be a teacher.

"It is not strange that in those days, when there were so many more men than young women, I received a great many proposals, but I was wedded to my profession, teaching, and for 14 years I continued it. I taught from the time I was 20 until I was 34. I taught my first school on the Molalla River when I was 18 years old. It was a three months' summer school, for which I was paid $25 a month. From there I went to the Pringle neighborhood, south of Salem. Later I taught at Silverton, where I became well acquainted with Mr. and Mrs. T. W. Davenport, and their charming infant, Homer, who became a great cartoonist. From Silverton I went to Jefferson. Next I went to Salem, where, for two years, I taught in Central School. I believe two of the worst youngsters I ever taught were in

Central School, and by the worst I mean the most mischievous. They were Abe McCully and George Wright. George is now a dentist at McMinnville. Also, one of my best pupils was in this school. Her name was Maggie Cosper. For many years she has been a teacher at Salem. After teaching at Salem I taught near Amity, then at Dayton, at Lafayette, and Forest Grove. From Forest Grove I returned to Salem and became a teacher in Willamette University and was a teacher there at the time of my marriage to W. S. Gilkey.

"In 1868 a schoolmate of mine, Fanny Case, who was then divorced and who later married Sam Moreland, told me Colonel Williamson had been making a survey of Mount Hood to determine its height. In a newspaper interview he had announced it was so steep no woman could climb it. Fanny Case and I decided we would show him he didn't know what he was talking about, so we climbed to the summit in 1868. I believe we were the first white women to stand on the summit of Mount Hood. I am an honorary member of the Alpine Club and, of course, eligible to membership in the Mazamas.

"I have given you here and there only a highlight of the past 75 years. Some time, if you will come to my ranch near Dayton and spend a day or two I will tell you enough to fill several notebooks."

Oregon Journal
February 21 & 22, 1922

Susan Piney Yeomans Angell

Mrs. Susan P. Angell of 794 Upper Drive, Portland, is the Queen Mother of Oregon. She was crowned Queen Mother at a recent meeting of the Pioneer Association here in Portland. When I visited Mrs. Angell recently, I said to her, "You are looking mighty well." She said, "Yes, I guess I look pretty well, but I don't feel as well as I look, for I have neuritis in my thimble finger and can't sew any more. The last real sewing to amount to anything I did was piecing a quilt when I was 92 years old.

"My maiden name was Susan Piney Yeomans. I was born in May 12, 1832, at Rome New York. My father, Prentiss Yeomans, was born in Connecticut, as was my mother, whose maiden name was Margaret McKinney. I was the youngest of their ten children. When I was six years old we went from New York State to Iowa, in a covered wagon. My father, when a young man, was a carpenter, but later took up farming. Father bought a farm about three miles from Lowell, Iowa.

"As a girl, I went to singing school and spelling school and occasionally in the winter had a sleighride, though, when I was a girl, there was so much housework to be done that girls and young women didn't get a chance to run around as they do nowadays.

"I was married when I was 15 years old. My husband, Thomas Angell, lived at Lowell. He was a descendant of Thomas Angell, who, with Roger Williams, settled in Rhode Island, where the townsite of Providence was later laid out. My husband was born in New York State. He was a school teacher when he was a young man, but when I married him he was running a grist mill and also a store in Lowell, Iowa.

"When word came of the discovery of gold in California, he said he thought a trip across the plains to the gold fields might help his asthma, so he bought a wagon and an ox team and started across the plains in the spring of 1849. He didn't find mining exactly to his liking, nor particularly profitable, so he took contracts to build cabins at Sacramento. In 1850 he came from San Francisco around the Horn to New York by sailing vessel and then home to Iowa.

"After coming home he seemed restless and discontented. He thought Iowa was too quiet, and there was too little doing, so, during the winter of 1851, he made preparations to cross the plains again to the Pacific Coast. We started on St. Patrick's Day, in 1852. Sarah, my baby girl, was still in long dresses. My brother, Ben, came with us to drive the stock, and my husband hired a man to drive the ox team, while he drove the family wagon, which was pulled by mules.

"My husband had provided a bed for me and a crib for the baby. He also brought along some milch cows, so that we not only had fresh milk, but we had butter, for the jolting of the wagon during the day's trip would churn the milk into butter. I think we were probably better provided than most of the emigrants, for we not only brought along plenty of flour, but my husband also laid in plenty of ham, bacon, cheese, dried fruits, sugar, tea, coffee, and a barrel of crackers.

"Shortly after leaving our home in Iowa we had to camp for a few days on account of the heavy snowstorm. Our wagon train was probably the first to start across the plains. It was a fortunate thing for us, for in 1852 the cholera swept the wagon trains. Those who came late found hundreds of graves beside the Old Oregon Trail. We had no trouble whatever from cholera or from the Indians.

"David McCully was captain of our wagon train. He and his brothers, Asa, Sam, and Ham, were all men of high character, and the longer you knew them the better you liked them. Dave, Asa, and Sam had their families along. Ham was not married. He was with his mother and sister. Dave's brother-in-law, J. L. Starkey, and his wife, were also along. Dave and Mr. Starkey had married sisters, Dave marrying Mary N. Scott.

"The reason we chose Dave McCully as captain was that he and his brother Asa had crossed the plains to California in 1849, and Dave was one of the most resourceful men you ever saw. There was hardly anything that the McCully brothers couldn't do when it came to work along mechanical lines. There was only one wagon train beat us to Oregon, and that was a wagon train drawn by horses.

"We reached the western slope of the Cascades on August 10, two months earlier than many of the other emigrants that year. While crossing a stream on a ferryboat the ferry broke loose from its fastenings and drifted down the stream. Our wagon and oxen were on board, and it looked for a while as though we were in for a pretty serious time, but the ferryboat lodged safely, so no harm came of it.

"We had two fatalities in our wagon train. A son of David McCully, about 12 years old, while riding on a mule and leading a horse to water, was caught in the rope when the horse became frightened, and was dragged to death. He was buried at Fort Kearney. Lawson Roberts, a young man in our wagon train, shot a bear on the other side of a swift stream and started to swim across to get the body of the bear. He was carried down the stream and was pulled under in an eddy and drowned. The men hunted for his body, but they were unable to find it.

"We laid over one day in the Grand Ronde Valley at a place the mountain men called La Grande. It was only an Indian village. I don't remember seeing a single white person there. In fact, I think no white people settled at La Grande till along about the time of the Civil War. While we laid over at La Grande, Mrs. John MacDonald gave birth to a little girl, whom she named La Grande. This little girl later became the wife of

Sam McCully.

"The McCully boys were good boys. The coming of the McCullys to Oregon was almost like one of the old-time tribal migrations, for, in addition to Dave and his family, his mother, and his brothers, Asa, Sam, and Ham, and various other relatives, were in the wagon train. When you travel with people for six months across the plains seeing them under all sorts of conditions, you get to know them pretty well. Some folks improve upon acquaintance. Others don't. The McCullys were the kind of folks that wore well.

"Most of the members of our wagon train settled in or about Salem, but we went down the valley, settling in the forks of the Santiam River. My husband bought a squatter's right on which was built a log cabin. Later we moved to Lebanon, where my husband ran a store. In 1861 we moved east of the mountains, taking up a stock ranch in Wasco County, not far from The Dalles. My son, Oscar, is now running this place. After living on the stock ranch for many years, we moved to The Dalles.

"My husband died in 1888. Of my eight children, three are still living. Homer is a lawyer here in Portland, Oscar is on the old farm, and Sarah, who married William Campbell, is at The Dalles. My son Fred has been gone for 25 years. I think he must have died or been killed shortly after leaving home or he would have written, but for years and years I kept hoping that I would hear from him.

"During the 40 years or more that I lived at The Dalles, I made many friends, of whom I am very fond: Mr. and Mrs. Joe Wilson and their son Fred, Z. F. Moody and his wife and children, Mrs. Elizabeth Lord, Lulu Crandall, and many others. I lived at or near The Dalles from 1861 until two or three years ago.

"As I look back over the 94 years of my life, insofar as my memory serves me, and particularly of the events of the journey across the plains, I am forcibly impressed with the change that time has wrought in the manner and mode of living and transportation. In the raw March day of 1852, when we left our homes in New London, Iowa, we thought we were especially well equipped for the trip across unknown land separating us from the Pacific Coast. And, indeed, we were—measured by the development of transportation as it existed at that time—

for we were able to successfully transport ourselves and equipage across this perilous territory without mishap and ahead of all other trains but one. But, measured by the standards of today, our oxdrawn wagons would be of little avail.

"However, we were contented with our lot and, with an abiding faith in God, who always shapes our destinies, ever kept our eyes toward the land which to us was to be our opportunity, and, with our advantages such as they were, we were able to bring success to our journey.

"As in memory I relive the past, I am reminded of my long journey through life, not unlike the journey across the plains, for life itself is but a great adventure. I am grateful to my Creator for the generous addition to the 'three score years and ten' he has granted me, but cannot but be mindful of the fact that all of my contemporaries, my relatives and friends of those other days when this great West was in the making, have one by one been called over the great divide, and I sit alone in the twilight of life. I am glad to have lived amid the stirring scenes during the formative period of the pioneer lands, and to have been permitted to remain to enjoy the wonderful achievements of this age of invention and of science. I have seen the ox team depart and the express train, the automobile, and the airship take its place. The tallow dip of my childhood is gone and the electric light is substituted. In place of the pony express we now have the telephone, telegraph, and radio.

"Time has indeed wrought wonders in the mechanics of life, but, without discounting the value of all these to the human race, I am mindful that the potency of the homely virtues and moral principles of our fathers and our fathers' fathers alone remain unchanged. Friendship, truth, honesty, loyalty, reverence for God, mother love—these are the eternal verities, and these remain unchanged, yesterday, today, and forever. When we lose our grip on these, the fabric of our existence as a nation will disintegrate as a garment corrupted by moths.

"I leave to my loved ones no heritage that may be inventoried and appraised, but pray I may be granted the privilege of leaving to them this admonition impressed upon me by my observations of life:
'Forget not the homely virtues taught at Mother's knee. Keep the faith of your fathers and live honestly before man and God, and all will be well in the end.'"

Mrs. A. N. Gilbert

"Yes, I am a Forty-niner. I was born July 4, 1849. My father was in the California gold fields at the time, though I was born in Iowa. My father was born at Sussexvale, New Brunswick, September 15, 1814. My father, John McCully, was born in Nova Scotia. When my father was eight years old the family moved to Jefferson County, Ohio, and 22 years later, they moved to Iowa. In 1849 my father, David McCully, with his brother Asa, crossed the plains to California. Late that year they came back by way of the Isthmus. There were six children in my father's family, five boys and one girl.

"Father and his brother were restless after returning from the California gold fields. They wanted to return to the west, so, in 1852, a family council was held and 40 members of the family decided to go to Oregon. Four of the family had gone west in 1849 to spy out the land. These four were my father, his brother Asa, their brother-in-law John Starkey, and William Scott, another brother-in-law. William Scott was murdered for his money on his way home, while crossing the Isthmus.

"The McCullys are of Scotch stock. They are clannish. The ties of family bind them very closely. That is why so many of them decided to go to Oregon in 1852. Among those in the party were the McCullys, the Starkeys, the Scotts, the Walterses, the Loves, and the Reddings. My father was the captain of the train.

"On our way across the plains my oldest brother Joseph, who was 14 years old, was leading the mules to water. Some of the other mules had already been down the stream and were coming back. The mule that my brother was riding became unmanageable and, whirling, tried to join the other mules. Joseph was thrown and a leg was broken. They fixed up a swinging bed in a hack and started for Fort Kearney, about 100 miles on the back trail, to secure surgical attention. Before they reached there they saw their errand would be fruitless, for gangrene had set in and my brother was suffering great agony. They told him he would probably die, so he asked to have the mules headed back for the party, so he could see his people before he died. They buried him on the plains. The next year

131

Uncle Asa went back to put an iron marker on his grave.

"We reached Salem, August 17, 1852. We camped just across the creek from the home of the Parrishes. My father and his brothers were mechanics. They were not only good brick-masons and tinsmiths, but they understood working in iron and could do bridge and boat building. They built the Starkey block, which is still in use here in Salem, for their brother-in-law, J. L. Starkey. It was the first brick building in Salem. I think the Griswold Building was next, and possibly the Moores building the third.

"After looking around at Salem for a short time, Father and Asa traveled up the valley until they came to a farming settlement in Linn County that they liked. Many of the settlers there had taken up 640-acre tracts as donation land claims, so that the land was all taken, but they agreed that if my father and my uncle would settle there and start a store they would reduce the size of their holdings so as to allow them to secure claims there. Father and Uncle Asa built the first house at Harrisburg and established the first store there. Harrisburg became the headquarters of the McCully interests, Sam, David, Asa, John, and Hamilton McCully all settling at Harrisburg or in its immediate vicinity, as well as John Love, a relative.

"In 1853 Asa went to Philadelphia and bought a stock of goods. The goods were shipped around the Horn while Asa returned to Oregon overland in the summer of 1853, to bring out some blooded stock to improve the stock in Linn County. In addition to running the store at Harrisburg, my father and his brother packed pork, made flour, manufactured tinware, and shipped goods to the mines. They furnished a good market for the produce of the farmers around Harrisburg and soon became the largest shipper of produce in that part of the Willamette Valley.

"In 1855 and 1856, when their business had become quite extensive, they were handicapped by having to freight all their goods from Corvallis to Albany by ox team. The town of Corvallis claimed to be at the head of navigation on the Willamette River. In 1855, Father arranged to ship 50 tons of merchandise from Portland to Harrisburg by water. The goods were taken from Portland to Oregon City on board the steamer Portland and from Oregon City to Harrisburg on the shallow-draft river boat Enterprise. My father was on board the boat with the goods.

"When the boat reached Corvallis a deputation of the merchants there came down to the wharf and served notice on Captain Jamison that if he attempted to take the goods to Harrisburg, thus making Harrisburg the head of navigation on the Willamette, they would boycott his boat and ruin his company. After prolonged discussion, Captain Jamison gave orders to dump the 50-ton shipment of my father's goods on the river bank. My father had to secure transportation by ox team from Corvallis to Harrisburg.

"My father was like the granite hills of Scotland. When he made up his mind to do a thing, he was not be swerved or dissuaded. He had decided to ship goods by water to Harrisburg, so he returned to Oregon City, where he purchased an interest in the James Clinton, which was being built to ply on the Yamhill River.

"The citizens of Eugene were very anxious to have a steamboat that would bring freight up the river as far as Eugene. They told my father they would buy $5000 worth of stock in the Clinton if he would agree to run up the river as far as Eugene. The Clinton was soon finished and was operated between Oregon City and Harrisburg, making occasional trips to Eugene.

"My father was still indignant at the treatment he had received from the captain of the Enterprise, so he bought the Enterprise and put it on the run with the Clinton. He then bought the Portland and the Relief and the headquarters of the company was established in a small store on the site now occupied by the Ladd and Bush Bank. The other transportation men decided to put the McCullys out of business, so in 1860 they formed a merger of the various rival lines on the lower Willamette and on the Columbia under the name of the Oregon Steam Navigation Company.

"My father and his associates saw that it was a life and death fight. My father took the matter up with E. N. Cooke and S. P. Church, both prominent and able men, residents of Salem. My father and his brothers, when they were young men, had traveled all over the country selling Seth Thomas clocks. Later they had acquired the state rights for Iowa to manufacture and sell the Champion fanning mill. This business experience stood them in good stead now. They had added to their various industries at Harrisburg not only the manufacturing of flour and the packing of pork, but a furniture factory, a tin shop, and a plant where fanning mills were manufactured. It was vital to their growth that they maintain their transportation interest on the river. S. T. Church had become a partner with my father and his brothers in the business at Harrisburg and had charge of the sale of goods to the mines. E. N. Cooke was the first state treasurer of Oregon. He had been a merchant in Ohio, and he owned a store at Salem. Later the firm name became Cooke, McCully & Co. My father, Asa McCully, Cook, and Church, organized the People's Transportation Company to fight their powerful rival, the Oregon Steam Navigation Company, and they waged an aggressive and successful fight."

Oregon Journal
May 23, 1923

Elizabeth Paschal Gay

"My maiden name was Elizabeth Paschal. My father, Isaac Paschal, was born in Virginia. His people were Huguenots. You remember that Henry IV, through the Edict of Nantes, gave religious liberty to the Protestants of France, in 1598. In 1685 Louis XIV revoked this edict, so my father's people, with thousands of other French Protestants, left France. Most of the Huguenots went to England or to Holland.

"My father's people came in the early days from England to Virginia. My father moved from Virginia to Ohio, where I was born June 5, 1838. I will be 90 years old if I live till next June. My mother's maiden name was Margaret McVicar. She also was born in Virginia. Her father was Irish, her mother Scotch. Father and Mother were married in Virginia and the first three of their five children were born in that state. I think I am the only one of the children now living. My brother William may be living. The last time I heard from him was during the Civil War, when he was fighting in the Union Army. The probability is, however, that he is dead.

"On December 4, 1859, I married Dr. A. R. Dillon of Virginia. We were married in Virginia. My husband was a skillful surgeon and a good doctor when he was sober. We started for Oregon in the spring of 1862. A widower with two small children wanted to come to Oregon. He told me that if I would do the cooking and take care of his two children he would bring my husband and myself across the plains for $200. We paid him $100 down and were to pay the other $100 when we reached the Willamette Valley. He started out with young cattle. One yoke gave out, so my husband had to buy a yoke to replace the ones that died. When we got to Fort Hall the man announced that he had changed his plans and was going to turn off there for California. This left us stranded. However, we found a bachelor who was headed for Oregon, so we arranged to go with him. When we got to Salmon Falls he sold his outfit and told us he was going to the mines, so once more we were stranded. I had to throw away my feather bed and all of our cooking outfit except a frying pan and a tea-kettle. My husband had to abandon his medical library. Our little girl, Jessie, was two years old. I paid a man $10 to let Jessie ride in his wagon. My husband and I struck out on foot with what food we could carry, and during the next 500 miles I only got to ride three miles. We were without money, and when my husband heard that a town had been started a few months before at a place called Auburn, near where the town of Baker City was later located, he decided that there might be a chance to practice his profession there, so we walked to Auburn.

"A great many of the emigrants who were on their way from Missouri to the Willamette Valley learned about the new mining camp at Auburn, and settled in Auburn, or elsewhere in eastern Oregon. When we got there, late in September, 1862, there were several stores, a livery stable, blacksmith shops, and quite a number of saloons. The houses were all log cabins, as there was no sawmill anywhere in that vicinity. Late that fall Mr. Leveredge brought some sawmill equipment up from Portland. He and Mr. Bowen set up their sawmill in the lower part of Blue Canyon and began sawing lumber, so the price came down to $60 a thousand. Next spring they moved their portable mill to the Boise mines. Theirs was the first sawmill in Baker County. In the summer of 1863 Carter and Davis started a waterpower mill just east of Auburn.

"We lived next door to a family named Peters. I remember Alice Peters very well. One of the Peters girls married a Mr. Cleaver.

"My husband started the practice of medicine in Auburn. Most of his cases were surgical cases, caused by accidents.

When he was not too drunk he had very good success. He spent all he made in the saloons. I took to washing to pay for our food. Food was high. I charged a dollar to wash and iron a boiled shirt, and 50 cents for a woolen shirt. I renember one day a saloonkeeper's wife gave me a big washing. She had not had any washing done for over three weeks. It took me all of one day to wash it and all of next day to iron it. It was really worth more, but I decided to charge her only five dollars. When I took the washing to her she said, "I'll have my husband credit the five dollars I owe you on the bill your husband owes at the saloon.'

"I felt terribly bad about it, and told her I needed the money. She wouldn't pay me, however, and as we were arguing, her husband, who was in the next room, said, 'Pay the woman the five dollars you owe her. She don't have to take in washing to pay her husband's bar bills. If I was fool enough to trust him, it's my fault, not hers.' He made her pay me the five dollars.

"You have no idea of the difficulty we had that winter. I had to melt snow in a pan over an open fireplace to do the washing. We had no stove. I boiled the clothes in a brass kettle and strung lines from the rafters all over the house, so the clothes could dry. I had to walk through the deep snow to deliver the washing, except for the miners, who brought their dirty clothes and called for them.

"We spent the fall of 1862 and the winter of 1862-63 at Auburn. In the spring of 1863 we moved to the mines in Boise Basin. I ran across a family there who were keeping a restaurant at Placerville. The man's wife and I had both taught school in the same district in Iowa.

"My husband, though a skillful surgeon, was unable to leave liquor alone, so he did not earn enough money to feed our baby, Jessie, and myself. The woman who was running the restaurant told me if I would wait on the tables and do the dishes, my baby and I could stay there and work for our board. The miners who boarded at the restaurant would frequently give me a nugget, or sometimes a half dollar, as a tip.

"When my husband was sober he was not only a capable doctor but a kindly, considerate gentleman, but when he was drunk, which was most of the time, he would worry Jessie till she cried, and then he would beat her for crying. Life with him was so impossible that I went to The Dalles to get away from him.

"He really loved me. He followed me to The Dalles and told me that he had had his lesson, that he was through with drink and would never, never touch another drop. I hoped he would keep his promise, so I took him back.

"An epidemic of smallpox swept over the mining district and my husband was put in charge of the pesthouse at The Dalles. In those days there were saloons on every corner, and the saloonkeepers and gamblers dominated politics and business. Men felt that they had to drink rather than offend the saloonkeepers. My husband said he would not get any practice from the saloonkeepers, gamblers, or their adherents unless he drank with them, so soon he was as bad as ever, being drunk most of the time.

"My father having been a doctor, and my husband being a doctor, I knew a good deal about nursing, so Reverend Ben Lippincott, the pastor of the Methodist Church in The Dalles, employed me as a nurse for his wife. The Methodist Church was organized at The Dalles in 1856 by Reverend H. K. Hines. In 1858 Reverend A. Kelly built a Methodist chapel costing about $200. He had succeeded Reverend J. W. Miller as pastor. He was followed by Reverend John Flinn. In 1861 Reverend J. F. DeVore became pastor and Reverend Lippincott, for whom I worked, succeeded him. When Mr. Lippincott was called as pastor of the Taylor Street Methodist Church in Portland in 1865, I. D. Driver became pastor of the church in The Dalles. Mrs. Lippincott wanted me to go with them to Portland to help with the work, as she was not strong, so I went down to Portland and lived at their home till I married my second husband. When Reverend Lippincott was pastor of the Taylor Street Methodist Church, they still occupied the old building that was built by Reverend J. H. Wilbur in 1850. It fronted on Taylor Street near Third. They replaced the original church building in 1869 and built a brick church. When I worked for Mrs. Lippincott the church had an old bell that had been given them by Stephen Coffin.

"When I was waiting on table at the restaurant at Placerville in the Boise Basin, M. B. Gay, a miner, boarded at the restaurant. From Placerville he went back to his home at Eugene. On his way back to the mines, in the winter of '64, he heard I was working in a boarding house at The Dalles, so he came there to board. He boarded there for six weeks. By this time I had found it was hopeless to try to live with my husband. Judge Woods, later governor of Oregon, secured a divorce for me in April, 1865. Mr. Gay and I corresponded after I had come down to Portland and, in June, 1866, he came down from the mines, and on June 17, 1866, Reverend Ben Lippincott married us in the Methodist parsonage here in Portland.

"My husband's brother, John Gay, owned a farm on Albany Prairie, seven miles from Albany. He was a bachelor. He asked us to come to his farm, and he paid my husband to work on the farm while I did the cooking and the housework. We were there two years and would have stayed longer, but John married Helena Pike, the daughter of a neighboring family. We moved to Albany and my husband took a contract to cut 500 cords of cordwood for Perry Spinks. Working on the river bottom, my husband got a good case of old-fashioned ague, so he had to throw up his contract. My husband's oldest sister had married John Cogswell, who had a place twelve miles from Eugene. He moved to his place and my husband worked for him for some time.

"My husband was considered a visionary by his friends. He always thought that the farthest fields were greenest. On our 14th wedding anniversary we figured that we certainly must be rolling stones, for we had made 21 moves in 14 years."

Oregon Journal
December 10 & 11, 1927

Iva Templeton Galbraith

"My father crossed the plains to Oregon in 1847. I was born at Brownsville on May 9, 1867, and was one of four children. My brother Charlie Templeton is a dentist in Portland. My father's name was James R. Templeton. My mother's maiden name was Martha Ritchey. After my mother's death Father married Mary Yantis. They had three children, two of whom are living—Mrs. Hattie Stites, at Lamont, Washington, and Mrs. Anna Kirk, at Halsey, Oregon. Father was 15 years old when he crossed the plains with his parents. His father, William Templeton, was born in Virginia in 1809. His mother, whose maiden name was Elizabeth Ramsey, was born in

Pennsylania in 1812. His parents were married on June 30, 1830. Father was the second child in a family of 13 children. There were ten children in the family when they crossed the plains, and three more were born after they reached Oregon.

"When they arrived at Portland, on November 1, 1847, almost every member of the family was sick with mountain fever and their total cash assets were 25 cents. They went out to Tualatin Plains to spend the winter, but Jonathan Keeney, an old-time neighbor in Missouri, heard they were here and came up from his cabin near Brownsville and invited them to spend the winter in his cabin. There was a big settlement of former friends and neighbors who had known each other in Missouri, who had settled around Brownsville. Among them were Hugh Brown, Riley Kirk, Jonathan Keeney, the Blakeleys and some others. They moved into the Keeney cabin a day or two before Dr. and Mrs. Whitman were killed by the Indians.

"Reverend H. H. Spalding, with his family, and Mr. Osborne and his family came down from the upper country and settled at Brownsville. Mr. Spalding had been an associate of Dr. Whitman, and was in charge of the Nez Perce Mission. Mr. Osborne and his family had escaped when the others were killed at the Whitman Mission. The Osbornes took up a place next to ours. Reverend Spalding preached at Brownsville and also taught school. My grandfather took up a donation land claim three miles east of Brownsville. When gold was discovered in California, my grandfather sent my father and my Uncle David to California with Jonathan Keeney. They were gone three months and they brought back $3000 in gold dust. Grandfather let each one of them keep $500 of it, he taking $2000. Father later mined at Yreka, California, and still later at Orofino and elsewhere in Idaho and eastern Oregon.

"My father was 24 when he was married on October 4, 1855. My mother, Martha Ritchey, who was born in Iowa, crossed the plains in '53. I had but little opportunity of going to school till I was 16 years old. When I was 16 I went to school at Professor J. B. Horner's at Brownsville for six months. For the past 25 years he has been a member of the faculty of Oregon State College. Professor Horner taught me enough in six months so that I could teach school. He gave me the teachers' examination and gave me a certificate.

"My first school was on my grandfather's old place. I was

paid $100 for a three months' term. I taught school at different places for the next six or seven years.

"There was an old wooden bridge over the Calapooia between Brownsville and Sweet Home. There was lots of travel on this road and they say that at least 200 wagons a day crossed this old bridge. On July 11, 1890, my sister-in-law, Mrs. Nanny Templeton, and myself drove onto this bridge just as another wagon drove off. The bridge collapsed and we fell 30 feet. Both horses were badly hurt. One had to be killed. My sister-inlaw was thrown over the dashboard and lit on the shoulders of one of the horses. The hames put out one of her eyes. She also had her leg badly hurt. My skull was fractured, my nose broken, four of my front teeth knocked out, my right arm broken at the elbow, my hand and wrist crushed, my right leg crushed at the thigh, both bones in my left leg were broken below the knee and the bone ran into the ground. The end of my backbone was broken and the bone came out through the flesh. I was unconscious for three weeks. For nine weeks the doctors declared I couldn't live. After nine weeks they moved me from Crawfordsville to my home, where I stayed for five months. I was then brought to a Portland hospital to see if my leg could be straightened. They put it in a cast. They failed to put a drain tube in the back of my leg so the pus could drain out, so my leg mortified and they had to amputate it at the thigh. Both my father and my brother mortgaged their homes to pay my doctor bills and the bill at the hospital. Nine years later the legislature passed a relief bill, giving me $5000.

"About a year after my injury I secured a school at Halsey. I would lie in bed till school time, then take my crutches, go to school, teach till four o'clock and then come home and go to bed again. Next winter I taught at Brownsville. Later I taught five years at Sweet Home and I also taught at Sand Ridge and Muddy Station.   "Three weeks after the legislature awarded me the $5000 I was married to George C. Porter of Halsey. Reverend Robert Robe performed the marriage ceremony. He had baptized me when I was a baby.

"I forgot to tell you I went to the Drain Normal School for about a year. I had saved money to go through school and I wanted to graduate, but a girl friend of mine, Mrs. Maggie Humphreys, was sick and asked me to come and nurse her, so I stopped school to be with her. She died in three weeks, leaving five children for me to take care of. John, Lester, Jesse, Sadie, and Willie always seemed like my own children. Lester studied law with George E. Chamberlain. He was a major in the World War. He lives in Portland. Jesse was shanghaied in Portland, quit the ship in England, enlisted in the British Army and served several years and later joined the United States Army. He is now a rural mail carrier at Roseburg. Willie served in the World War. He is a railroad man in California. Sadie married a railroad man and lives at Klamath Falls.

"My husband and I adopted two children. Our little boy died when he was 15 and our daughter, who is 23, lives in San Francisco. My husband died in the summer of 1919 at Washtucna, Washington. I went back to teaching, so as to send my daughter through high school. On September 15, 1921, I married J. N. Galbraith of Sweet Home. Reverend J. L. Yantis, who organized the First Presbyterian Church at Portland, was my stepmother's uncle."

Oregon Journal
April 9, 1928

Mrs. M. J. Allen

"My parents were married a few days before they started across the plains for the Willamette Valley in the spring of 1845. My father and mother, Mr. and Mrs. Benjamin Walden, were with my mother's parents, Mr. and Mrs. John Lemmon.

"When the wagon train reached the Malheur marshes my grandmother said she could go on no longer, so they camped there and let the rest of the wagon train go on. That night my grandmother gave birth to a baby, whom they named John. You used to live in Salem, so you undoubtedly knew him. He was four feet, four inches high when he got his growth, and he weighed 180 pounds. His arms had no forearms, each hand being attached at the elbow. He also had no legs below his knees, his feet being attached at the knee. He had tremendous strength. He was offered what in those days was a very large salary to go in a sideshow, but he preferred raising horses in Marion County to making an exhibition of himself.

"At about dusk on the second day that my people were camped on the Malheur marshes, another wagon train came, in which there was a doctor. He decided that my grandmother could go forward next morning with her newborn baby. They left with the other train at four o'clock in the morning and joined the train in which my people had been traveling. Dr. Whitman, with his Nez Perce Indians, guided the train through the Powder River and into the Grande Ronde Valley.

"That evening a large number of Walla Walla Indians, in war paint, arrived with the intention of forbidding the train to go through their country. They were surprised to find Dr. Whitman, who held a council with them, but they were sullen and unfriendly. The next morning a Nez Perce chief, with a large number of followers, arrived from Reverend Spalding's mission at Lapwai. They brought fresh and dried deer meat, so they all had a feast.

"Dr. Whitman, with some of the Nez Perces, went with the train as far as The Dalles, which they reached September 14, 1845, two days before my mother's 17th birthday. They attended church at the mission and heard Reverend A. F. Waller preach.

"Indians from across the Columbia brought over turnips, potatoes, and onions to sell to the emigrants. They spent a week there, the Indians supplying them with plenty of game. My grandfather had brought a herd of 100 head of stock. He hired two Hudson's Bay boats and three Indian canoes to take the family and the goods down the Columbia.

"When the wagon train was camped on Bear River, some of the emigrants wanted to strike north. Others thought best to follow directions given by Captain Kearney. Both sides were determined. Finally the train, of over 90 wagons, with 200 men who could bear arms, divided. Part of the train bore north, following Bear River to the Snake. They believed they would have an easier time by following the Snake to the Columbia and the Columbia to The Dalles, rather than by taking the regular trail, for their leader claimed they would have a water grade all the way.

"They had a trip full of hardship and danger. One of the men who had taken this route, Mr. Hull, made his way to The Dalles on foot and reported that his wife and five other women had died and that the party was camped on the Columbia without food and their cattle were so exhausted they couldn't travel. My grandfather and others started at once with food, while still others followed, and the survivors of the party who had left the main train were brought in. Mrs. Sam Parker, one of the women who had died while taking this short cut, left a large family of children.

"My mother and father, with the three Welch boys and my Uncle Lemuel, drove the stock, while the rest of the party came down the river in boats. A man named Carson went along with his stock. Because he was the oldest in the party, he was selected as guide. Marion Poe, my grandfather's hired man, volunteered to take charge of the pack horse with provisions. He fell behind, and some Indians took the pack horse and provisions away from him, so the party was left without food. Carson mistook an Indian trail that led to the huckleberry patches on the slopes of Mount Hood for the trail down the river, and for an entire day they climbed steadily, till they found they were on the slopes of Mount Hood. A storm came on and in the thick snow they lost their way. They were held several days by a raging snow storm above timber line. For eleven days they wandered through the snow. All the food they had was nine hard-tack biscuits and four slices of bacon. After 14 days they reached the home of Peter H. Hatch. Mrs. Hatch took them in and allowed each a small amount of food, for she was afraid that in their famished condition it would kill them if they ate too much. After a night's sleep she gave them a substantial breakfast, and during the day gave them four more meals so they would catch up from their long fast.

"My father secured work on the Tualatin River. Mother's father got work at Oregon City. Later, Father and Mother moved to Oregon City and spent the winter. Their next door neighbor was Mrs. Welch, who later moved to Astoria. My father and my mother's father in the spring of 1846 took up donation land claims on French Prairie, near where the town of Brooks was later established. In the fall of 1849 they sold their squatter's right and their improvements and took up donation land claims six miles east of Salem. My father taught school there several terms.

"In the fall of 1848 my mother's father, John Lemmon, went to California. The next spring he and his companions struck a rich bar and panned out a considerable amount of coarse gold. My mother's father put his share of the gold into a coffee pot and brought it home. At $12 an ounce he realized $1900 from his dust and nuggets. In the spring of 1850 my father and mother once more sold the improvements on their claim and moved up into the Waldo Hills. My father was the first county judge of Marion County.

"In 1858 my father's parents came to Oregon and settled in the Waldo Hills near my father and mother. One of their sons, Smith Walden, with his family, who had come with them, took up a claim on part of which the town of Halsey was later built. Grandfather Walden died in the spring of 1864, aged 94. My mother's father died in the summer of 1870 and her mother in the spring of 1875. In 1871 my father and mother moved to Weston, Oregon. My father died November 16, 1887, and some years later my mother married Dr. R. Cummins of Touchet, Washington."

Oregon Journal
July 18, 1925

Rebecca Heater Hess

Mrs. Hess was born in Iowa in 1848. She was interviewed at her home in Sherwood, Oregon.

"During the 66 years I have lived on that farm I have managed to keep busy, taking care of my ten children, cooking for harvest hands, and milking six or seven cows night and morning besides making bread, doing my housework, and keeping the children's clothes mended."

Oregon Journal
January 6, 1933

Amanda Gardener Johnson

Calapooia Street is in Albany, Oregon. In the center of a block, beside a crystal-clear stream, stands an oldfashioned house—a house of the middle '70's. Thick-branched odorous cedars surround the house. beside the walk, like green-painted golf balls, are newly fallen black walnuts, still in their protective coverings, which, when crushed, smell like woodland incense. I knocked at the door. A pleasant-faced woman answered the summons and, responding in the affirmative to my question as to whether Amanda Johnson lived there, she invited me into the parlor, where enlarged photographs hang on the wall, and called to someone in the kitchen, "Amanda, there is a gentleman here to see you." A moment later Mrs. Johnson came in, with brisk step. Her eyes were clear, her hair was white, and she was the personifica-

tion of neatness.

"I am not much accustomed to being interviewed, but I will do the best I can to answer your questions. I was born at Liberty, Clay County, Missouri, August 30, 1833. My father and mother were born at Louisville, Kentucky.

"No, sir. I was never sold nor bartered for. I was given as a wedding present to my owner's daughter. I belonged to Mrs. Nancy Wilhite. She was married, after her first husband's death, to Mr. Corum. Mrs. Corum was the grandmother of Miss Maud Henderson, who answered your knock at the door, and the great-great-grandmother of Mrs. E. M. Reagan, whose husband owns the **Albany Herald.**

"I have known seven generations of the family. I knew my owner, Mrs. Corum, and her father. Mrs. Corum gave me to her daughter, Miss Lydia, when she married Anderson Deckard. My new owner was the third generation and I helped rear her children and grandchildren. That is five generations, and yesterday I held a baby in my arms that is the grandson of one of these grandchildren, so that makes seven generations I have known.

"I had five brothers and six sisters. None of them was sold like common Negroes. They were all given away as wedding presents to relatives of the family when the young folks got married.

"The thought of being 'sold down South' was always a cloud that shadowed the happiness of the slaves. A man would drink and lose his money or he would be unlucky at cards and would have to sell some of his slaves. I have often attended auctions of slaves when I was a girl, back in Missouri. They are very much like auctions of any other stock, except that the men that were buying the Negroes would ask them questions to see what they had done and were best fitted for. They would feel their muscles and look them over to see that they were sound. Usually the slaves sold for $500 to $1500, depending upon age and condition. A strong young field hand would bring $1000 to $1200, while a handsome young Negro woman would often sell for $1200 to $1500 if she had attracted the liking of some white man. Usually house servants commanded a better price than field hands.

"In 1853 my owners decided to come to Oregon. A merchant, hearing that my master was to go to Oregon Territory, where slaves could not be held, came to Mr. Deckard and said, 'I will give you $1200 for Amanda. You can't own her where you are going, so you might as well get what you can out of her.'

"I had been given to Miss Lydia, his wife, when I was seven, and I was 19 then. Mr. Deckard said, 'Amanda isn't for sale. She is going across the plains to the Willamette Valley with us. She has had the care of our four children. My wife and the children like her. In fact, she is the same as one of our family, so I guess I won't sell her.'

"Mr. Deckard asked me if I wanted to be given my freedom and stay where I had been raised, and where all my people lived, but I was afraid to accept my liberty, much as I would have liked to stay there. The word of a Negro, even if a free Negro, was of no value in court. Any bad white man could claim that I had been stolen from him and could swear me into jail. Then, in place of keeping me in jail, he could buy my services for the time I was sentenced for, and by the time I had served my time for him he could bring up some other false charge and buy my services again, and do whatever he wanted to me, for Negroes were the same as cows and horses and were not supposed to have morals or souls. I was afraid to accept my liberty, so I came to Oregon with my owners.

"It took us six months, to a day, to travel by ox team from Liberty, Missouri, to Oregon City. We started from Clay County, March 13, 1853, and got to our destination September 13.

"When I think back nearly 70 years to our trip across the plains I can see herds of shaggy-shouldered buffaloes, slender-legged antelopes, Indians, sagebrush, graves by the roadside, dust and high water and the campfire of buffalo chips over which I cooked the meals.

"Lou Southworth, also a slave, crossed the same year I did. So did Benjamin Johnson, another slave, who later became my husband. There are two women living in Albany now who were in our emigrant train—Mrs. Mary Powell and Ella Blodgett. They were little girls then and their name was Summerville. We camped at Oregon City until October, while Mr. Deckard went on horseback down through Linn County looking for a donation land claim. He took one between Albany and Peoria. In those days, when the boats ran on the river, Peoria looked as if it would be a good-sized town.

146

"I went to work for a man named James Foster. He was a merchant, but later started the Magnolia Mills and made flour. When I left Missouri you could buy eggs for three to five cents a dozen, bacon at five to six cents a pound, butter at twelve to fifteen cents a pound, and corn for twenty cents a bushel, and you could hire men for fifty to seventy-five cents a day, so when I was paid $3.50 a week I decided I had come to the land of promise, a land that was flowing with milk and honey.

"I was baptized when I was 14 years old by Mr. James, a Baptist minister. You have often heard of his son Jesse. Jesse James got into trouble holding up trains and doing all sorts of other mischief.

"On April 12, 1870, a little over 50 years ago, I married Ben Johnson. The Reverend T. J. Wilson, who now lives at Eugene, performed the ceremony. I was married at Mr. Foster's house and they gave me a fine wedding.

"Yes, I never get over feeling that my first duty is to my family. Whenever any of the Deckards are sick I always go to nurse them and take care of them, for, you see, they are my people, and the only people I've got. I am 88 years old, but I am strong and well. Most of our family have done themselves proud. Mr. Reagan, the editor of the Albany Herald, married into our family. I ate dinner there a few nights ago.

"No, I don't suppose there are many other colored people in Oregon who have been slaves, but I have been free since I was 20, and that's nearly 70 years ago."

Oregon Journal
undated

Sophia Ellen Tibbetts McKinney

Mrs. McKinney was ten years old when she crossed the plains from Indiana to Oregon in 1852. She was married in 1858, after which she and her husband lived in Washington and California before returning to Oregon to take up a homestead in Shoestring Valley in Umpqua County. She and Mr. Lockley met in a Cottage Grove candy store. The interview was conducted over a bowl of ice cream.

"When we took up our homestead in Shoestring Valley the country was pretty wild. We built a log cabin and put up a big stone chimney at the end of the cabin. Our hogs used to like to lie in the corner made by the big chimney.

"One night we heard one of our pigs squealing, so my husband grabbed his gun and told the hired man to bring the light so he could see to shoot the bear or cougar that was killing the pig. The hired man said it wasn't healthy to tackle a cougar after dark when they were eating, so I grabbed up the candle and went out to where the cougar was. My husband said, 'Hold the light near him,' so I held the candle bout six feet from him. My husband couldn't see the sights on his gun, so I stepped a little closer. This made the cougar provoked, so it jumped on me and rolled me over and over. Knocking me down that way put out the light, so the cougar got away. My husband was disgusted with the hired man, the cougar, and also a little with me for not holding the candle so he could see the sights on his gun.

"Next evening at dusk the cougar caught another pig. My husband followed the cougar and set the dogs on it. The cougar climbed out on a pile of drift over the stream. My husband followed it out. It was too dark to see the sights on his gun, so he followed the cougar, which jumped on a low limb that hung over the water. My husband followed it till he could press the muzzle of his gun against its shoulders and then he shot.

"The cougar fell off the limb and crawled into a cave. My husband crawled in after it. The entrance to the cave was so narrow that the cougar couldn't get out as long as my husband was there. It tried to but when it came my husband put his gun against its throat and fired and killed it. He dragged it out of the cave. The cougar measured over ten feet from tip to tip and had a fine skin. We made a rug of it."

Oregon Journal
undated

Corinda Davis Ames

Mrs. Ames was born on her father's donation land claim, "about a mile south of Silverton," in 1858. She was interviewed at her home in Silverton.

"Father and Mother had 13 children. All of us were so strong and healthy that only one died before the age of 50. Most of us lived to be fairly old."

Oregon Journal
March 9, 1933

Mrs . Da Gaboin

In a small two-room frame cabin with a kitchen leanto at Brooks,

Oregon, there lives a woman who came to French Prairie before the first log cabin was built on the site of Portland. I visited her recently and, sitting in the kitchen with her, asked her about early days on French Prairie. In answer to my questions, she said:

"You speak the French, some?"

I shook my head.

She sighed and said, "I speak the English not so good. My father, Lucius Gagnon, was French. My mother was what you call the half-breed—her papa was English, her mamma was a squaw.

"Yes, I am old—a good deal old. Eightynine years I have come to already, but 90 not yet.

"In Canada I was born. When I came here there was no Portland—only trees—no Salem, only Fort Vancouver and a trading post at Walla Walla—Wallula they call it now. First my mother have a baby. Louis was his name. Next there came Antoine. Me, I am the next one. Three brothers, my sister and me, that is all in the family. In those days there were no white women in this country, so the Hudson's Bay men, Dr. McLoughlin, Peter Skene Ogden and all of the others had squaws for wives.

"For many years my father worked for Dr. McLoughlin and the Hudson's Bay Company. When beaver were so hard to catch because there were few of them, he settled near St. Louis on the Willamette River, not far from Champoeg. Eighty-five years ago I came to French Prairie. I was a little girl—only so high—maybe six years old, when I went to live with Andre La Chapelle. Bishop Blanchet came to French Prairie and established a mission at St. Paul. Etienne Lucier, Joseph Gervais, and Louis Labonte were French, like my father. Also, like my father, they had worked for the Hudson's Bay Company. They sent a petition to have a priest come to French Prairie. They built a log church at St. Paul. This was the first church on French Prairie. Later they built one at St. Louis. My father helped haul the logs and put the heavy logs under for the church to rest on.

"When I was a little girl we used to go to Fort Vancouver. I used to see Dr. McLoughlin, Mr. Douglas, Peter Skene Ogden, Dr. Forbes Barclay, and many of the other head men of the Hudson's Bay Company. Bishop Blanchet confirmed me and gave me my first communion. Often, when I was a little girl, I used to see Monsigneur Modest Demers and Father Langlois.

149

Father Demers started the Catholic Church in Oregon City in 1844.

"When I was a little girl and lived at the home of Andre La Chapelle we did not have furniture like today. He made all of his furniture with an auger and an ax. The beds were made of poles. The chairs were home-made, and so were the tables. I married young. I married Peter Depot. He had two boys when I married him. We had five more children. All are dead now. When my husband died I married Mr. Da Gaboin. When he died he left me the house and farm, but he left a lawyer a mortgage. I did not know about this, but they told me the mortgage was a writing that meant they could take the farm away, so I had to leave the farm and my house. Joe Martel, he has lived here a long time. He helps me. I live in this little house for nothing. They said I could live in it till I die."

Oregon Journal
April 18, 1926

Mary Ann Taylor Baker

"I was about six months old when we started across the plains, in the spring of 1845.

"Though I knew nothing about it at the time, I came very near not coming to Oregon. The wagon train had stopped on the banks of a river so that the women could wash the dirty clothes that had accumulated and so that the oxen could graze and rest. A squaw came to where Mother had put me on a blanket on the ground. Some babies are afraid to go to strangers, but I was not, so when the squaw offered to pick me up I was perfectly willing to go to her. She said to my mother: 'How much you want for your papoose?'

"Mother said, 'My baby is not for sale.'

"The squaw said, 'I will swap you my papoose for yours.'

"Mother said, 'I'm afraid you couldn't take care of my baby, and I don't want your baby.'

"The squaw said no more, but watched her chance, and a moment or so later Mother saw the squaw headed for the timber as hard as she could go, with me in her arms. Mother set up a commotion and some of the men ran and overtook the squaw just as she got into the timber. The squaw protested vigorously but they took me away from her and brought me back to camp."

Rhoda Quick Johnson

If you are at all familiar with the history of Tillamook County, you have heard of Aunt Rhoda Johnson. She lives in a small cabin a mile or less from the western boundary of Tillamook City. When I visited her recently she said:

"It's about time you were getting round to see me, even if you did pick a bad day for your visit. I have invited the Rebekahs here to lunch today. They are going to eat lunch under the trees, and I am afraid we shan't have much time to talk.

"I was christened Rhoda Ann, but everybody calls me Aunt Rhoda. My father, James Quick, was born in the Shenandoah Valley in Virginia. My mother, whose maiden name was Martha Ann Pitzer, was born in Ohio. My people on both sides, as you can tell by their names, are Dutch—Dutch as sauerkraut. My father's mother came from Holland, and though she lived in America for years, she never learned to speak English though her children picked it up in no time.

"I was born March 23, 1844. We started for Oregon in the spring of 1851, when I was seven years old. There were five of us children when we started across the plains: Libbie, Will, Thad, Ellen, and myself. I remember when we were coming through Iowa we stopped and asked two girls we met what county we were in. One of them dug her bare toes in the mud by the roadside, and, pushing back her sunbonnet, drawled, 'You are in Pottawatomie County, Iowa.' That was too much for us children. We went off like a bunch of firecrackers, and by the time we were about ready to subside one of us would drawl 'Pottawatomie County', and off we would go again. It doesn't take much to amuse a bunch of children.

"It wasn't all fun, though, by a long shot, for we had gone only a few days' travel beyond Kanesville, as Council Bluffs was then called, before our oxen were stolen. Along the border outcast white men dressed as Indians used to make a business of stealing cattle from the emigrants and driving them off to sell later to other emigrants. The Indians also drove off the stock, so many an emigrant bound for Oregon was left high and dry, as we were, with no means to buy more oxen. The only thing for us to do was to go back to Kanesville, which, by the way, was in Pottawatomie County, and winter there.

"Brigham Young and his Mormons had settled on the banks of the Missouri in 1846, the government giving them permission to settle there for five years till they could find a place to suit them. They started a town across the river from the present city of Omaha, which they named Kanesville for their friend, Colonel Thomas L. Kane. A year or so later the Mormons pulled out and sold their interests to the Gentiles, who changed the name of Kanesville to Council Bluffs.

"Father met a man who had a log cabin 30 miles north of Kanesville, in the timber. He told Father we could stay in his cabin that winter. I shall never forget that winter. Father trapped timber wolves, killed deer and wild turkeys and worked at what he could get to do. We lived on wild turkeys, deer meat, and corn bread. Father smoked the hams of the deer to use as provisions on our trip across the plains the next season. He tanned the deerskins and from them Mother made fringed shirts and buckskin gloves. She outfitted her own family with buckskin suits and got good prices for those she sold. Father cured 52 deer hams during the winter, so we were well provisioned when we started out once more for Oregon, in the spring of 1852. In addition to the venison hams, Mother had fried out a lot of the oil for lard from the fattest of the raccoons Father had trapped, and had molded a lot of tallow candles from the tallow of the deer.

"I guess 1852 was one of the worst seasons for coming across the plains the Oregon-emigrants ever experienced. We traveled pretty much by ourselves, but we were always passing camps where the people had pulled to the side of the road to bury their dead. The cholera was bad that year, and you could follow the Oregon Trail by watching for newly made graves. There were hundreds and hundreds of them.

"We reached French Prairie on my brother Will's birthday—September 14, 1852. Money was plentiful in the Willamette Valley in the winter of 1852 on account of the gold fields of California proving so rich. Father got work teaming, and we wintered near Gervais. Father was paid in gold dust and other kinds of money but he changed his money and dust for the big eight-sided $50 gold 'slugs' from California, because they were handy to carry. During the summer of 1853 Father made a trip across the Coast Mountains into Tillamook County, though at that time there was no Tillamook County as what is now Tillamook County was included in what were then Clatsop and Yamhill Counties. Tillamook County was created December 15, 1853.

"Father gentled our oxen so they would wear pack saddles, and in October, 1853, just 70 years ago, we struck out for the claim Father had picked out near Tillamook Landing. Cad Eiler, Al White, John Higgenbotham, and our family made the trip. We went by way of Grande Ronde, the Salmon River, past the cape and Sand Lake, and on to the mouth of the Tillamook River. In those days there were no roads—only Indian trails or game trails—to follow. From the mouth of the Tillamook an Indian rowed us up to Tillamook Landing. From there we walked to John Tripp's place.

"When we came here there were only two families in this neighborhood and six single men. Joe Champion, the first settler in here, came in 1851. He and two other bachelors, John Tripp and Henry Haynes, lived on the prairie, and three other bachelors, Warren Vaughn, Peter Morgan, and Sam Howard, lived on the bay. Then there were the Trasks and the Doughertys, and that was all.

"Father and Mother took up a donation land claim of 640 acres next to Trask's claim on the west. We couldn't bring much in the way of equipment for farming or housekeeping over the trails on the oxen, so we lived off the country. The settlers made homemade furniture and the women cooked in the fireplaces. We children went barefoot the year round. When I used to turn out early on frosty winter mornings to do the milking and other chores my feet would get so cold I would make the cows that were lying down get up so I could stand on the ground where they had been lying, to warm my feet. The first winter we were here we lived on milk and butter, deer meat and other game, for we didn't have a dust of flour in our cabin, and, strangely enough, we didn't seem to miss it. Mr. Trask had a shop for his tools near his cabin, so every night his children and we children would go into the tool house and by the light of a tallow dip or a whale oil lamp we would study the school books Mr. Trask had. The first sure-enough teacher in Tillamook County was Mrs. Esther Lyman. She taught in the Dougherty house, and I was one of her pupils.

153

"The Indians were mighty good to the whites when we came here. They used to bring us clams, salmon, game, and big bladders of whale oil for our lamps. The whales would strand on the shore and the Indians would try out their blubber. The men folks would give the Indians a chisel or an ax head as a present, in exchange for the things they brought us. The Indians were promised annuity goods by the government in exchange for their lands, but the agent wouldn't give them the goods unless the Indians worked in exchange for the goods or paid for them in some way, and the Indians used to feel very bitter against the agents.

"We had only one sure-enough Indian scare. One night early in July, 1854, one of the Trask family came to our place and told us the Indians had broken out and were on the warpath. It was a beautiful moonlight night. Mother roused all of us children and told us to dress in a hurry. I hurried so that I got Sister Libbie's dress on and she ran around hunting for her clothes and finally put on my dress. We hurried over to the Trasks and pretty soon the Doughertys drove up. Mrs. Dougherty had wrapped her children in a big mattress to keep them from being shot with arrows. The men put out guards, and the rest of them began molding bullets.

"I can't help seeing the funny side of everything. I guess I would have to laugh at a funeral if something funny happened. Mr. Dougherty was trying to pour the melted lead into the bullet mold, but his hand was shaking so that the lead would go both sides of the opening in the mold and the more he tried to steady his hand the more the lead splashed on the floor. His wife saw him, and said, 'Look after the children. I will mold the bullets.' Her hand was as steady as a rock. The way she said, 'You look after the children,' and the way he was shaking as though he had buck ague, was too much for me, and I went off into a spell of giggles.

"Finally the men folks sent a courier to Tillamook Landing for help. He came back after a while, completely disgusted. It was the night of July 3, and it seemed a sloop had come in and the men aboard it had got hold of some liquor and had decided to celebrate the Fourth of July, so they had started firing their guns and pistols at midnight to celebrate the Fourth. The Indians, hearing the firing, took to the hills, and it was a week or more before they could be coaxed to come back. They

154

thought the whites had started a war against them. They never did understand what ailed the whites, for they didn't seem to understand about the Fourth of July.

"My father, James Quick, like most Of the other early settlers, had gone into the stock business, but we didn't succeed in raising a single calf the first three years, as the wolves or the bears got them all. Father trapped a good many of the wolves and put out poisoned salmon and got a good many more, but he decided to go into something that had more money in it, so he built a boat, which he called the Champion, after Joe Champion, the pioneer settler in this neighborhood. Later he built another boat, called the Ellen. He made good money bringing in freight with his boats. He built a toll road over the mountains along the Trask River. This also proved a good money-maker. He hired a man to run it for him, paying him $10 out or every $100 he took in, to keep the road clear, collect the toll and work on the road. Father also ran a hotel here in Tillamook, which made good money.

"When I was a girl Judge Olney wanted to keep company with me. He was a lot older than I. He was a widower with several children, so I didn't like the idea of marrying him. Every white girl in those days had plenty of suitors, for there were a lot more young men than young girls. Judge Olney didn't seem to have good luck in getting a girl to marry him, so he became disgusted and took two squaws, one of whom was just a young girl. He was like U. S. Grant and Phil Sheridan, both of whom lived with Indian girls when they were officers here in the '50's, only he went them one better by having two squaws, while they had only one apiece. Later, when white girls were more plentiful, the judge married a white woman. On January 3, 1861, Judge Olney performed the ceremony that united my husband and myself.

"My husband, William Johnson, died in 1892. We had seven children. Our son Lewis lives in California. Henrietta married Ben Higginbotham. Ed died. Jessie married John Embum. Eva, who is now Mrs. Henry Leach, lives on Wilson River. Tom lives in California. Lottie married Jim Hunt and they live on Trask River. Most of the pioneers that lived here before the Civil War are gone now. There are not many left who have been in Tillamook County as long as I have.

"What about my sisters and brothers who came here with

me 70 years ago? Well, Libbie married Henry Haynes, one of the earliest settlers here. My brother Will married a widow here. Thad never married. Ellen, who was born in Illinois in 1849, married James Sanders. She lives on the east side in Portland. Mandy was born November 25, 1852, a few weeks after we reached Oregon. She married Joe Davidson. Warren died in California. Charley married Alice Graham. After my brother Charley's death his widow married my brother-in-law Joe Davidson, and after my brother-in-law's death she married Captain Dodge. My sister Nellie first married Minne Stillwell and after his death she married Mr. Stimpson and when he died she married her present husband, Howard Drorbaugh.

"What do I remember hest about my girlhood? There are a heap of things I remember, but I believe one of the things that gave me most pleasure when I was a girl was a little black pullet that Mrs. Trask gave my sister Libbie and me. I was ten years old, and I set a lot of store by that little black pullet. Mother gave an Indian a silver quarter for a rooster he had got in some way and that gave sister Libbie and me our start in the chicken business. A heap of things happen in 80 years, so I don't lack for things to think of as I sit by my fire of an evening."

Oregon Journal
September 11 & 12, 1923

"Aunt Phoebe" Newton

Among the pioneers I interviewed at Myrtle Creek was Aunt Phoebe Newton. Aunt Phoebe had never been interviewed before and was rather doubtful if it would be just the right thing to have her name "right in the paper where everyone could see it...Just the thought of it makes me break out in a sweat," she said. "I have been here in or near Myrtle Creek for .more than 65 years and I have never done anything yet to get my name in the papers."

"Do I remember our trip across the plains? I should say I do. I was a woman grown. I was upwards of 15 years old when we headed our oxen westward from Missouri for the Willamette Valley. I was born in Missouri, September 29, 1848. My father, Samuel Hulser, was born in Iowa. My mother's name before she was married was Finnetta Phillips, but I don't recollect hearing her say where she was born.

"Women had to work so hard when I was a girl that most men had two or three broods of children. When my mother

156

died she left four children. Father married again and had seven more children by his second wife.

"We started from Caldwell County, Missouri, in the spring of '64. We had four yoke of cattle on one wagon—three yoke of oxen and one yoke of cows. Both the women and the cows had to work hard in those days. The cows not only furnished us milk but they had to help pull the wagon. We milked the cows till we struck the alkali country, where the pulling was hard and the feed was poor, so we had to go without milk on our corn meal mush after that. We had upwards of 100 wagons in our wagon train for a while, till the train began splitting up. One of the men while standing guard over the cattle at night killed himself outright. They figured his gun went off by accident.

"That was 66 years ago when we crossed the plains, but I can shut my eyes even today and almost hear the songs we sang around the campfires made of sagebrush, cottonwood, or greasewood.

"When we got to Idaho City, Father decided to winter there and make some money. We ran a hotel for the miners. I waited on the table. Yes, there were dances, but my father didn't hold with dancing, so I couldn't go.

"Next June we yoked up our cattle and once more headed westward. We had to leave our wagon at Camas Valley and pack in over the mountains to Day's place on the Coquille. From there we packed our stuff in a boat and went to La Neves where we wintered. We came out to Myrtle Creek in the spring of '66.

"My father liked old Missouri better than Oregon, and as the Civil War had simmered out and quit, he decided to go back to Missouri, so he went. I had met James G. Newton, from Randolph County, Missouri, so I stayed. He was carrying the mail between Canyonville and Scottsburg. We were married November 13, 1866. We lived for a spell on the Calapooia, but for the most part I have lived here in Myrtle Creek ever since I was married. My husband died eight years ago. My son William lives at Eugene, and Walter works in a logging camp at Coquille.

"Can I tell you about the early days here? Yes, I could, if I took a notion to, but I believe a still tongue makes a wise head, so I ain't going to. Lots of people, the more they talk the more they show what they don't know. Lots of people that don't say much, even if they haven't anything worth saying, get the reputation of being wise, so you can't get me to do any talking."

Oregon Journal
October 4, 1930

Mary Eliza Buxton

Miss Buxton was born in Portland in 1855. She was interviewed at her home in Portland in 1930.

"No, I have never been married and neither has my sister Nancy. Nancy says the reason she was never married is the men that she wanted she couldn't get and the ones she could get the devil wouldn't have, so she stayed single."

Oregon Journal
July 23, 1930

Martha J. Bowers Frederick

Mrs. Frederick was interviewed at her home in Ashland, Oregon.

"My grandfather, Meaders Vanderpool, never spent a dollar for medicine or on a doctor till he was 99 years old. Not long before his 100th birthday he wasn't feeling as pert as he generally did, so someone persuaded him to call in the doctor. I guess he figured that if he was sick enough to have a doctor, he must be pretty sick. In any event, the doctor only came to see him two or three times before Grandfather died."

"My father, Thomas Bowers, was born in Missouri, January 22, 1826. He went across the plains to California in 1844, as his lungs had gone bad on him and the doctor didn't think he could live long. In 1845 he got a job with Jim Bridger. The first year he was trapping with Jim Bridger, practically all he ate was wild meat. He never had bread but once during the entire year. He weighed 115 pounds when he left home, and after living outdoors for three years he weighed 175 pounds. Father came back home in the fall of 1847, and the next spring his brother, Benton Powers, started across the plains for Oregon. No, my father was never wounded by the Indians, though during the three years he was with Bridger they had quite a few skirmishes. One night when he and another man were sitting by the campfire, the other man suddenly fell forward. An Indian had crept up close to the campfire and shot an arrow completely

through him."
Oregon Journal
April 26, 1928

Lilly Caldwell Blackwood
Mrs. Blackwood was born in Phoenix, Oregon, in 1863. Mr. Lockley interviewed her at her home there in 1933.

"Father came here to Phoenix in 1853 and started a drug store. There was a woman who lived here at that time who was quite a gossip. They called her 'Gassing Kate', so, out of revenge, she called Phoenix 'Gasburg', and the name stuck to it for years."
Oregon Journal
August 18, 1933

Kate Pringle Miller
Mrs. Miller was born in the Pringle neighborhood, just south of Salem, Oregon, in 1852. Her parents, Clark Pringle and Catherine Sager Pringle, crossed the plains to Oregon in the 1840's. She was interviewed at her home in Creswell, Oregon.

"I happened to be visiting my grandmother on their place south of Salem early in January, 1865. It was about a week or ten days after New Year's Day when word came to us that Daniel Delaney, a lone man 70 years old, who owned a farm near grandmother's, had been killed for his money. He had come across the plains in 1843. A young man named George P. Beale, with a man named Baker, had gone to his place at night. Beale knocked on the door, which was locked. When Delaney recognized Beale's voice he opened the door and Baker and Beale killed him.

"Some months later, while I was staying with my aunt Mrs. Smith, I was on my way to Willamette University one morning, accompanied by some girl friends. Some men were putting up a platform while a crowd stood around watching. We crossed the footbridge across Mill Creek and saw that a tall frame had been erected. I asked one of the men what it was. He said it was the gallows on which they were going to hang Baker and Beale for murdering Delaney. It gave me the shivers. We hurried on to school as fast as we could go.

"Hangings were public in those days and people drove in from 20 miles around to see Beale and Baker hanged. They were executed May 17, 1865. I saw the crowd assembled on Mill Creek. It was as big a crowd as a circus would have brought out, only they were quieter."

Oregon Journal
November 25, 1931

Clarissa Asineth White Dunbar

"My maiden name was Clarissa Asineth White. I was born in Portland, Oregon, June 28, 1852. My father, William White, was born in Indiana. My mother's maiden name was Margaret Stewart. My father was a cabinet maker. My oldest sister was born in Springfield, Illinois. In fact, the eight oldest children were born back east. I was the first child to be born here in the west, and my brother Lee was the next. He was born on Chambers' Prairie, near Olympia. My half-brother was also born out here.

"Father came across the plains in 1850. He liked it and wrote back to Mother saying he would come back and settle up the business, or she could do so if she would. Mother sold the place, bought a wagon and oxen and an outfit for crossing the plains. With her children, Elizabeth, William, George, Ellen, and Anson, she started for Oregon in the spring of 1851. My mother's sister, Eliza Ross and her sister Mildred, who married Dr. Charles Spinning, captain of the wagon train, came with her.

"While on the plains they made a dry camp one night and when they were ready to pull out next morning a widow who had a young son was so sick she could not travel. The captain of the wagon train felt they should go on, so she said, 'Put me by the side of the road and go on, for I can't last long.' Mother would not consent to this, so she and the woman's son stayed with her till she died. They buried her in a shallow grave and hurried on and caught up with the wagon train. My mother's sister Eliza Ross had a baby on the plains.

"The cattle got poisoned with alkali. They fried out a lot of bacon and forced the hot grease down their throats and most of them recovered.

"At one place the river where they had to cross was high. The ferryman refused to take a chance on crossing. My mother's brother, William Stewart, with some other men, pointed their guns at him and told him that if he did not take the women and children across on the ferryboat they would kill him, so he decided he might as well be drowned as shot and he ferried them over.

"Father worked at his trade as a cabinetmaker in Portland in the fall and winter of 1850. In the fall of 1851 he started out to meet Mother. They met at Lee's Encampment, in the Blue Mountains.

"Shortly after my birth, on June 28, 1852, in Portland, Father took up a place on the Chehalis River, near where the town of Chehalis is now located. Father built a cabin and got all fixed up for winter, then the Chehalis River rose and drove us out of the cabin. Next spring Father moved to Chambers' Prairie, 12 miles from Olympia. Father built the first weatherboarded house on Chambers' Prairie. He cut a big cedar tree, rived out the boards, and planed them by hand. Our place was heavily timbered with big cedar trees. He worked hard to cut down and burn these cedar trees, so he could raise timothy hay.

"During the Indian War of 1855-56 my father and mother, with my mother's sister, Mrs. Stewart, went to church one Sunday. My mother and her sister each had a baby in their arms. They were riding in a cart. My father was walking just behind the cart. Just as they passed some heavy timber on the trail some Indians stepped out of the timber and tried to stop the cart. My father grappled with them, and when they fired at him it scared the horse, which ran away. They killed my father. Next morning the men went to where Father had the fight with the Indians. The Indians had broken his arm and shot him through the body. Mrs. Jane Pattison lived not far from where Father was killed. They took Father's body to her house. The Indians had taken all of Father's clothing, so that all he had on was a pair of boots. Mrs. Pattison washed his body and spread a sheet over him and the men carried him to a house owned by Andrew Chambers, for whom Chambers' Prairie was named. My mother and the neighbors went to the house where Father was. They buried Father in the little cemetery on Chambers' Prairie.

"After Father's death, Mother married Stephen Douglas Rudell of Missouri. Their son, Rigdon Rudell, my half-brother, lives at Baker, Oregon. My brother, Anson White, lives at Yakima.

"The first school I attended was on Chambers' Prairie. I

was four years old and I sat on a bench without a back. I went to sleep and fell off on the floor and I was humiliated beyond expression when the teacher called me 'Clara-come-tumble-bug'. I attended Miss Slocum's school at Olympia six years. During summer vacations I taught school I was 15 when I taught my first school, on Tenalquat Prairie, 15 miles from Olympia. I was paid $25 a month and boarded at the homes of the scholars. Later I taught school at Oakland, on the bay. There were only three families there and I had only 12 pupils. For a while I attended the young ladies' academy taught by Miss Churchill and Mrs. Case. Mrs. Case later married Mr. Hale, and Miss Churchill married Judge Wingard. The second year I attended the academy I earned my way by teaching the primary grade in the school. My brother William married Emma Dunbar.

"I met my husband, Ralph Oregon Dunbar, in Olympia. He studied law with Ellwood Evans. We were married on October 18, 1873, at the home of my oldest brother in Yakima. A Methodist minister, Rev. W. F. Kennedy, author of the book **Pioneer Campfires**, married us. We lived at Yakima till 1876, when we moved to The Dalles. My husband practiced law there, but times were hard, so we moved to a place on the Columbia River 20 miles from The Dalles. Later we moved to Klickitat County, not far from Goldendale. We ran stock here several years, later moving to Goldendale where my husband edited the **Goldendale Sentinel** and practiced law.

"My husband was born in Illinois, April 26, 1845, and came with his parents across the plains in 1846. The Donner Party, who met such a tragic fate in the Sierra Nevada Mountains of California traveled with the Dunbars as far as Fort Hall. My husband's father, Rice Dunbar, settled in the Waldo Hills, east of Salem. My husband was a member of the territorial legislature and for one session was speaker of the house. He was a member of the state constitutional convention and for 23 years was judge of the Supreme Court of Washington.

"Three of my children—Wells, Chester, and Trot—died within a week of diphtheria. Fred lives in Seattle. Ruth lives here with me. She is the author of a book entitled **The Swallow,** and also contributes articles and short stories to the **Saturday Evening Post, the Woman's Home Companion, the Century,** and other magazines. My son John is attorney general of

162

Washington. We have lived in Olympia for the past 37 years."

Oregon Journal
January 26, 1928

Sarah Fidelia Gray Abernethy

Mrs. Abernethy, whose father, William H. Gray, came to Oregon with the Whitmans and the Spaldings in 1836, was born on Mission Bottom, just north of Salem, Oregon, in 1843. She was interviewed at her home in Forest Grove, Oregon.

"Father practiced medicine then. A doctor in those days had a rather strenuous life. Once while Father was on his way to attend a young man who was suffering from stricture of the bowels, which was the name by which they called appendicitis in those days, he was attacked by a bear. His dog attacked the bear, while Father hurried on to attend his patient. The dog was badly crippled and did not return to our home for over two weeks...

"In 1852 Father decided to bring a herd of sheep to Oregon. He mortgaged his ranch for all he could get and went to San Francisco, whence he sailed by way of the Isthmus of Panama for New York City. At Washington he stopped to visit General Joseph Lane, Oregon's territorial delegate. He visited at Washington, D. C., and New York City and then went to Cincinnati and thence to St. Louis.

"The next spring he bought nearly 400 sheep and a two-horse wagon and a team of horses. As soon as the grass would furnish pasturage to the sheep he started across the plains. He hired three men to drive the sheep and also bought a good shepherd dog.

"He drove his sheep to Independence, Missouri, thence up the Kansas River and across the South Platte and on to Fort Laramie, the Sweetwater, and South Pass. From there he followed the regular Oregon Trail to Fort Hall, from which point he went to the Whitman Mission. He averaged 20 miles a day.

"He reached The Dalles safely, where he purchased a scow, 16 x 60 feet, on which he put his 360 sheep. He made the trip down the river safely to the mouth of the Willamette. From there to Astoria he was towed by one of the Portland-Astoria steamboats. Putting up a sail at Astoria he sailed across Youngs' Bay and reached the shore, the end of his journey.

"While fastening a line from the scow to the shore a

sudden squall sprang up, which carried them out into the bay. A moment or two later and the lines would have been fast and they would have been safe. Instead of this, they were carried across the Columbia River to Chinook Point, where the waves dashed over the scow and sank it, drowning every one of the 360 sheep.

"Instead of making a fortune, as he would have done if he had been able to get the sheep ashore, Father, through the loss of his sheep, was unable to pay off the mortgage, and lost his farm."

Oregon Journal
September 7, 1922

Clara C. Munson

Miss Munson was born in Oysterville, Washington, "on the last day of the oyster season," in 1861. She was a resident of Warrenton, Oregon, at the time of this interview, which Mr. Lockley conducted on the train en route from Astoria to Portland. When Miss Munson wae elected mayor of Warrenton, she became the first woman elected mayor of any city west of the Rocky Mountains.

"My father was fond of hunting and boating. He used to kill lots of elk and deer when I was a little tot. He had an Indian canoe of which he was very proud. He got it in a rather unusual way. He bought it from a dead Indian.

"It came about in this way. All Indians—in fact, all so-called uncivilized peoples, unlike many white people, believe in a future existence. When a plains Indian died they would kill his horse and put it on his grave so he would have his favorite steed when he arrived in the happy hunting grounds. They would put his blankets, ornaments, spear, and bow and arrows on his grave, for his use in the land of the hereafter. The coast Indians used to bury a chief or a warrior in his best canoe, so he could ply the dark river to the land beyond the setting sun.

"One day Father was hunting. This was when we lived at Oysterville, in the early '60's. He saw lashed in a treetop a very fine canoe. He climbed up the tree, examined the canoe, and found its former owner in it. That night Father returned with a spade and dug a shallow grave in which he buried the Indian. Then, cutting the elk skin thongs that bound the canoe to the tree, he carried it home. He put it into our boatshed and locked the door so no inquisitive Indian would discover it. He painted the canoe so it would not be recognized as a memaloose canoe and began to use it. A few days later a delegation of Indians came to our place and demanded the canoe. Father told them he had bought it. They pointed out certain marks by which they identified it as the property of the dead chief, and intimated that Father handled the truth recklessly.

"They are very superstitious about white men taking the property of dead Indians, for, to them, a 'memaloose', or death, canoe is sacred.

"Father asked them what he had better do about it. He offered to trade two quarts of whiskey to the dead Indian for his canoe. The Indians went into council, and after considerable discussion decided it was a trade, and as the dead chief could not drink the whiskey, they drank it for him, regarding it as a 'potlatch' from the dead chief."

Oregon Journal
May 31, 1925

Mrs. George Applin

Mrs. Applin was born at Fort Vancouver in 1837. At the time of her interview, she was one of the "few surviving members of the old regime under Dr. John McLoughlin, the grand old man of Oregon, who was virtually governor of the entire Pacific Northwest."

"I married George Applin. We had ten boys and three girls. All of my children are dead but five of my boys. In these days the women do not have but one or two children, but when I was young we took what the good God sent, without complaint."

Oregon Journal
May 5, 1922

Mrs. J. F. Galbraith

"My mother and her people were with the train that tried to cross the Cascades to the Willamette Valley by Meek's cutoff. After great hardships and suffering they finally reached The Dalles. At The Dalles my grandfather, Daniel Bayley, hired a bateau to take Grandmother and the children to Portland, while he should drive the oxen down to the Willamette Valley by the old Indian trail. The first night out the bateau was drawn up beside the camp. The next morning when they got up they found that someone had stolen the bateau, blankets, and provisions.

"My grandmother, Betsey Munson Bayley, came of Revolutionary stock. She had been a teacher, and was a woman of great resolution and courage. To be stranded with her family on the banks of the Columbia without food and without money to hire another bateau was enough to discourage the stoutest of hearts. My grandmother hailed some men who were going down the river and told them of her plight. They took the family aboard and took them to Linnton. When they reached Linnton two of the children were sick with mountain fever. My mother was about 15 or 16 years old at this time.

"They lived on salmon for several weeks while Grandfather was looking for a claim in the Tualatin Valley. The Indians would trade them a good-sized salmon for one needle or three pins. Mother found where there was a heifer about half a mile away, and twice a day she walked there and milked this heifer.

"When Grandfather came back he went to Dr. McLoughlin and told him he must have some meat. Dr. McLoughlin said, 'Yes, every immigrant who comes here must have something and none of them has money to pay. I furnish it, and that is the end of it.' He let my grandfather have some beef and flour. When my grandfather took the money to him later, Dr. McLoughlin seemed much surprised and said, 'I have helped scores of immigrants and you are the first one to come in and want to pay for what I furnished.'

"Grandfather had failed to locate a claim to his liking in the Tualatin Valley. Someone told him there was an old bachelor named Sidney Smith living on the Ewing Young place in Chehalem Valley who had a good cabin and would probably take them in for the winter. My grandfather went to see Sidney Smith, who said he would be glad to have the family spend the winter in his cabin, and that in lieu of the rent they could furnish him board, as he was tired of doing his own cooking.

"Grandfather came back to get Grandmother and the family. When they got to the Ewing Young Place my grandmother found a quarter of beef hanging in the tree near the back door, with big crocks of cream and milk, lots of fresh eggs and a big panful of fritters that Sidney Smith had made. Grandmother could not keep the children out of the pan of fritters. They had been living on salmon straight, and they were famished for something good to eat. Pretty soon Sidney Smith came in, with Phil Thompson and Bill Doty. Grandmother said she would get supper for them, but Sidney Smith said, 'Do not bother. I made up a whole pan of fritters. We can eat those.'

"Grandmother said, 'The children have already eaten those.' So she got out the Dutch oven and made a lot of biscuits and fried two or three pans of meat.

"My father, Sidney Smith, was born in 1809. My mother was born in 1829. My mother was 17 and my father 37 when they were married. On May 6, my mother's 17th birthday, she and Sidney Smith were out walking, when they picked up an acorn. They sat down to talk beside Ewing Young's grave, and Mother planted the acorn at the head of the grave. A huge old oak that is a landmark in that part of the country today grew from that acorn that Father and Mother planted there 78 years ago.

"My grandmother, Betsey Munson Bayley, was the midwife for the whole Chehalem Valley in the late '40's and early '50's. Caroline, the oldest girl of the family, married Felix Dorris. After his death she married Dr. J. W. Watts of Yamhill County, a well-known temperance lecturer of the early days. The next girl, Miranda, my mother, married Sidney Smith. The next child was named Bishop Asbury Bayley. The next child, Zarulah, married Frank Large. She died a year or two ago at Forest Grove. Iola, the next girl, married Morris Wolfe, a merchant of Lafayette. After his death she married T. B. Handley of Tillamook. Delphine, the next child, married Robert Nixon.

"My father went to what was then called New Helvetia, at Sutter's Mill, when gold was discovered in the mill race in 1848. We have letters he wrote to my mother in the fall of 1848 telling about the richness of the gold fields there.

"Father and Mother had eight children, five boys and three girls. I was their first child. Then came Almira, who married Andrew Hurley of Salem; then Sidney and Henry, both of whom died while children. Then Gustavus Hines, who married Lillian Getchel, then Ethan Allen, who died when he was young; and last of all, my brother John, who married Mattie Rroutz and lives on the old home place in Chehalem Valley, Yamhill County.

"I went to St. Mary's Academy and graduated in the first class, in the '60's. I was a teacher at Oregon Agricultural College

167

in the '70's. Professor Arnold, Professor Hawthorne, Professor Emery and I were the teachers at that time. I married Dr. J. F. Calbreath. When we were married he was a physician at Lafayette. He is now associated with Dr. Williamson here in Portland. My husband was superintendent of the state hospital at Salem for eight years.

"On March 6, 1843, a meeting was held at the home of Joseph Gervais, midway between the Methodist Mission settlement and Champoeg, which was known as the 'wolf meeting'. They met to decide how to protect their stock from attack by wild animals. A committee of 12 was appointed, consisting of Dr. Elijah White, Joseph Gervais, Etienne Lucier, W. H. Gray, I. L. Babcock, George Gay, my father, and one or two others. This was the meeting that led up to the assembly of the citizens on May 2 at Champoeg, when the provisional government was formed. During this meeting Joe Meek was appointed sheriff and my father and two other settlers were appointed captains.

"My grandfather on my mother's side, Daniel Dodge Bayley, crossed the plains in 1845. There were 66 wagons in his wagon train. Solomon Tetherow was captain of the train. At Fort Hall a considerable number of the immigrants took the advice of a man named Greenwood and turned off for California instead of going to Oregon. At Hot Springs, near Boise, Dr. Elijah White met the Oregonbound wagon trains and told them of a cutoff that would save a good deal of hard traveling to get to the Willamette Valley. He met
several wagon trains, including the one led by Barlow, Knighton, and McDonald; also the one led by General Joel Palmer, and the Tetherow train.

"Stephen H. L. Meek, who was a brother of Joe Meek, had met and married one of the young women in one of the wagon trains, and when he heard the talk of the cut-off he said he could guide the party by this cutoff, which was used in early days by the mountain men and the Hudson's Bay trappers. About 200 families decided to take what was later known as the Meek cutoff. It was while trying to find the shorter way to the Willamette Valley that one of the immigrants picked up the gold that was the origin of the Blue Bucket Mine story. For years parties of miners were organized to hunt for the Blue Bucket Mine.

"For several weeks the Oregon-bound immigrants wandered in the country beyond the Malheur mountains. In a place called Lost Hollow one of the women of the party died. Her husband swore he would kill Steve Meek on sight for leading them on this wild goose chase and causing the death of his wife. Grandfather Bayley concealed Meek and helped him get away.

"Some days later, when they were in the desert country, the party met an Indian. They asked him how far it was to water. The Indian did not understand. Finally, one of the men in the party told the others to be still, as he could talk to the Indian. He spoke very loudly and distinctly, beating time to each word as in music and said, 'How far-is-it-to-water? We are thirsty.'

"This amused the Indian and he laughed. Finally someone made a motion as though drinking. The Indian in sign language told them it was two days on horseback, or three days by ox team, to water. This was on a ridge between John Day and the Deschutes River. They traveled all that day and all night, and finally came to a stream that flowed into the Deschutes River.

"Meek reached The Dalles and told the missionaries about the immigrants being lost, but they apparently had no way of sending aid. A mountain man there named Moses Harris, who was called 'The Black Squire', got some salmon and other food from the Indians and, leading several horses with it, went to the help of the other immigrants. They were near the mouth of the Tygh, about 35 miles from The Dalles. More than a score of the party had died from mountain fever and from hardships while lost in the rough country of central Oregon.

"Grandfather Bayley came through with every one of his oxen. He had two yoke on each wagon. He would not allow them to be whipped or goaded, and he used to wash their eyes when the alkali dust got into them, and also washed out their mouths and washed their tongues with the family drinking water when there was no water to be had for the oxen. He was a good provider. He spent two years getting ready to go to Oregon. He made his wagons of selected hickory. He boiled the hickory in oil. He fixed up cupboards and beds and every convenience in the wagons. I have often heard my mother talk about Buck and Bright, Figure 4, and the rest of the oxen, and of the hardships they endured while wandering through central Oregon while trying to find their way across the Cascades

169

by the Meek cut-off."

Oregon Journal
undated

Mrs. John L. Barlow

Mrs. Barlow was born in Maryland in 1834, and crossed the plains to Oregon with her family in 1850. She was interviewed at her home in Oregon City.

"I didn't tell you how near I was to failure to reach Oregon, did I?

"Coming across the plains, I, with a girl named Lizzie Dickinson, used to walk ahead of the train, to be out of the dust. One day when walking thus in advance, an Indian rode by and threw his lariat at me to catch me. I dodged and it fell on Lizzie's shoulder. She shook it off and we began to call for the men folks. The Indian rode off in a hurry."

Oregon Journal
April 8, 1922

Kate Summers Holman

"Frances was about four years old when they crossed the plains. One day an Indian came to their camp and threw a beautifully tanned buffalo robe over Frances. Mother was very much frightened, but the Indian explained he was giving the buffalo robe to Frances."

Oregon Journal
August 31, 1927

Julia Frances Miller

Mrs. Miller was born in Arkansas in 1842, and celebrated her fifth birthday crossing the plains to Oregon in 1847. She was interviewed at her home in Portland.

"One of the things I remember on the plains was seeing an Indian wearing what looked like a heavy linen bedspread. It had clay on it. We found out that he had dug up the body of some emigrant who had died and been buried by the side of the Old Oregon Trail. He was wearing the shroud that was taken from the dead person. I thought that's what they meant when they spoke of Digger Indians. I thought they meant Indians who had dug up the bodies of dead people and wore their clothes."

Oregon Journal
March 22, 1935

Issaphena Waldron Collard

Mrs. Collard was interviewed at her home in Portland.

"A lot of people that started for Oregon in 1852 didn't get here. That was the cholera year. Mother died on the plains—I think somewhere on the Platte. My oldest sister, Samantha Jane, was only eight years old. I was just over three. With four little girls on his hands and the oxen to care for and drive, my father had his work cut out."

Oregon Journal
December 17, 1932

Ida J. Davis Oakerman

Mrs. Oakerman was born on Robertson Hill, in Yamhill County, Oregon, in 1859. She was interviewed at her home in the Corinne Apartments on the west side of Portland.

"Kamiakin, chief of the Yakimas, against whom Father had fought in the Yakima War of 1855-56, was a good-hearted Indian. He had suffered many wrongs and much injustice at the hands of the whites, but nevertheless he helped Father get his ground ready to be planted, and, with some other Indians, helped plant the crop. Father planted corn, and I can still remember what a heavy crop we had and how long and large the ears were.

"The Indians used to bring us gifts of salmon, deer meat, and huckleberries. When you get acquainted with Indians they are very jolly. I soon learned to speak their jargon, and because there were practically no white children in that part of the country, I played with Indian children.

"One time Father had to drive to The Dalles to get provisions. The trip took about a week or ten days. Some of the younger Indians came to our place while Father was gone, and one of them said, 'The whites stole our land. We have come to kill you.'

"Mother said, 'I can't prevent your killing me. I have no way to defend myself. But I want you to promise that before you kill me you will kill the children first. I can't bear to think of them being left motherless.'

"The Indians didn't seem to know quite what to do about

it, so they left, and said they would come back next day. Next day a large number of Indians came and brought pine nuts, fish and huckleberries, and one of the Indians said to Mother, 'You are very
brave. You need not worry, for as long as there are any Indians in this part of the country we will protect you. You will be in no danger from the Indians, and we will protect you from the bad white men.

"One day, when Chief Kamiakin was there, I asked him if he had ever been hurt when he was fighting against the white men. He opened his shirt and showed me his chest covered with scars."

Oregon Journal
June 12, 1935

Emma Warfield Howard

"My maiden name was Emma Warfield. I was born near Junction City, Oregon, on June 21, 1857. My son-in-law, Lewis P. Love, was born in Portland on April 2, 1851. My father, Sam Warfield, was born in Illinois. My mother's maiden name was Melinda Morgan. I am one of a family of 11 children.

"My parents crossed the plains in 1853. When my father married my mother he was a widower with four children— Tom, Phoebe, Melinda, and Jess. Phoebe married John Hill of Albany. Melinda married Tom Vinson of Benton County. They went to Yaquina Bay, and later moved up into the Eight Mile country, near The Dalles. All four of these children of Father's first wife are dead. My mother was a bride when she started across the plains. Mother 's first child was born at The Dalles as they were on the way to Oregon. His name was Alfred and he was born in the fall of 1853.

"My father volunteered in the Indian war of 1855 and 1856. J. W. Nesmith of Polk County was the colonel of the regiment, which was called the First Regiment of Oregon Mounted Volunteers. My father enlisted at Portland on October 22, 1855, and was a member of Company H, commanded by Captain Dayton.

Late in November, when the volunteers were up in the Walla Walla country, a party of about 20 Indians approached the white troops, which were commanded by Lieutenant Colonel Kelly, about 15 miles from the mouth of the Touchet River. These Indians were under the command of the chief of the Walla Walla Indians, named Peu-peu-mox-mox. They had a flag of truce.

Nathan Olney, the Indian agent and interpreter, with some others, met the Indians and Peu-peu-mox-mox asked why the soldiers had come into his country. Colonel Kelly said the soldiers were there to chastise the Indians for what they had done to the whites. Peu-peu-mox-mox said his tribe of Walla Wallas had done nothing against the whites and he didn't wish to fight. When Colonel Kelly told him how some of the Walla Walla Indians had stolen cattle and burned houses of the settlers, Peu-peu-moxmox said this was done by some of the young men against his orders. He said he would see that payment was made for any damages, but Colonel Kelly said that in addition to paying for all property injured or destroyed his people would have to surrender their arms and ammunition, furnish cattle for beef, and give the volunteers horses to pursue the hostile Indians.

Peu-peu-mox-mox agreed to Colonel Kelly's demand and said he would deliver the arms the following day. Colonel Kelly refused to allow him to go and said if he did so the volunteers would at once attack the Indian village. He told him further that if he and six of his followers would stay as hostages until his promises had been made good the volunteers would not attack the village of the Walla Wallas. Peu-peu-mox-mox consented to this arrangement.

That night Peu-peu-mox-mox asked permission to send one of the six men with him to instruct the people to gather cattle and horses for the volunteers and also to bring in all guns and ammunition to be surrendered.

On December 6, Colonel Kelly marched toward the Indian village, but found it deserted. They tied Peu-peu-moxmox and the others during the night to prevent their escaping. Next morning, December 7, there was a skirmish with the Indians. The volunteers kept up a running fight until they arrived at the farmhouse of a French-Canadian two miles from Dr. Whitman's former station at Waiilatpu. During the fight near the laRoche farmhouse, Captain Bennett of Company F and some others of the volunteers were killed.

When the sergeant who was guarding Peu-peu-mox-mox asked Colonel Kelly what to do about the prisoners, Colonel Kelly said, "Tie the prisoners, and if they attempt to escape, kill them."

When Sergeant Major Isaac Miller and the members of the guard attempted to tie the prisoners, one of the Indians wounded Miller in the arm with a knife. Peu-peumox-mox attempted to seize the gun of Sam Warfield, but Warfield struck him on the head with it,

173

knocking him to the ground, and he and the other prisoners, with the exception of a Nez Perce boy, were at once killed.

The volunteers scalped Peu-peu-mox-mox, cut off his ears, and cut a number of razor strops from the skin of his back and sides.

"When my father came back from the war, he gave me the scalp that he had cut from the head of Peu-peu-mox-mox. Mother used to make rag dolls for me and would sew the scalp of Peu-peu-mox-mox on the doll's head for hair. This scalp served as hair for several of my dolls. As the dolls would wear out I would change the scalp to the new doll. Finally we left the scalp in our farmhouse in the Willamette Valley when we moved to Yaquina Bay."

Oregon Journal
May 5, 1935

Jennie Stevenson Miller

"I had my first offer of marriage when I was 13, and from then till I was 24 I had numerous proposals. But I had a pretty strong suspicion that many of the men who wanted to marry me wanted the extra land they could get if they were married. Under the donation land act a single man could take up 320 acres, but if married he could have 640 acres."

Oregon Journal
May 18, 1933

Margaret LaFore Folsom

Mrs. Folsom came to Oregon with her family in 1852. She was interviewed at the Oregon State Fair in Salem, Oregon.

"Do I approve of elopements? Well, that's a rather leading question, for I did the same thing that my brother Eb did, only wasn't as old as he was. I was 14 when I ran away to Albany and was married to Freeman Folsom. We settled on Howell's Prairie, east of Salem. Father bought out a man's claim there in the winter of 1852."

Oregon Journal
October 2, 1923

Tina Zumwalt Howard

Mrs. Howard crossed the plains to Oregon with her parents in 1854. She was interviewed at her home in Ashland, Oregon.

"When I was a little tot, eight or nine years old, my father took me on horseback all over the country, to dances. Sometimes we would go 40 miles to a dance. He would make from $10 to $15 a night, playing for a dance. I learned a jig when I was about nine years old, and I also learned to play the violin, banjo, piano and accordion.

"In those days the dances started right after supper. A good substantial meal was served just before midnight, and refreshments were served at about four a.m. Refreshments in those days didn't mean a cup of tea and a sandwich. It meant all the deer meat and potatoes you could eat, as well as cakes and pie, and coffee made out of burnt rye or burnt bread crust."

Oregon Journal
March 17, 1927

Mrs. Boone Johnson

Mrs. Johnson was the lone survivor of the fifteen children of Samuel Hink and Carrie Busley Hink. She was born in Missouri on March 10, 1836.

"Boone Johnson was a neighbor. He was 19 and a likely lad. He got a job driving a wagon across the plains for Reverend Joab Powell, 75 years ago. I was nearly 16, and Boone and I had been going together some. I didn't like him going clear out to Oregon and me staying, for I was afraid we would never see each other again. We decided to get married, but my father absolutely refused permission. He said we were both too young.

"My married sister and one of my brothers had joined the wagon train, so I didn't say anything to my folks, but when the train pulled out I joined it. I wanted Mr. Powell to marry us. He said he couldn't on the east slde of the Missouri, but when we got out on the plains, he would. We were married on May 3, with more than 500 people at our wedding. Mr. Powell performed the ceremony and all the train combined to give us a fine dinner. We had cake and pie, roast chicken and vegetables, bread and coffee, and an honest-to-goodness wedding cake. My husband drove Joab Powell's wagon for his board and I did the cooking to pay my way. We wintered at Oregon City. In the spring of 1853 we went out to Damascus, where my husband built a mill. We lived there 50 years. We had 11 children and I have a good many grandchildren."

Oregon Journal

Cordelia Caroline Hubbard Staats

"My father was married on March 29, 1946, to Cordelia Caroline Forrest. They had become acquainted while crossing the plains. Father and Mother were the first white people to be married in Polk County. Mother says their wedding dinner consisted of boiled wheat with plenty of milk. My father's clothes had worn out while crossing the plains, so he was dressed in buckskin."

Oregon Journal
April 13, 1933

Mary Gilmore Hoeye

"While we were crossing the plains the Indians attacked us, and while none of the people in our train were killed, the Indians stole almost everything we had."

Oregon Journal
October 13, 1923

Mrs. Wilson M. Barnett

"My father, John Golden, was the founder of Goldendale. He was born in Pennsylvania. His father's father, John Golden, and his mother's father, Mr. Williamson, served in the Revolutionary War.

"My father crossed the plains to Oregon in 1853. He spent the winter of 1853 in Polk County. In the spring of 1854 he went to Yreka, California, where he ran a pack train for some time and later started a store. His store burned down about 1857, so he came back to Oregon and went in with Louis Parrott in the cattle business. He traveled all over the Willamette Valley buying cattle.

"While visiting at his partner's home he saw Jane Parrott, who was nearly 14 years old. Shortly thereafter he proposed to her and on May 17, 1858, he and my mother, Jane Parrott, were married. At the time of her marriage she was 14 and he was about 35.

"I was their first child. When I was in my teens I looked more like my mother's twin sister than her daughter. In fact, we looked so much alike that a young man who came to see me, when Mother answered his knock at the door caught her in his arms and tried to kiss her, under the impression that it was I. My mother was 15 years old when I was born.

"About a week or ten days after their marriage, Father and Mother went up to The Dalles and after spending a few weeks there, on July 6, 1858, crossed the Columbia River at the Rockland Ferry and settled in Klickitat County. Rockland was a small community just across the Columbia from The Dalles. My father took up a place on the lower swale, not far from where Centerville was later located. Centerville, as you know, is about ten miles southwest of Goldendale. Louis S. Parrott, my mother's father, took up the adjoining place. My mother's father and her husband put all of their money into cattle, and by the fall of 1861 they had a big band.

"The winter of 1861-62 was one of the most severe the Inland Empire had ever seen. The cattle pawed the snow away and ate bunch grass, but that winter a heavy snow fell and was followed by a long-continued cold spell, which caused the snow to crust over so that the cattle could not paw it away. Here and there some of the stockmen built V-scrapers and scraped the snow away so the cattle could get something to eat, but for the most part they were unable to do anything to help their starving cattle. When a chinook finally came and took the snow off, my father had only six cattle left. That winter wiped my father as well as my mother's father off the map financially.

"Father decided to go into some other business, so he built a sawmill on Spring Creek, at the Blockhouse, five miles from Goldendale. This, I believe, was the first sawmill in Klickitat County. Later he built a sawmill on the Little Klickitat, five miles east of Goldendale. He hauled his lumber by ox team down the bed of the canyon to Columbus, on the north bank of the Columbia River, for shipment. He shipped his lumber on flatboats and scows, operated by sail, up the Columbia to Umatilla Landing, where it was used locally or freighted to nearby points.

"Columbus, you know, is now called Maryhill, and instead of the rough 17-mile road down the canyon from Father's old mill there is a beautiful paved highway; and, by the way, Klickitat County owes a debt of gratitude to Sam Hill for the value of highways in that district.

"One of my early recollections is of being at Columbus, when I was a little tot, and seeing two men having a fight at

Father's sawmill. One was a Northerner and the other a Southerner. They were fighting over whether Mrs. Surratt should be hanged for the part she had taken in the assassination of President Lincoln.

"I was born on our place in Klickitat County, December 8, 1860. When Father and Mother first went to Klickitat County there were only six white families in the county, but there were lots of Indians. I learned to speak the Chinook jargon almost as soon as I learned English. Mother, who had come to Oregon in 1847, could talk the jargon as well as the Indians themselves.

"When I was a little tot the few families in Klickitat County were all neighborly. For example, my father would kill a beef and would divide it among the neighbors. Later, one of the neighbors would kill a beef and send it around to all his neighbors. By taking turns in this way they were able to eat a beef without having it spoil.

"The Indians kept close track of whose turn it was to kill a beef and always turned up to get the heart, liver, entrails, and the other waste parts. I can remember, when I was four or five years old, my father sitting in the doorway sharpening two butcher knives to cut up a beef that he was going to kill. Half a dozen or more Indians rode up, left their ponies standing in front of our gate, glided in past my father, and sat solemnly on the floor to await developments. As my father continued to sharpen his butcher knife, he said to my mother in jargon, 'These Indians think I am going to kill a beef. Instead, I am going to kill that big Indian sitting next to the wall, but I want to get my knife sharp enough first.' The big Indian next to the wall looked rather nervous.

"My father said, 'Where do you think I had better stick him first--in the throat or in the heart?' My father kept up a running fire of comment about how he would kill this Indian, till it got on the Indian's nerves. He straightened up from a sitting position as if he had been a piece of bent whalebone, jumped clear over my father's head, and lit running, and the other Indians, with apprehensive glances, followed him to their horses and away they went. My father explained to them, later, that it was all a joke, but they were quite dubious of him for some time thereafter.

"My mother was a small woman, but utterly without fear. One day when she was baking some salt-rising bread a big

178

Klickitat Indian, with several other Indians, came in. She heard the big Indian say something of an insulting nature about her. Without a moment's hesitation she grabbed a broom and hit him over the head. As he ran out of the door she followed him up, hitting him at every jump till, with one tremendous jump, he leaped on his horse and at his best speed departed. The Indian did not turn up for two years, and when he did my mother recognized him and, grabbing up a heavy length of stovewood, threw it at him. The other Indians were nearly convulsed with laughter at the speed with which he got away.

"One of the pioneer families of Klickitat County was the Bunnell family. There were nine boys in the Bunnell family and nine girls in our family, of which I was the oldest. Later mother had two more children, both boys. Of the 11 children in our family, six are still living.

"I married W. M. Barnett of Wasco. My sister Mary married C. O. Barnes of Goldendale. Florence, my next sister, was Mr. Barnes first wife, before he married my sister Mary. Florence, Clara, and Annie are dead. My sister Flora married C. M. Shelton and lives at Goldendale. Dora married Andy Bunnell. She lives here in Portland. Her husband is one of the nine Bunnell brothers who were born in Klickitat County. Almeda married Thomas Hill. Luella married George Ponting of Goldendale. My brother John lives at Goldendale, and Paul died some years ago. Mary, Flora, Dora, Almeda, John Wesley and I are the only ones now living.

"When I was a little girl—it could not have been over two or three years after the close of the Civil War—I awoke one night in our little two-room log cabin and saw my mother sitting by the fireplace with her gun within easy reach. I asked here what time it was. She told me it was two o'clock in the morning and to go to sleep. I asked, 'Why don't you come to bed, Mother?' She told me she had to sit up and watch. This alarmed me greatly, so I got out of bed and went to her and, putting my arm around her neck, said, 'Why do you sit up tonight?' She told me not to wake the other children, that a friendly Indian had come and told her that some of the bad Indians were out making trouble and had threatened to come to our house and burn the house and kill us, so she had to sit up and watch. I shall never forget how long the rest of that night seemed, and how glad we were when daylight came.

"Goldendale, county seat of Klickitat County, is named for my father, John Golden. Thomas Johnson, a native of Canada, who came to Klickitat County in 1863, surveyed the townsite of Goldendale in 1871. He settled in 1863 at Rockland, just across the Columbia River from The Dalles, and for several years ran the ferry between Rockland and The Dalles. He built the first store in Goldendale.

"Klickitat County was organized in 1859, but as there were only three or four white families in the entire county the organization of the county was allowed to go by the board. When the county was first organized the county seat was located on Albert Allen's land claim. The first county commissioners were Albert Allen, Richard Tartar, and Jack Halstead. Willis Jenkins was probate judge, James Clarke was sheriff, Nelson Whitney was auditor, Edwin Grant was assessor, William Murphy was county treasurer, and John Nelson was justice of the peace. In 1861 the boundary of the county was changed and the county seat was located on the land claim of G. W Phillips. In January, 1867, the county seat was changed to Rockland and a new set of county officials was elected. Rockland continued to be the county seat until Goldendale was selected.

"Our place was on the main traveled road to the Indian reservation. Father Wilbur was agent at Simcoe. He was a fine man and was very popular. He frequently stopped overnight at our place coming or going from Simcoe to the Columbia River, where he caught the boat for Portland.

"On July 14, 1878, I was married to Wilson M. Barnett. Judge Stapleton's sister, now Mrs. Mary Denton, was my bridesmaid. Judge A. L. Miller of Vancouver married Judge Stapleton's sister. I was the first one to be married in the new church at Goldendale. The day after our marriage, my husband opened a small furniture store in Goldendale. As there was not much demand for furniture, he added groceries and clothing and made a general merchandise store. In the fall of 1880 we moved to Spanish Hollow, near where the town of Wasco was later built.

"Sherman County was formed from Wasco County in 1889. The old emigrant road passed through Sherman County. You can still see traces of the old road about a mile and a half north of the town of Wasco. The emigrants used to cross the

180

Deschutes about a mile north of Sherar's Bridge. If the water was high they ferried over in their wagon boxes.

"The first settler in Sherman County came there in 1859. William Graham took up a place between John Day and the Deschutes River along about 1858 or 1859. D. G. Leonard settled on the John Day River in 1861. He ran a hotel and a ferry there and later put a bridge across the John Day. Jesse Eaton settled about a mile and a half from Wasco in 1864. He served meals for travelers on his claim in Spanish Hollow. He grew the first grain of any kind in Sherman County. He planted rye for hay for his horses.

"Shortly before the close of the Civil War a stage road was built between The Dalles and Walla Walla. This came past the mouth of the Deschutes, on through Fulton's Canyon, past Poplar Grove, then through Locust Grove and on past Jesse Eaton's place. From there it went through where the town of Wasco was later built, to Klondyke and on, by way of Webfoot Springs, to Leonard's Bridge on the John Day River. Practically all the travel from the valley to the Idaho mines went by way of The Dalles and on to Walla Walla and then on to the Idaho mines. When the railroad was built, in 1881, it cut down the heavy travel.

Among the pioneers inSherman County were A. J. Price, the Finnigans, John Gilland, Mr. Gould, James Pierson, James Jenkins, Mat Ingleman, James Mackin, John Harrington, Tilford Moore, J. H. Smith, a sheepman, James Frazier, who also ran sheep, John Fulton, William Walker, and some others. At the time of my marriage in 1878 there were but 42 white people living in Sherman County. When we moved to Sherman County, two years later, quite a number of others had moved into the county. In the fall election in 1880 there were 62 votes cast at Eaton's place, near the present town of Wasco. Most of these people had come into the county during the preceding two years. In 1882 Annie Fulton, sister of Judge Fulton, took up a place near Wasco and operated her ranch successfully.

"The only post office in 1880 between the Deschutes and the John Day Rivers was the post office at our store, in Spanish Hollow, and my husband, Wilson Barnett, was the postmaster.

"The ground on which the town of Wasco is now located was at that time owned by several different settlers—Dunlap, Biggs, MacPherson, and Armsworthy. When Sherman County was about to be cut off from Wasco County the county was to be called Fulton County, after Colonel James Fulton, but the name Sherman was substituted and the county was named in honor of General William T. Sherman. The county was created on March 12, 1889. Wasco was the first county seat. In the summer of 1892 Moro became the county seat. We moved from Spanish Hollow to Wasco, where my husband built the first store in Wasco. It was a two-story building. He used the lower part for our store and the upper floor was used as a meeting place for lodges and public meetings. The next firm to locate in Wasco was MacKenzie and Somers. They started a machine shop. They were followed by Tozier and Holland, who started a blacksmith shop. This same year, in 1883, the Methodists built a church.

"Wasco township was platted in the summer of 1885 by Clark Dunlap. The second store built in Wasco also was put up by my husband. He rented it to Josiah Marsh for a drug store. The first hotel, called the Oskaloosa Hotel, was built in 1887 by Levi Armsworthy. The first schoolhouse was built in 1888. My husband was the first postmaster of Wasco and was succeeded by Jeanette Murchie. Then came Mary Jory, William Henrics, Clark Dunlap, W. E. Tate, and many others since then. My husband, in addition to his store, operated a warehouse and started a bank. He also built a flour mill. He died seven years ago.

"Of our ten children, eight are still living. My oldest son, Corwin Barnett, moved to Eugene so that his children could go to school. My next child, Florence, married H. W. Turner, chief dispatcher of the O. W. R. & N. They live here in Portland. My next child, Marie, married Madison Cooper. She is president of the bank at Wasco and conducts the various business enterprises operated by our family. My son Owen lives at Oak Grove. Ira is at Salem. Golden Barnett, my next son lives here in Portland. Both Ira and Golden saw service in France during the World War. Lois married Ormand Hilderbrand. They live at Wasco. Dorothy lives with me at Wasco and here in Portland.

Oregon Journal
January 5 and 6, 1925

Dr. Mae H. Cardwell

Dr. Cardwell entered the medical profession at a time when there were very few woman physicians. She was interviewed at her home in Portland.

"My husband was a fine mechanic. He made many of his own dental instruments. He also, in the early 1850's, made the plates
for sets of teeth from 20-dollar gold pieces, for in those days, most of the plates were made of gold. Occasionally, he would hammer
out one of the old-fashioned, eight-sided 50-dollar slugs. When he made silver plates he usually made them out of Spanish dollars,
beating them out on a blacksmith's anvil. Later, however, he purchased the rollers that had been used to make the Beaver gold pieces at Oregon City, and on these rollers he rolled the gold to the necessary thickness for plates.

Oregon Journal
undated

Mary Jane Cline Turnstall

Mrs. Turnstall was born on Sauvie Island, in the Columbia River, in 1852.

"When my people crossed the plains in 1844, they had two wagons. Father drove one and the hired man drove the other. The hired man got sick, so Mother had to drive the wagon, in addition to caring for her five children and doing the cooking.

"One time Mother broke her arm. This was years and years after she came to Oregon. The doctor gave her chloroform when he set her arm. All the time she was having her arm set she thought she was driving the oxen. She would say, 'Haw there, Buck. Get up, Berry. Gee a little, Buck."

Oregon Journal
undated

Olive El izabeth Knifong Hussey

Mrs. Hussey was born in Missouri in 1851. Her mother died of cholera while the family was crossing the plains to Oregon in the summer of 1852. She was interviewed at her home in Willamina, Oregon.

"Father married Mrs. Polly Owen White. She was a widow with one child, a girl. She and her husband started across the plains with their little baby. Her husband was driving a team for their keep. When he died on the plains, the family for whom he had been working didn't feel like taking his wife and baby on to Oregon for nothing, so they made them get out, saying that maybe she could walk on to Oregon with her baby or she might pick up a ride. She had no outfit, no money, and no way to come on to the Willamette Valley when she was abandoned, about half-way of the journey.

"A man named Woodin saw Mrs. White, with her little baby, sitting beside the road, crying, so he stopped to see what was the matter. She told him she had been abandoned and had no money and no food. She told him that her husband's brother, Mr. White, lived at Salem, and that if she could get to Salem she could get enough money to pay for the rest of her trip across the plains. Mr. Woodin took her along with him to Salem and wouldn't charge her anything for it. Father met her in Salem and married her along about 1853 or 1854. She and Father had four pairs of twins—that makes eight—plus a number of singles."

Oregon Journal
September 17, 1930

Elizabeth Matlock Joerger

Mrs. Joerger was born two miles east of Goshen, Oregon, on the coast fork of the Willamette River, in 1863. Her father, Joseph DeWitt Matlock, and her mother, Elizabeth Millicent Rutledge Matlock, both came to Oregon in 1853. Mrs. Joerger was interviewed at her home in Eugene.

"As you know, Columbia College (in Eugene) had a pretty stormy career. It was opened in the fall of 1856, D. P. Henderson being the president. Some of the supporters of the school believed that the exercises should be opened with a prayer, and others didn't, so they had a big fight about it and a few days after the school was opened it was burned down.

"Another building was secured and this also was burned. They then built a building of stone so it couldn't be burned, but they were still scrapping about whether they should have prayers or not, so Professor Henderson resigned as president and Professor Ryan was elected, but within a few months the school broke up, partly on account of debt and partly on account of the big fight they had been having over whether they should pray or not."

Oregon Journal
October 30, 1928

Laura C. Caldwell

"I was two years old when I came across the plains with my parents to Oregon. We started from our home in Arkansas in the spring of 1846. I was so young that I only remember three incidents on the entire trip, which took a year, for we started from Arkansas as soon as spring opened and we went into our winter camp in southern Oregon just before Christmas, staying there until spring before we came to the Willamette Valley.

"The first incident I can remember was being left out of our covered wagon. I was frightened. Mother told me to go to Father. He reached down from the wagon, told me to hold my arms up, and lifted me into the wagon. The next incident I remember was while we were camped near Umpqua Canyon, where Father killed a black cow and they caught the blood to make a pudding. The third incident was going out from our cabin on Cabin Creek, in southern Oregon, to meet my brother Joseph and my cousin, Israel Stoley, who had been hunting. Each of them took one of my hands and led me back to camp.

"My next childhood recollection is of going out to the woodpile while we were living in a log cabin on the Tualatin Plains and trying to cut wood with my brother Joe's axe. I cut myself in the ankle, and when I saw the blood flowing over my foot, I was very much frightened.

"When my brother George was eight years old he got hold of Cousin Israel's gun and said he would show my sister and myself how to shoot it. He didn't know it was loaded, but it was, so he pulled the trigger and it went off with a terrific roar. I screamed. The squaws ran to where we were and Mother rushed out and said, 'Are you hurt?'

"I said, 'I am shot.'

"She said, 'Where are you shot?'

"I said, 'I am shot through the head. The gun nearly killed my ears.'

"Another very early recollection of my childhood is seeing my sister, Elizabeth, standing up with Dr. Geiger while Reverend Harvey Clark was marrying them. This was in 1847. My brother-in-law, Dr. Geiger, was born in New York in 1816.

He was 31 years old and my sister 16 when they were married. He was appointed missionary teacher to the Indians in 1833, but it was found that the missionary board had insufficient funds to send him to what was the foreign mission field in Oregon. He crossed the plains on horseback to Oregon in 1839. He was employed by Jason Lee as a teacher at the Methodist mission, north of Salem, in the winter of 1840. That spring he went to Monterey, California, but he found he would be unable to travel through California without a passport and that he would have to secure it from the Sandwich Islands. He went to Honolulu, where he secured his passport, and, returning to Yerba Buena, he went up the Sacramento River to Sutter's Fort. General Sutter employed him as a surveyor for the next year.

"Purchasing mules and horses, he started east, but at Fort Hall he found the Indians were said to be hostile, so he turned back, going to Dr. Whitman's mission. Dr. Whitman employed him as a teacher, and when Dr. Whitman made his trip to Washington, D. C., in the winter of 1842-43, Dr. Geiger took his place while he was absent. In the late fall of 1843 he took up a place not far from where the town of Cornelius was later built. He was later elected county surveyor of Washington County and also county clerk.

"Another early recollection was of being with my sister when an Indian came to our cabin. My sister ran away and hid, leaving me alone. I was a little tot, probably seven years old. I slammed the door shut and rolled a backlog that had been brought for the fireplace against the door.

"Father took up a place in the spring of 1848 on the South Yamhill River, about three miles from McMinnville. In those days the entire country was unfenced. Tom Owens had some wild cattle that roamed all over the country. These Spanish cattle were as fleet and as wild as a deer. It was dangerous to be caught out on foot when a band of these cattle were around. The schoolhouse was two miles from our house. My sister, Angelica, was about three and a half years old and I was seven years old. Mother had made Angelica a new dress out of bright red cloth. When we were about a mile from home and the same distance from the schoolhouse, I saw the cattle beginning to gather toward us. Father had told me that in case of danger always stand my ground and never to run. Taking Angelica by the hand I told her to stand perfectly still. From all directions the cattle began running up until they had formed a circle around us. They put their heads down close to the ground and bawled and pawed the ground. They pressed closer and closer until I could almost touch their horns by putting my hands out. They sniffed and smelled at us and snorted, but we stood as still as two little mice, and finally the cattle went away. I am sure that if we had started to run we would have been pawed to death and trampled into the earth.

"Father built a new cabin on our place. The sill of the new cabin was raised about two feet from the ground at one corner. It was my job to gather the eggs. One day I heard a hen cackling under the house, so I ran to get the egg she had just laid. My mother happened to be away. My father and a young minister named Ben Music, who was staying with us, were talking in the room where Father had his books. I stooped down and put my head under the house and reached where the hen had her nest to get the egg. For a second I was almost petrified by terror, for in the hen's nest was a coiled rattlesnake, with its tail up and its rattle vibrating and its head drawn back to strike. I tumbled back and ran screaming into the house.

"My father said, 'What is the matter, Laura?'

"I said, 'There's a rattlesnake in the hen's nest.'

"He said, 'Hush crying. Don't bother us, we're busy. It's probably only a mouse.'

"I insisted that it was a rattlesnake. To satisfy me, Father went out to see and I heard him say, 'Why, Brother Music, it is a snake after all.' he got the pitchfork and killed it. For years after this I would wake up, cold with terror, when I dreamed of that snake."

Oregon Journal
July 21, 1926

Martha Jane Spencer Janney

"I was born at Little Falls, on the Mohawk, in New York state, November 27, 1835. My father's name was Asobel C. Spencer. He was born in Vermont, of English and Scotch ancestry. Spencer Butte, at Eugene, is named for his brother, Seth Spencer. My father was one of the early-day school teachers at Springfield, near Eugene. He taught at various places in Lane County in the early '50's.

"My mother's maiden name was Lucina Dye. She was

born in New York state and was of English ancestry. I am the only one of the nine children now living, although six of the children were younger than I. Although I am spry and able to do a good day's work, I am getting along in years, for I shall be 90 this fall.

"No, I didn't bob my hair to be in style, but because I believed it would be easier to care for if I bobbed it than if I left it long; and it is, too. There is no reason why a woman should be a slave to long hair or long skirts.

"My father crossed the plains to Oregon in 1852. My mother joined him later. I was attending the Presbyterian Academy at Danville, Illinois, and as I wanted to graduate I did not come out to Oregon when my parents did. After graduating I taught school at South Danville and other points in Illinois. When I was a little girl I carried a banner for James K. Polk for president.

"I served as assistant postmaster in Baker County under President Grover Cleveland. Governor Oswald West—and they don't make any better men than Oswald West—appointed me on the reception committee when President Wilson spoke at The Auditorium. Wait a moment, and I will get you a letter that President Wilson wrote me. He writes a very cordial and friendly letter, and he signs it himself instead of having someone do it for him.

"My uncle, J. C. Cooper, was a captain on a canal boat on the Erie Canal. A horse walking along the towpath pulled the boat. When the Erie Railroad started running it spoiled my uncle's business.

"When the railroad train first started to run, the engine ran into a cow and killed it. The cow belonged to a widow we knew. She wanted the railroad company to pay for killing her cow, but they refused. Right near her house there was a slight grade in the railroad track. She told the lawyer for the railroad company they would be sorry if they didn't pay for her cow. He refused to pay her anything, and said maybe this would teach people to keep their cows off the railroad track.

"She cut the cow up, tried out all of its fat and made soft soap. She poured soft soap on the rails for a few hundred yards on this grade. When the train came next day it started up the grade, got part way up, stopped, and slid all the way back. It made the engineer and conductor awfully mad. They had to borrow shovels and shovel dirt on the rails before they could go on. It delayed them pretty nearly an hour. That night she went out, washed the dirt off the rails and put on a lot more soft soap. The next day they slid down the grade again, and were madder than ever. After she had done that half a dozen more times the lawyer came to see her, to threaten her. She told him she would watch her chance and do it for the rest of her life, or until they paid for her cow. The lawyer asked her how much she paid for the cow, so she told him, and he decided it would be cheaper to pay for the cow than to have her put soft soap on the track for the rest of her life.

"I took the Thompsonian temperance pledge 83 years ago. I am a past president of the Portland W. C. T. U. I was its first life member, but I yielded this honor to Narcissa White Kinney, who was very anxious to be No. 1 on the list, so my certificate is No. 2.

"I was married on New Year's day, 1856, to Emory G. Howard. He had gone to California in 1849, stayed a year or two, and returned to Illinois. Three years after our marriage we went to Kansas. That was in 1859. We settled on Cherry Creek. Later we moved to Fall River, in the Big Osage country. We gave the Indians flour and tobacco as rent. They called me their white sister.

"We got along in a very friendly way with the Indians. They brought us all of the tenderloin of venison and of buffalo that we could eat. They also gave me a number of very fine buffalo robes. I used them for rugs for the floor and also as covers on the bed.

"Later my husband took up a homestead and I bought a section of school land at $2.25 an acre. That was in Woodson County, Kansas. He helped raise a cavalry company in 1861, and was elected first lieutenant of Company B. Ninth Kansas Cavalry. I made my home at Fort Belmont, Kansas, 60 miles from Fort Scott. I boarded the commissary officers at the fort. When the Union men would come home on a furlough the bushwhackers would watch their chance and kill them. It was almost as dangerous to come home on a furlough as it was to stay at the front.

"In 1867 I came out to visit my parents in the Willamette Valley. From Ogden, Utah, to Umatilla Landing, on the Columbia River, I traveled in a freight wagon. From Umatilla Landing

189

to Portland I came by boat. In Portland I took a boat to Salem, where I caught the stage for Eugene. When I returned I went as far as Corinne, Utah, in the stage operated by Uncle John Hailey.

"In 1869, after my husband's death, I came back to Oregon and lived for a while at Springfield. In 1871 I moved to Baker City, where I ran a hotel for some years. My father gave me a 44-acre farm on the island between the McKenzie and Willamette Rivers in Lane County. I sold this place and bought a ranch 20 miles out from Baker. Here I ran a hotel, putting up travelers and supplying meals to the stage passengers, and also supplying hay and feed to emigrants and freighters.

"On October 16, 1882, I was married to George B. Janney, who was born in Missouri. We ran a store in Baker City. Frank Swan, Clark Tabor, and my husband owned the Eureka and Excelsior Mine, or the E. & E. Mine, as it was usually called. They sold it to Jonathan Bourne, who made a lot of money from it.

"In 1903 I moved to Portland and at the suggestion of Abigail Scott Duniway, I moved into her house, and for a year or more we shared the expense of living together, which was a very satisfactory arrangement. We lived at the corner of Clay and Fifth Streets. My son, Sylvester Howard, lives at Durkee, in eastern Oregon."

Oregon Journal
August 22, 1925

Abigail Hathaway King

Mrs. King was born in Union Ridge, Washington, on September 13, 1854. Union Ridge today is known as Ridgefield. She was interviewed at her home in Vancouver, Washington.

"My brother Hile, who lives with me here, was six months old when they crossed the plains. Nadah, who was three years old, died and was buried between The Dalles and the Cascades. Mrs. Knapp, one of the members of the wagon train, died of cholera, and Mother laid her out. Mother took the cholera. Father didn't know what to do, so he had her drink a cupful of spirits of camphor. The other people thought it would kill her or cure her. It cured her."

Oregon Journal
May 14, 1928

Elizabeth Kelly Biles

"My father, Major William Kelly, was born in England. He served in the Mexican War. My father married Mary Ann Louise Wright at Halifax, May 15, 1837. My parents had seven daughters and one son. I was born June 16, 1841, at Montreal. My father was a music teacher. He moved from Canada to the United States in 1843. At the breaking out of the Mexican War he enlisted as a private and was promoted to sergeant.

"We came to Fort Vancouver by way of the Isthmus in 1852. The Fourth Infantry, to which my father belonged, was ordered to assemble at Governor's Island in the spring of 1852. On July 5, eight companies of this regiment sailed for Aspinwall aboard the steamer Ohio, commanded by Captain Schenck. Seven or eight days after sailing we dropped anchor at Aspinwall in the midst of a torrential downpour of rain. We traveled on the Panama Railroad for a few miles to the Chagres River. From there we went in bateaux up the Chagres to Gorgona. These bateaux were propelled by native boatmen, who walked up and down a plank along the side of the boat, pushing the boat forward with poles. The boats held from 25 to 40 people each. There was no danger of our being arrested for exceeding the speed limit, for the best time these boatmen could make poling the boats up the stream was a mile an hour.

"Most of the soldiers and all of the passengers went from Gorgona to Panama, about 25 miles distant. The soldiers marched while the passengers rode on mules. One company, and the soldiers who had families, went a few miles up the river from Gorgona to Cruces. It was there that our family learned to love Lieutenant U. S. Grant, who was the quartermaster of the regiment. My father was orderly sergeant.

"Lieutenant Grant was as much loved as Colonel Bonneville, who was in command of the regiment, was disliked. Colonel Bonneville wore a white silk hat. Cholera had broken out on board the Ohio. The soldiers were dying like sheep. When Colonel Bonneville would come along the deck the soldiers would call out in chorus, 'Who made our coffee out of salt water?' and then, in chorus, they would say, 'The man with the white hat.' Then they would call out, 'Who neglected the soldiers so they got the cholera?' Then would come the chorus, 'The man in the white hat.' If one man had said it, or if a dozen

191

had said it, they could have been punished, but the soldiers, knowing there was strength in numbers, would call out in concert and Colonel Bonneville would flush with annoyance and ignore their remarks.

"My father was the only first sergeant in the regiment who did not take the cholera. The other sergeants had examined the knapsacks of their men and thus caught it. When it came to Company G, of which my father was first sergeant, the men were ordered to throw their knapsacks, with all the contents, overboard.

"Because there were a good many passengers aboard the Ohio in addition to the troops and because they had a good deal of freight, there was great delay in crossing the Isthmus. Grant, who had been detailed to stay with the equipment at Cruces, ordered the company of soldiers with him to march on to Panama, thinking it might be more healthful there. Grant, with the soldiers who were sick with cholera, and with the women and children, stayed at Cruces till arrangements could be made to take us across the Isthmus. More than one third of the sick soldiers and the others who stayed at Cruces died of the cholera. There were five of us children and my mother was expecting another child shortly. She could not cross the isthmus on a mule, so Grant hired some natives to carry her in a litter. He also arranged to have a native carry my 2-year-old sister on his shoulders. I was 9 years old, so I was old enough to ride on a mule.

"After reaching Panama we were quarantined for three weeks on Flamingo Island. Some of the sick soldiers were taken care of in tents on the beach, while others were taken out to an old ship that was converted into a hospital. Several of our family had the cholera, including myself. More than 100 of the soldiers died of it and were buried on the Isthmus.

"While we were on Flamingo Island my sister Fanny, who later became Mrs. Hiram Cochran and lived at Oregon City, saw two soldiers carrying a body wrapped in canvas to be buried. Fanny was 14 years old—a tender-hearted little thing—and she thought it was too bad there were no mourners, so she decided to go with the soldiers and act as mourner. When they got to the grave and were about to lower the body my sister thought she saw the canvas move. She told the soldiers she had seen the man move. They said, 'It must be your imagination,' but she insisted and finally one of the soldiers took out his knife and cut the stitches. The fresh air revived the man, so they took him out of the canvas and carried him back to his cot. He was a Scotchman named Thompson. For years afterward he was at Vancouver Barracks and much of the time he drove the water wagon that brought fresh water to the post. Whenever he saw Fanny he would say, 'You are the little girl that I owe my life to. If it hadn't been for you I would be lying in a grave on the Isthmus, where the other soldiers are buried.'

"When the cholera was at its height on the Isthmus, Grant was like a father to the men. He seemed to have no regard for his own safety, and was up day and night with the dying soldiers, doing everything he could for them. One of the officers whom I remember well was Lieutenant W. A. Salguther, later killed by the Indians in the Yakima War.

"After six weeks' delay on the Isthmus and after the loss of more than one seventh of our soldiers, we went aboard the steamer Golden Gate for San Francisco. Just as we were opposite San Diego my brother was born. We reached San Francisco early in September and from there went to Benicia Barracks, where, after staying a few weeks, the regiment received orders to go to Fort vancouver, which, in those days, was in the Oregon Territory.

"I was married September 3, 1860, to John D. Biles. When I first met Mr. Biles he was justice of the peace at Vancouver. He was the first American judicial officer to serve north of the Columbia River. Governor Lane appointed him justice of the peace for Vancouver in 1849. He was in charge of the squad that went in 1849 to arrest the men who had deserted at Oregon City from Colonel Loring's command. They overtook them in the Cow Creek Mountains. He was Speaker of the House in the legislature of Washington Territory in 1850.

"Mr. Biles became interested in the Peoples' Transportation Company and served as purser on many of their boats, particularly on the run from Portland to the Cascades. He was purser on the Alert and later on the Senator.

"Not long after our marriage we moved from Vancouver to Portland, to a house on the corner of Clay and Front Streets. This was before the Civil War. In those days Portland had little or no street improvement. The teams used to bog down in front of our house, and often the planks that served as sidewalks were submerged in deep, chocolate colored mud.

"When my husband went into the Peoples' Transportation Company, David McCully of Salem was president, L. S. Parrish was vice president, T. MacF. Patton, later ambassador to Japan and still later a bookseller in Salem, was secretary. David McCully, J. S. Parrish, E. N. Cook, S. T. Church, T. MacF. Patton and my husband were directors. When Captain Joseph Kellogg built the Senator, my husband became the purser of the company, with which the Peoples' Transportation Company sold out to Ben Holladay and my husband became a director of the company. Still later Henry Villard bought the Oregon Steam Navigation Company, with which the Peoples' Transportation Company had been merged, and my husband became secretary of the company. Mr. Villard was one of the most affable and courteous men I have ever met.

"I am 80 years old and, while I am keenly interested in what goes on today, nevertheless, I like to think back to the early days and of the friends and acquaintances of my girlhood days. While my father was stationed at Fort Vancouver in the '50's, I met many young officers who later became famous. One of these was Lieutenant Philip Sheridan. He was rather small, not very good looking, very retiring and reserved, and had the reputation with his brother officers of being a very capable and courageous officer. Another officer there at that time was Dr. J. K. Barnes, who later attended Lincoln when he was assassinated. Still others were Captain Hodges, who later became a general and Captain Slaughter. Captain Russell and Lieutenant Grant, who was quartermaster of the regiment and who became a captain in the summer of 1853.

"When Grant was making his tour of the world he came to Vancouver Barracks from The Dalles aboard the Wide West, one of the swiftest, handsomest, and most powerful steamboats on the river. I went to Vancouver, where I boarded the boat to meet General Grant and his party. Shortly after I went aboard the boat left Vancouver for Portland. The distinguished guests, with the reception committee, went to dinner shortly after leaving Vancouver. I sat in the stern of the boat to wait until the party came on deck. Presently General Grant came up. Looking at me closely, he said, 'This ought to be Lizzie Kelly.' he hadn't seen me for 28 years and I thought it was remarkable that he should remember me. He said, 'You were ten years old when you crossed the Isthmus with us in 1852.'

"I said, 'I was eleven years old at the time.'

"He smiled and responded, 'I was giving you a year the best of it. In any event, you were small for your age. Does your father still own his farm near Vancouver?'

"I told him my father had long ago sold the farm and had remained in the army as a captain.

"He said, 'I want you to meet my wife.' he returned in a moment or two with Mrs. Grant and introduced us saying, 'I want you to meet this young lady. We crossed the Isthmus together in 1852.'

"I found Mrs. Grant very charming. We all then sat down together and had a most pleasant visit.

"I have been a member of Trinity Episcopal Church for more than 50 years. There are now very few of the charter members of this church alive. I have six children: four daughters and two sons. My son Norman would have been heard from as an artist had he lived. He studied art abroad, but died of pneumonia while still a young man."

Oregon Journal
undated

Sarah Booth Hockett

Mrs. Hockett was born on her parents' donation land claim, near Fort Yamhill, in Yamhill County, Oregon, in 1854.

"As I look back to my girlhood I realize how busy my mother was rearing her large family of children and doing all of the work of the home, for in those days there were no labor-saving conveniences. Mother carded and spun the wool and made the clothes for all of us children. She also made Father's overcoats and made his white shirts. She did all of the sewing by hand and at first did the cooking over the fireplace. She molded all of the candles we used, and knitted socks and stockings for all of us and also knitted socks for sale. Mother knitted lots of socks and mittens which she sent to her brother, John, who was a soldier in the Union Army. He was wounded twice. When he was finally discharged he told Mother that he had never received a single pair of socks or a single pair of mittens.

"I can remember as a little girl sitting on a box beside Mother for hours at a time as she sewed. Some of the Indians who had been captured for going to war in Southern Oregon were moved to a reservation. They were warlike and occasionally they got hold of whisky. They would come past our house sometimes, giving the war whoop, and Mother was afraid they might kill us. Whenever she heard the drunken Indians around our house she would put out the light. She had a pie pan in which was some melted lard and in which there was a twisted piece of cloth for a wick. She would light this dim lamp and I would go up to the attic and look through the peephole to see what the Indians were doing. No matter how late the Indians stayed, none of us went to bed till they had left.

"Father was gone on his preaching trips most of the time, so Mother had to oversee the boys, who did the work of the farm. One of the Indian boys, named Moses, who was about 16 years old, became very fond of my brothers. He would often visit at our home. One day he came running to the house and said, 'Go quick. Some bad Indians coming to burn your home and kill you. I will have to run back or they'll kill me for telling.' We hurried away from home and stayed at a neighbor's house that night. Wext morning there were the moccasin tracks of Indians all around our house; but they didn't burn the house.

"One time Indian Dave's squaw came to our house to trade a beautiful white silk shawl with long fringes. I was crazy to have it. She also had a silver tea service to trade. In spite of my ardent desire to have Mother get them, she wouldn't trade for them. She explained to me that it didn't become a minister's family to have silk shawls and silverware, and moreover, these articles had undoubtedly belonged to people the Indians had killed."

Oregon Journal
April 19, 1934

Esther Louise Dempster Adams

Mrs. Adams was born in Scotland, and came to this country when she was three years old. She was interviewed at her home in Sherwood, Oregon, where she had lived for the previous 40 years.

"I was married when I was 14 years old and before long I had a family of 11 children—eight girls and three boys."

Oregon Journal
May 26, 1932

Marianne Hunsaker Edwards D'Arcy

Recently I received a letter from Marianne Hunsaker D'Arcy. She is a pioneer of Park Place, near Oregon City. In her letter, Mrs. D'Arcy said:

"I have just read your article about early state fairs. There was a fair held on the north bank of the Abernethy in 1860. I am under the impression that it was a county fair. I entered a loaf of bread—very poor bread it was, too—but it took first prize. There was no other entry. The next year a fair was held on the north bank of the Clackamas at what is now Gladstone. My father took first premium for his model orchard. While this is not of great importance, nevertheless, it is history.

I decided to acknowledge the receipt of the letter in person, so I dropped in at No. 835 Lovejoy Street and spent an hour or so with Mrs. D'Arcy.

"On New Year's morning, 1842, my father got up at about daybreak and built the fire. My parents were living in a log cabin that had not yet been chinked. Father said some of the logs were crooked, which resulted in making chinks large enough to throw a cat through, providing the cat was not too large. The snow had sifted in upon the floor. As he turned to get the broom to sweep out the freshly fallen snow from the floor he saw that Mother was awake, so he said, 'New Year's gift, Emily.'"

"She said, 'You had better hurry over to our neighbor's and bring her back with you or I will have a New Year's gift for you while you are gone.' He hurried into coat and cap and went for the neighbor. Shortly after her arrival I also arrived, so Mother made good on her promise of presenting Father with a New Year's gift. I celebrated my eightieth birthday last New Year's Day.

"My mother bore 12 children, worked hard all her life, and died a comparatively young woman. It usually was the second or third wife that enjoyed the improved farm and the comforts that the first and second wives had worked so hard to help earn.

"My father, Jacob T. Hunsaker, was born July 20, 1818, in Pike County, Illinois. My mother, whose maiden name was Emily Collins, was born October 3, 1820, in Kentucky. They were married December 7, 1837. Their first child was born February 10, 1837, so, you see, my father was the father of a man

197

child before he himself was of age. I was the third of their 12 children.

"We started for Oregon when I was four years and four months old, which was in the spring of 1846. Two of my earliest recollections are of asking Father what Oregon was. Everyone seemed to be talking of it. Father said, 'It is a place. We are going there. It is in that direction,' and he pointed toward the fireplace, which happened to be toward the west.

"After that, wherever I happened to be I would point to the fireplace and say Oregon is in that direction. Sometimes I was right, but more often I was wrong. I thought the grown people were very stupid. Sometimes when I pointed to a neighbor's fireplace and announced that Oregon was in that direction they would nod their heads and say how smart I was, and when I repeated the performance at some other neighbor's they would correct me and point toward the setting sun and tell me that was the direction of Oregon.

"My next vivid recollection was of having our relatives, friends, and neighbors gather at our place, and as we drove westward they waved their hands and said, 'Farewell, farewell.' Most of the women began to cry, saying, 'We shall never see you again.' I wondered what that word 'farewell' meant, so finally asked Mother, and she told me it was a more stylish way of saying goodbye.

"My mother's grandfather was of English ancestry and believed in leaving all of his property to the eldest son. My mother's father was one of the younger sons. When all of the land and the slaves were left to his eldest brother he felt humiliated to have to work with his hands and compete with slave labor, so he left Kentucky and went to Illinois.

"Mother said that when she was a little girl in Kentucky she had two playmates. Both of these little girls had blue eyes and golden curls. Mother supposed they were white girls, but it seemed they were the daughters of a neighboring plantation owner by a slave girl who had but a small infusion of Negro blood. The father of the children died. In his will he had provided that these children by his slave should become free. Instead, they were taken down the river and sold as slaves. Mother could never learn whether they were sold to pay the debts of their father and owner or were stolen and taken down the river.

198

"When Father was a boy a colored boy of about 18 or thereabout used to let him ride in his rowboat. The colored boy was free. One day a couple of strangers hired the boy to row them across the river. He told Father to jump in and go along. When they got pretty well across the river one of the strangers poked a pistol in the side of the Negro and said, 'If you call for help I Will pull the trigger. We need money, so we are going to say you are a runaway slave. We are going to sell you. We are in slave territory now, so there is no use of resisting.

"Father began to beg the men not to steal his friend. One of the men said, 'Any more out of you and we will knock you in the head and throw you overboard.' The Negro boy told Father not to cry or make trouble. They landed, and the white men grabbed the Negro and took him away. After a while Father got a chance to get a ride across the river, but when he got home he was afraid to tell about the Negro boy being stolen for fear the white men might come back some day and kill him.

"Long after Father was grown and had a family he was in the South and met this Negro. The Negro cried for joy when he saw Father, for he was afraid he might have been killed by the white men who had stolen him, on the theory that dead men tell no tales. The Negro boy had been sold and never again saw the men who had stolen him.

"The first school I ever attended was in a log school house that my father helped build in the fall of 1846 on the banks of the Molalla. It was all home-made, furniture and all. The floor was made of puncheons, the benches were puncheons with auger holes in each end into which pegs were driven for legs. The fireplace was of rock and clay. The chimney was of sticks plastered over with clay.

We used copies of the Oregon Spectator, printed in Oregon City, for our readers. We children went to school barefoot until Father could get some tanned leather and make shoes for us. Mr. Snyder, the teacher, gave us a treat of gingerbread, which he had bought at Oregon City. I thought it was food fit for the gods.

"The next year Father built a sawmill on the Columbia near St. Helens. The place where he built the sawmill was named Milltown, or Milton, as it was soon called. Mr. Knighton was the leading man at St. Helens. When he started the town in

199

1848, he called it Plymouth Rock. In the fall of 1848 Captain Crosby bought all the lumber Father had, to take to San Francisco, for it was believed the discovery of gold at Sutter's Mill would cause a building boom at San Francisco.

"Father was offered and accepted a good price for his mill, so he made up a raft of lumber and by the aid of a sail, some long sweeps and a hired man and my eldest brother, we came up the Columbia into the Willamette and sailed and rowed up to Green Point, just below Oregon City. It took us several days. One night we camped at Vancouver.

"Father told us to watch out for the city of Portland as we came up the Willamette. Presently he called, 'There it is.'

"I asked, 'Where?'

"He pointed to a cabin on the bank of the river and to one farther back, and said, 'There it is. Don't you see the man with the boy and the dog on the bank? That's where the new town is.'

"I was dreadfully disappointed. I thought it would look different, and more like a city.

"The Sisters of Notre Dame had started a school at Oregon City, so Father arranged for us three girls to go to school there while he and Mother and the two babies went to build and operate a sawmill on the Washougal. I cried myself to sleep every night. One of the older girls said most of the girls at the school were orphans. I wanted to know what that was and she said, 'Their folks are dead, or gone to California to the gold fields. I guess your folks have decided to abandon you and have given you to the sisters.' I was so panic-stricken and homesick that I nearly died, for I thought I should never see my mother again.

"We had not been there long when Dr. John McLoughlin and Dr. Forbes Barclay came to the school. Dr. McLoughlin said, 'I hear you have some new little girls as boarders. Where are they?'

"The sister called us to her and, putting her hand upon my head, said, 'Here are our new little girls.'

"That was too much for me. The sister had said we were 'their' little girls, so I burst out crying at having my worst fears confirmed. Dr. McLoughlin put his hand upon my head and tried to cheer me up, but I only cried the more, so I was taken away.

"In November, 1849, Father and Mother with the two little ones came back from Washougal and a few days after their arrival my brother Lycurgus was born. He lives at Needles now, where he runs a rooming house.

"One of my sisters decided to be a nun. Mother decided that for a good Baptist to become a nun would never do, so they took us out of that school. The next school we went to was Ezra Fisher's school, kept in the Baptist Church in the lower end of town, near the sister's school. Lucy Jane, Mr. Fisher's daughter, was our teacher.

"After we had been going to school there a while our class missed the definitions in one of the reading lessons. The definitions were so much more difficult than the words they were supposed to explain that we couldn't master them. Mr. Fisher had no patience with poor scholarship. I can remember yet how he faced our class and scolded us. In our class were Robert and Davis Caufield, Joseph Parrot, Gus Kilbourne, and Medorum Crawford, with some other boys, and I was the only girl in that particular class. He said with a frown, 'If you are not able to recite correctly tomorrow I shall see that you boys take off your coats and I shall flog you thoroughly.' Turning to me, he said, 'As for you, Miss, I shall ferule your hands well.'

"I was terrified. I cried all the way home. I couldn't eat any supper. I cried until my pillow was wet, and I prayed that I might know the lesson so I wouldn't be disgraced by being punished. I looked forward to the next morning with dread.

"The next morning Father said, 'Mother, the new teachers from the states are to start their school this morning. What do you say to sending the girls there and letting Horton stay at Mr. Fisher's school?'

"I held my breath, for it looked like a direct answer to my prayer. Mother asked him a few questions and agreed, and what a load of care rolled from my heart. Miss Lincoln, the new teacher, met us at the door, kissed us, and introduced us to Miss Smith, her assistant. Miss Lincoln was really very plain, but she looked beautiful to me.

"Several spinster teachers came out from New England, but they did not last long, as the unmarried men snapped them up and made them wives. Miss Lincoln married Judge Skinner. Miss Smith married Mr. Beers of Salem, and Miss Vaughn married Reverend Vacier, an Episcopal clergyman. At first the school was held in the church, but the seminary building was soon finished and the school was moved into it.

"Judge Shattuck and his bride came soon as the teachers. They lived in rooms in the seminary. I remember we girls were allowed to tiptoe into their rooms and see the new baby when she arrived.

"The sisters' school closed in the early '50's. Reverend George C. Chandler and also Professor Matoon taught in Mr. Fisher's Baptist school until it was moved to McMinnville. Professor Post went with the others to McMinnville. I was not married until September 24, 1861. I was 19 and was considered an old maid. Most of my school girl friends had been married for some time, for in those days girls were usually married at 13 to 15 years of age.

During our visit, Mrs. D'Arcy showed me some of her girlhood treasures. Amorg them was an autograph album in which many of Oregon's well-known pioneers had inscribed their names. Here was a verse written by David P. Thompson on May 6, 1859, and next to it an original poem by Harvey W. Scott, written July 4, 1860. Here is what he wrote:

To Mary

Joyous hopes forever beaming,
Enchanting as the land of dreams,
Brighter far than e'er fabled
Fair Olympus' dazzling beams.
Mary! Hope the wish expresses
That I your friend may always be,
And Hope again assurance gives me
That you'll be a friend to me.

"Before Harvey Scott went to Forest Grove to school he stayed with his sister at Canema," said Mrs. D'Arcy. "He used to keep company with my sister Araminta in those days. She liked him, but I couldn't see what she saw in him. He acted so condescending, so patronizing, and so superior to me that I couldn't abide him.

"Once I said, 'I just adore dancing.'

"He shook his head and said, 'I can't approve your judgment. Danclng panders to the baser passions.'

"It made me so mad I would have licked him then and there if I had been larger and he not so large. He was always a good student, though, in spite of being so serious.

"When Father and Mother and we five children reached Oregon City in the fall of 1846, Father decided to take up a place on the Molalla. We had hurried on ahead of the other emigrants, crossing the mountains by the newly-opened Barlow trail, as Father wanted to get on a place as soon as possible, for Mother was expecting the arrival of another member of the family at any time. A settler on the Molalla who had a double log cabin allowed us to move into one room of it. Father got in his crop and then, with some of the neighbors, built a log schoolhouse.

"When I was a girl we knew but little about the danger of contagious diseases. When a child had what they called putrid sore throat the neighbors all came with their children to visit, and when the child died, as it frequently did, the neighbors for miles around came to the funeral and took the germs of diphtheria home to their children, and the minister was kept busy preaching funeral sermons for the children of the neighborhood.

"In 1852 my father's sisters came across the plains to Oregon. When they reached the Willamette Valley they were suffering from 'mountain fever', as they termed typhoid in those days. We took them in, and, of course, we children soon came down with the same disease. The doctor said my brother Horton, my sister, Josephine, and I could not recover, so they dug three graves. They buried Horton and then Josephine, and left the grave between them for me. It was almost 25 years later, to a day, that I buried my boy in the grave that had been dug for me. Seven of the 12 children in our family have crossed to the land of the hereafter.

"One of my sisters, Mrs. H. B. Nicholas, lives here in Portland. Another sister, Mrs. E. E. Arnold, lives in Oregon City. Still another, Mrs. E. P. Waite, lives at Seattle. My brother, Lycurgus Hunsaker, lives at Needles, not far from Death Valley.

"When I was 19 I married A. C. Edwards, a cabinetmaker, Universalist clergyman, and Eorty-niner. Of our three children, but one is now living—Mrs. Emily Sanford, with whom I am living. My second husband, J. E. D'Arcy, was a lawyer. We moved up to eastern Oregon, where we ran a stock ranch on the John Day for ten years or more. of our children, one is living.

"You asked me how the early settlers earned money

before the discovery of gold in California made money so plentiful all over the west. In the winter of 1846-47 we lived in a double log cabin on the Molalla. The Gordons lived in one room and Mother and Father and we five children lived in the other room. Mother made soap, which she took to Oregon City and sold, and with the money she bought a hen. Together with Eliza Gordon, who later married Mr. Starkweather, she bought a rooster. They raised chickens, taking the little chickens from the hens as soon as they were hatched so the hen would go to laying sooner. We never ate an egg. They were all saved to be hatched. Mother raised 102 chickens the first year from her hen and the daughters of the hen. Mrs. Gordon raised nearly 100. This gave them money to buy cloth to make dresses for themselves and their girls.

"One of the tragedies of our first year was my mother's making a good dress and, after washing it, hanging it out on a bush to dry. The cow discovered it and ate part of it. You don't know what a tragedy that is, unless you have made soap and done washing to earn the money to buy a dress.

"Later, when the gold diggings in California had been discovered, the men from the Willamette Valley went down there, and when they returned they were flush and gold dust was abundant. Mother gave meals to travelers. They would usually give her gold dust or nuggets In payment. She saved all the nuggets until she had a large sardine box full. In 1852, when we were all sick, Father took them to Dr. McLoughlin, who weighed them and gave him $1200 for them.

"One thing I remember very distinctly was Father's being paid a large amount of gold dust for some lumber. This must have been about 1850. He put the gold dust into a small sack and started home with it. When he reached home he discovered there was a hole in the sack and that most of the gold dust and nuggets had leaked out. He retraced his steps, looking carefully, and found a good many of the nuggets, but the dust, of course, was gone beyond recovery."

Oregon Journal
October 30 and 31,
November 1, 1922

Laura Million Howard
Mrs. Howard crossed the plains to Oregon with her parents in

1854. She was interviewed at her home in Ashland, Oregon.

"My father drew a pension for fighting in the Indian wars. If he hadn't been a good runner, though, he wouldn't have drawn a pension, for the Indians ran after him for two or three miles. He finally got to the river, swam under the water, hid in the brush, and got away from them.

"Father was 94 when he died. Mother was 86. Father and Mother had twelve children. Six of us were born before they came across the plains, and the other six were born here in Oregon. There were seven girls and five boys in our family. They always used to say that Father was pretty well fixed, with seven Million girls and five Million boys."

Oregon Journal
April 19, 1928

205

206

Index

218

221

222

Walters family   131
Warfield family   172
Warfield, Sam   172, 173
Warm Springs Indian Agency
98
Warm Springs Indians   73
Warren, H. K.   105
Warrenton, Oregon   164
Wasco County, Oregon   98,
99,129, 180, 182,
Wasco Indian   85
Wasco, Oregon   179
Washburn, Alfred   113
Washburn, Henry   114
Washington Territory   98
Washougal, Washington   200
Watts, Dr. J. W.   167
WCTU   189
Weber Canyon   58
Webfoot Springs   181
Webster 33, 34
Welch boys   143
Welch, Sam   40
Wells, 'Daddy'   12
Wells, Giles   53
West, Gov. Oswald   19, 188
Weston, Oregon   144
Wexford County, Ireland   50
Whitaker, Rachel 105
White family   160
White Salmon   118
White, Al   153
White, Anson   161
White, Clarissa Asineth   160
White, Dr.   124
White, Dr. Elijah   70, 168
White, Polly Owen   183
White, William   160
White, William Wesley   84
Whitman Massacre   1, 3,
29, 40
Whitman Mission   31,33
Whitman Mission   139
Whitman, Alice   39
Whitman, Dr. and Mrs.   139,
142

Whitman, Dr. Marcus   1, 2, 5,
31, 34-39, 79, 104, 173, 186,
Whitman, Narcissa Prentiss
1, 2, 5, 32, 36, 37, 38
Whitman, Perrin   33
Whiton   62
Wide West (boat) 194
Wilbur, Father   123, 180
Wilbur, Oregon   70
Wilbur, Rev. J. H.137
Wilhite, Nancy   145
Willamette River 90, 98, 119, 149,
190
Willamette University   105,
124,159
Willamette Valley   31, 34,
58, 77, 87, 92, 94, 99, 102, 109, 113,
176, 185, 189, 203
Williams, Helen   125
Williams, John A.112
Williams, Roger   127
Williamson, Colonel   126
Williamson, Dr.   168
Williamson, Mr.   176
Willits, Docia   52
Willits, Edna   52
Willits, J. Quinn   52
Willits, Rush   52
Wilson River   155
Wilson, J. Q.   26
Wilson, Mr. and Mrs. Joe   129
Wilson, Mrs. H. H.   41
Wilson, Rev. T. J. 147
Wimple, Adam   4
Wingard, Judge   162
Wolfe, Morris   167
Woodin, Mr.   184
Woods, Governor   105
Woods, Judge   137
Woodson County, Kansas 189
Wright, Ben   23, 24
Wright, George   126
Wright, Mary Ann Louise 191
Wyatt, Douglas   76
Wyeth, Dr.   124
Wyeth, William   125

224

What they say
About the
Oregon Country Library:

Conversations with Bullwhackers, Muleskinners,
Pioneers, Prospectors, '49ers, Indian Fighters,
Trappers, Ex-Barkeepers, Authors, Preachers, Poets
& Near Poets & All Sorts &Conditions of Men
by Fred Lockley
Compiled and Edited by Mike Helm

"...fascinating, full of memories of buffalo galloping across the prairie, prairie schooners, campfires of buffalo chips or sagebrush, frying antelope steaks, peaceful and warlike Indians, early schools, frontier missionaries, gold mining, encounters with grizzly bears, moonshine, ripoffs, legendary drunks and hard work."

> *The Delta Paper*
> Delta Junction, Alaska

..."contains enough colorful wind to sail a ship filled with bulls and all they produce..."

> *Northwest Magazine*
> Sunday magazine of *The Oregonian*
> Portland, Oregon

"...Mike Helm gets a gold star for following through on the brilliant idea of resurrecting the Lockley papers from archives and making them available to readers, historians, and writers interested in recapturing the patchwork quality of the Northwest as it was..."

Oregon Territory
Sunday Magazine
of the *Statesman-Journal*
Salem, Oregon

"...full of stories of human interest, sacrifice, and endeavor, a most vivid recreation of the life and times of the early settlers.
Kliatt Paperback Book Guide
Newton, Massachusetts

Tracking Down Coyote
by Mike Helm

"**Tracking Down Coyote** is a wonderful book...Many have walked, stomped, hiked, biked, or horsed their way across Oregon, and some have written about it, but none yet with quite the personal approach taken by Helm, a man of 47 who has tender feet as well as a tender, romantic heart...Helm is a storyteller, historian, and writer of worth. His Coyote tales are delightful, depictive of the Indians' interpretations of the mysteries of this beautiful country."
The Oregonian

"In **Tracking Down Coyote**...Mike Helm recounts a personal odyssey in search of the soul of his territory. His predecessors are Edward Abbey, Edward S. Curtis, John Muir, Henry Thoreau, W. P. Kinsella, with an echo of Carlos Castaneda...his scholarship approaches the religious..his best writing recreates journeys into the mind and legends of Coyote and his fellow Oregon deities, bringing ancient stories to life..."
San Francisco Chronicle

"**Tracking Down Coyote** (is Mike Helm's) heartfelt, roughhewn and lyrical ode to his native state...Helm's journeys to the outback of Oregon are also Coyote tales. His search for the spirit of Oregon's wild places is metaphorically a hunt for the totem figure that personifies that spirit.

"**Tracking Down Coyote**...is a unique, flavorful mix of inner quests, outer struggle, and recaps of local lore.

"Coyote would dig it. He likes it when we let go with a few howls of our own."
What's Happening
Eugene, Oregon

"**Tracking Down Coyote** is one of the best books of its kind I have ever read. Mike Helm is an excellent teller of tales and a fine hand at weaving experience, fact, legend and myth into an engrossing whole.

"...it is an honest, clear-sighted and in some places angry book. It sounds a warning we will ignore to our sorrow."
Eugene Register Guard
Salem Statesman-Journal

ISBN 0-931742-16-1

Visionaries,
Mountain Men
&
Empire Builders
They Made a Difference
by Fred Lockley
Compiled and Edited by Mike Helm

"A treasury of intriguing tales about not-too-remote pioneer citizens..."
Eugene Register Guard

"...profiles of such legendary figures as Dr. John McLoughlin, Joe and Stephen Meek, Ewing Young, Abigail Scott Duniway, Simon Benson, Sam Jackson, and Lockley himself, to name only a few included in this biographical pantheon."
Northwest Magazine
Sunday magazine of *The Oregonian*

"A more colorful cast of characters would be hard to find..."
Salem Statesman-Journal

"I doubt if Fred Lockley ever met a stranger. The people he writes about were his friends and he simply expects you too will want to meet them."
The CorvallisGazette-Times
ISBN 9 0-931742-09-9

Oregon's Ghosts and Monsters
by Mike Helm

"...familiar tales of regional phantoms and haunted buildings...(and) some bloodcurdling newer ones that sent shivers down the spine of at least one late-night reader."
The Register Guard

"For readers fascinated by Oregon lore, the book will be hard to resist."
The La Grande Observer
ISBN 0-931742-03-X

The Oregon Country Library

1. Conversations with Pioneer Women
By Fred Lockley, compiled and edited by Mike Helm. 310 pages.
ISBN 0-931742-08-0

2. Conversations with Bullwhackers, Muleskinners, Pioneers, Prospectors, '49ers, Indian Fighters, Trappers, Ex-Barkeepers, Authors, Preachers, Poets & Near Poets & All Sorts & Conditions of Men
By Fred Lockley, compiled and edited by Mike Helm. 358 pages.
ISBN 0-931742-09-0

3. Visionaries, Mountain Men and Empire Builders
By Fred Lockley, compiled and edited by Mike Helm. 395 pages.
ISBN 0-931742-10-2

4. A Bit of Verse: Poetry (&Etc.) from the Lockley Files
By Fred Lockley, compiled and edited by Mike Helm. 165 pages.
ISBN 0-931742-10-2

5. Oregon's Ghosts and Monsters
By Mike Helm. 158 pages.
ISBN 0-931742-03-X

6. Tracking Down Coyote
By Mike Helm. 218 pages.
ISBN 0-931742-16-1

What they say about the Oregon Country Library:

"...an amazing oral history collection..."
Small Press Review

"...engaging, meaningful documentation of women's experiences on the frontier..."
Seattle Post Intelligencer

"...preserves something today's Oregonians forget at their peril—the human dimension."
Corvallis Gazette-Times

"...enough colorful wind to sail a ship."
Portland Oregonian

"...highly recommended."
Kliatt Paperback Book Guide

"...a rare treasure..."
Corvallis Gazette Times

"I highly recommend this book."
Wyoming Library Roundup

"...vivid view of those obscure lives..."
Western Humanities Review

A special offer for lovers of Pacific Northwest
Literature

The Oregon Country Library
discounted 10%.

Please send me:

____copies of **Conversations with Pioneer Women**, by
Fred Lockley, compiled and edited by Mike Helm. 310 pages.
ISBN 0-931742-08-0. $17.95 each. $_____

____copies of **Conversations with Pioneer Men**
(originally published as Conversations with Bullwhackers,
Muleskinners, Etc.), by Fred Lockley, compiled and edited
by Mike Helm. 358 pages. ISBN
0-931742-09-0. $20.00 each. $_____

____copies of **Visionaries, Mountain Men & Empire**
Builders by Fred Lockley, compiled and edited by Mike
Helm. 300 pages. ISBN 0-931742-10-2.This book is presently
out of print. $_____

____copies of **A Bit of Verse: Poems (&Etc.) from the**
Lockley Files, by Fred Lockley, compiled and edited by
Mike Helm. 166 pages. ISBN 0-931742-13-7. $7.95 each.
                                                  $_____

____copies of **Oregon's Ghosts and Monsters**, by Mike
Helm. 158 pages. ISBN 0-931742-03-X $9.95 each.
                                                  $_____

____copies of **Tracking Down Coyote**, by Mike Helm. 232
pages. ISBN 0-931742-16-1. $14.95 each. $_____

        Subtotal $_____
        less 10% discount   -$_____
        Plus postage & handling $_____
        ($1.20 for the first book,
            $.40 for each additional book)

    Total
                                                  $_____

Name_____
Address_____
City_____State_____Zip_____

Rainy Day Press
PO Box 3035
Eugene, OR 97403